BYRON'S
WAR

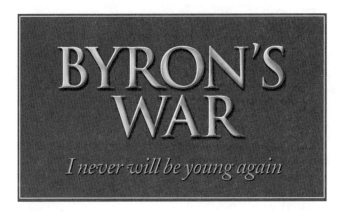

BYRON'S WAR

I never will be young again

Byron Lane

CENTRAL POINT, OREGON

Byron's War
I never will be young again

Published by Hellgate Press, an imprint of PSI Research, Inc.
Copyright 1997 by Byron Lane

For information or to direct comments, questions, or suggestions regarding this book and other Hellgate Press books, contact:

> Editorial Department
> Hellgate Press
> P.O. Box 3727
> Central Point, OR 97502
>
> (541) 479-9464 *telephone*
> (541) 476-1479 *fax*
> psi2@magick.net *email*

Designer and editor: Constance C. Dickinson
Compositor: Jan O. Olsson
Jacket designer: Steven Burns

Lane, Byron.
    Byron's war : I never will be young again / by Byron Lane. — 1st ed.
        p.   cm.
    A chronological compilation of the author's letters home and journal entries written between Oct. 1942 and Mar. 1945.
    Includes index.
    ISBN 1-55571-402-1 (hdbk)
    1. Lane. Byron—Correspondence. 2. World War. 1939–1945—Aerial operations, American. 3. World War, 1939–1945—Personal narratives, American. 4. United States. Army Air Forces—Biography.
    5. Bombardiers—United States—Correspondence.   I. Title.
    D790.L265 1997
    940.54'4973—dc21   97-27688

Printed and bound in the United States of America
First edition 10 9 8 7 6 5 4 3 2 1 0

 Printed on recycled paper when available.

Contents

Illustrations vii

Foreword ix

Preface xii

Prologue   Happy Birthday? 1

Chapter 1   A Student Joins Up 9

Chapter 2   A Buck Private in Miami 15

Chapter 3   Back to the University 29

Chapter 4   Getting Classified 39

Chapter 5   Ground Gremlin Training 49

Chapter 6   Aerial Gunnery School 69

Chapter 7   Bombardier School 87

Chapter 8   The Crew Comes Together 123

Chapter 9   Flying the North Atlantic 141

Chapter 10   And Now to War 155

Chapter 11   Taking the Lead 179

Chapter 12   New Year, Same War 219

Chapter 13   Countdown to Home 245

Epilogue   Closing the Box 261

Glossary 263

Acknowledgments 279

Index 281

Illustrations

Prologue   1944 portrait, Kings Lynn, England 7

Chapter 1   With Dad and Mom at U. of Illinois 14

Chapter 2   Winter uniform at U. of Cincinnati 28

Chapter 3   First flying lesson in Aeronca trainer 38

Chapter 4   Cadets marching at Ellington Field 48

Chapter 5   B-24s on the ramp 68

Chapter 6   AT-6 training planes in formation 86

Chapter 7   Ticket to graduation exercises
             Bombardier's wings 122

Chapter 8   Summer uniform in Tuscon 140

Chapter 9   Eighth Air Force patch 154

Chapter 10 392nd Bomb Group patch 178

Chapter 11 B-24 Bombers in formation* 218

Chapter 12 B-24 Bombers over target* 244

Epilogue   Ribbon bar consisting of (from left to right):
            Distinguished Flying Cross,
            Air Medal with four Oak Leaf Clusters,
            European Theater of Operations with
            two Battle Stars 262

* Courtesy of The Mighty Eighth Air Force Heritage Museum, Savannah, Georgia.

Foreword

Back in 1943, 1944, and 1945, the Army Air Force combat fliers assigned to the Eighth Air Force in England had the best of worlds and the worst of worlds.

On the plus side, they were stationed in a friendly, civilized country among people who spoke the same language — after a fashion. The food and lodgings, compared to those of a combat foot soldier, were incredibly good. And, there was a plentiful supply of beer and ale to be had, either in a nearby village or in cosmopolitan London, along with a goodly number of pretty girls to share it with.

On the flip side, this pursuit of happiness was regularly interrupted by day-long flights over enemy occupied Europe. As soon as the English Channel was crossed, the plane and crew became "clay pigeons" for the hundreds — and often thousands — of anti-aircraft guns lying in wait below. The Luftwaffe, with its ME-109s and FW-190s, was also a deadly menace early in the air war, but was for a time reduced to a comparative nuisance as our fighter pilots and gunners shot them down and our bombardiers hit their airfields and plane factories. The flak, on the other hand, only continued to get worse — or so it seemed.

Ernie Pyle, the premier wartime reporter who followed the action with the fighting foot soldiers, declined to write about those who were fighting in the air war, because "they slept between sheets every night — not in a muddy foxhole." He had a good point, but for many of us, it still hurt. Seeing a plane in your formation, carrying ten of your comrades, explode in a big ball of flame and smoke made sleeping between sheets that night no bed of roses. The bottom line is that, overall, the Eighth Air Force was the most dangerous place for any serviceman to be during WWII. Of the estimated 200,000 combat crew personnel serving with the "Mighty Eighth," 26,000 were killed and 28,000 became POWs — a rate of loss that far overshadowed those of all other United States military components.

The author's day to day account takes the reader through enlistment, training, combat, and finally to kissing the ground after completing his final mission. He may come across at times as a brash, cocky young kid — one of the best. But, at the same time, he admits to making his share of dumb mistakes, both in training and in combat — and the truly honest admission of being damned scared at times in combat. His writing style is reminiscent of one of the best-selling wartime books, *See Here, Private Hargrove*, which was also a good read.

Mr. Lane's story will be of interest to anyone involved, directly or indirectly, with the Army Air Force in WWII. And, to all those who are interested in the air war, it provides an excellent insight into what went on back then.

GLENN HOUGHTON

Glenn Houghton served on a B-24 crew as a radio operator with the 704th Squadron of the 446th Bomb Group, 2nd Air Division, Eighth Air Force from May into December 1944. Even though he began his tour three months earlier than the author and was in a different bomb group — situated less than 20 miles away — they were assigned to the same division of the Mighty Eighth and flew most of their tours on lead planes. Mr. Houghton was lead radio operator on the crew that flew the Eighth Air Force lead plane on D-Day.

Although their paths never crossed, many of Mr. Houghton's World War II training and flying experiences closely paralleled those of the author. They were close to the same age, enlisted within weeks of each other, and went to gunnery schools in Texas — only 90 miles apart. Also, they both arrived in England aboard the new B-24s they and their crews flew via the more dangerous of the Atlantic crossings — the northern route.

Preface

Like many others of my generation, much of my youth was given to fighting a war. When I returned home after three years of service in the Air Force and 30 combat missions as a bombardier on a B-24 air crew in Europe during World War II, I tried to regain some semblance of a normal life by closing my mind to the craziness of those times.

Several years later, when my mother died and I discovered among her possessions a box of more than 300 letters I had written to my family during the war years, I was not anxious to read them.

I am not a person who saves things; if something is not of immediate use it goes out. But there is one box full of mementos, labeled "Byron's War," that has remained closed, yet has followed me through my many moves over many years. My mother's box of letters was labeled "Letters from Byron's War" and placed alongside the other in a closet.

I have a place in my memory where I shove all unpleasantries and I rarely peek in. One brief lapse came when, on a trip to England, I decided to retrace my years there with the Eighth Air Force. Not many landmarks remained to jog my thoughts until I came upon the American Military Cemetery in Cambridge, where many of my comrades are buried. The memories that came rushing back were so painful that I left, vowing not to revisit such scenes ever again.

Memories of the war might have remained in the nether regions of my mind and the boxes of historical artifacts on the shelf forever were it not for my granddaughter. When she was very young she sent me a mostly blank book titled *The Grandparent Book*. It asked a lot of questions about my past, for which I was to provide answers — a gift of roots, the book said. I actually wrote three lines before I decided I didn't want to revive the past. Thereafter I would take the grandfather book down about once a year, write two more lines, get uncomfortable and put it back on the shelf.

Now I am getting older, the world changes, some of my friends die, and each event opens up a section of my memory that I had hidden from view. Since I have a harder time each year remembering things like where I went yesterday and where I put my glasses, it's at least comforting to know that my earliest memories remain very sharp. Recently, looking once again at the grandparent book, I decided that it was only right for me to get some of the events down on paper so that my granddaughter would have some connection with my past.

One day I pulled down the boxes marked "War" and discovered that this part of my personal history I hadn't thrown out was an amazing chronicle of the U.S. heavy bomber forces in Europe during World War II, as seen through the eyes of a very young air crew officer. After several days of reading and reflecting, I decided to do more than filling in blanks in the grandparent book, for here was a story that could be of interest to others as well.

While the letters substantially cover the experiences of a teenager in war-time training, combat, and duty overseas, there are many private thoughts not suitable for letters home. Fortunately, some of these thoughts are captured in a small journal that was part of the contents of my "Byron's War" box. Other items from the box, such as pictures, army orders, and aerial strike photos completed the memory joggers and helped fill in the blanks.

Although I am now willing to look deeply into my boxes marked "War," I cannot assume that my former comrades and their families feel the same, so I have scrambled the names. Aside from this, everything written here is substantially as it happened.

So, this book is for you, Ilana, and for your generation. My prayer is that you will never know these things first hand. Millions of young men and women, those who survived, had their lives changed forever by the events of the greatest war in human history, and I was among them.

Happy Birthday?

Sitting in my home office with a television, fax machine and computer keeping me in instant touch with the world, I struggle to bring up the image of America as it was over half a century ago — an America when the only medium of mass communication was the radio. In that dimming past, America was one cohesive nation united in fighting a war on two fronts — a war that engulfed most of the world.

Our involvement in that war began with a devastating strike from the air by the Japanese on December 7, 1941 and ended with an even more devastating strike from the air delivered by Army Air Force B-29s on the Japanese homeland in August 1945. In the intervening years, hundreds of savage air battles were fought around the globe.

One very important part of our global air offensive was the Eighth Air Force operating out of England. At full strength, 200,000 American airmen were stationed there. The mission of the bombers of the Eighth was to destroy the industry and vital installations of Nazi Germany. The men of the aircrews were the shock troops sent against Hitler, carrying the war to the German heartland long before the invasion by ground forces. Early raids were carried out by just 50 bombers, but D-Day saw 1,350 bombers of the Eighth strike the European beaches in support of the invasion.

In propeller-driven planes — about the size of today's 30 passenger commuter aircraft — they flew 250 miles per hour at altitudes over 20,000 feet and braved numbing cold, vicious attacks by enemy fighter planes, and deadly fields of anti-aircraft fire. In the end, they completely derailed the Nazi economy.

While the raids of the Eighth saved thousands of lives in the ground forces, they came with tremendous sacrifice. Casualties among the bomber forces were the worst for any arm of service. More than 26,000 American airmen were killed in action, 18,000 were wounded, and 28,000 were captured and held prisoners of war. Less than 25 percent of the aircrews survived the 25 to 35 missions that were required to complete a combat tour of duty.

These young men had to meet rigid requirements to join the Aviation Cadet Corps. Physical and psychological standards eliminated all but the healthiest, the best conditioned, and the best able to withstand extreme emotional trauma. The capacity to learn and retain complex technical data further narrowed the field. Those who satisfied these demanding criteria were educated, highly motivated young men — most in their early 20s. It was not unusual for the squadron commander, a captain or major, to be 25 years of age and referred to by his airmen as "the old man."

This is the story of one airman, like so many others, a patriotic, committed, sometimes brave, and often very scared young man.

October 27, 1944

Dear Mom and Dad,

It's my twentieth birthday — not exactly the one I had envisioned a few years back. Here's the way my day went:

"It's 3 A.M., sir. Briefing is at 4 A.M. Coffee and eggs at the combat mess." It's cold in bed, but much colder out. Someone in the far corner of the hut curses as he hops out into the wintery night. One of the fellows who isn't flying today mutters, "Hit it hard, guys." It starts off like many of the other days.

We leave quietly so as not to disturb the crews who are standing down, and head for the mess hall. Our usual breakfast is powdered eggs and powdered milk, but today, like the condemned's last meal, we get our pre-mission special breakfast of hotcakes with syrup, a real egg, and real milk.

At 4 A.M., with sleep still in our eyes, we walk into the briefing room. The S-2 officer has been up all night preparing target information; he's hollow-eyed and grouchy. He pulls up the screen covering the big map of Europe. All eyes follow the red string that goes way into Germany, marking our route into the target and out. There are a few groans, the lights go out, and a detail map is flashed on the screen.

The S-2 officer points to the map and speaks, "Our IP is here. The run is forty-six miles to the target. We have a river and autobahn here, which serves as the first check point. A double track railroad follows your route in, three miles to the left of course. You'll have to watch yourselves at this point and stay well on the briefed route as there are six heavy flak batteries that may bring you in range should you deviate. The target is well defined by this point of land jutting out into the Rhine, a double track railroad spur, and a patch of woods directly north of the target area."

The target chart flashes on the screen. "Here we can plainly see the target area. This building is well camouflaged and we have reports of smoke screens. So, you should synchronize on this point here and advance your cross-hair."

Now comes the high altitude photo. "You can see that your mean point of impact is clear so there should be no trouble on that score. The target was hit a month ago by three combat wings, but the damage has since been repaired. This is a first priority target and must be destroyed.

"Oh, yes, your fighter support will consist of five groups of P-51s that will pick you up at this point, take you within fifty miles of the target area, and bring you back to here. There will be another group of P-38s flying top cover in the target area, and a group of P-47s sweeping the general vicinity of attack. Flak is heavy at the target, but the route has been designed to take you through the minimum concentration (some laughter here from the men). If there are no questions, that's all."

I take Bill, our navigator, aside and we discuss check points on the route more thoroughly and decide at what point I'll be able to see the target. He'll talk me in to the target until I pick it up. We're both familiar with how the other works, so we should have no trouble.

Outside it's still dark. We get on our bicycles and ride down to the locker room. I fumble through my clothes, sleepy eyes now a thing of the past. Into my flying bag goes my equipment, each item carefully checked: heated boots, heated gloves, electric cord, gauntlets, helmet with earphones, throat mike, oxygen mask, sun glasses, scarf, .45-caliber pistol in a shoulder holster, ammunition, an extra jacket, flak vest, flak helmet, and Mae West. Then, Bill and I head for the navigation room to draw up our maps. On the way, I check out my bombsight and bring it along.

We're the last ones in and usually the last ones out. Other crews are already busy on their charts. We get the various coordinates, times, control points, altitudes and go to work. Finally, we have everything well in mind. Then I check where the known flak batteries on the route are located. I'm also the pilotage navigator today and, if we have visual contact with the ground, I'm responsible for getting our formation around them. Out into the cold morning again, there's a truck waiting to take us to our ship.

The crew is all out there and the armorer has the guns in place throughout the ship. I check my turret, recheck my equipment, and then we're ready to go. The officers have one last talk about the route and target and we climb aboard.

I check the bomb bays. We have thousand pounders aboard, the first time we have used them. On a whim, I write on one of the bombs, "Regards from the 392nd." The engines sputter and come to life and we taxi out onto the runway. The others in the squadron line up behind us, throttles jam forward, and we're off.

Now we're airborne, climbing and circling, allowing the rest of the squadron to get up and into formation. With the entire combat group of 30 Liberators stretched out behind us, we head out over the North Sea.

I give the order to check guns and, from the waist positions and turrets, there's a chatter of .50-calibers. I climb into the nose turret and clear my own. Over the intercom we check in, note that all is OK, and we're ready. Our route takes us over the coast of Holland. It's clear and calm as our P-51s come up to meet us and waggle their wings in greeting.

We're not far from the target when the Luftwaffe fighters appear. The Mustangs take them on, but a few Germans get through and are peppering us. Now everyone is firing. An ME-109 is in my sights and I let go with a long burst. I see my tracers hit back of the canopy, he flips over and heads down. This is my first probable kill as a gunner.

We're coming up on the bomb run and now I'm out of the turret, over the bombsight, and I'm in charge of the ship. It's the job of Mac and Deke to just hold the altitude. We're on auto pilot and any small corrections in course are made by me through the bombsight. There are no fighters now but the flak comes up in big, black puffs. Behind us the other bombardiers in the squadron are waiting to toggle their bombs on my signal.

I open the bomb bay doors, everything else out of mind. I struggle to concentrate on the target as the bursting flak makes the plane bounce around the sky. The hairs cross and the bombs are gone. I slam the button that closes the bomb bay doors and give the command to turn.

As we head for home, the flak comes up with all the anger the Germans can muster. I see the number three engine of our right-wing plane take a hit and burst into flames. I watch it lose altitude as the crew fights to put out the fire and feather the prop. Another plane from our formation is missing; it must have gone down while I was concentrating on the bomb run.

Mac asks for a position check and each member of the crew calls in. We have sustained some damage to the aircraft, but no casualties.

Soon the Dutch coast disappears beneath us and we're clear of anti-aircraft and fighters. I run through my checklist, and my work is done. It's up to Mac and Deke now to get us back to the base.

As we descend to the field, my mind goes back over the day, and the days that have gone before, and I wonder: Mom, am I really only 20, or could I be 40 — I have lived through so much. Or, maybe I'm just 17 — in many ways I have lived so little.

Chapter One

A Student Joins Up

In 1940 and 1941, the Royal Air Force was fighting daily battles against the German Luftwaffe for the survival of England. Although the United States was officially neutral, President Roosevelt had us sending munitions, ships, and other supplies of war to the valiant British. Still, to me, it was all so far away — it was their war, not ours.

A few German Jewish refugees came into our neighborhood bringing tales of the horrors inflicted on them and other members of the Jewish community by the Nazis, but they weren't "us," they were Germans. As a 16-, then 17-year-old, I was preoccupied with such important issues as how to cut the high school science class to go boating on the lake in the park without getting caught and how to qualify for graduation without really doing the required work.

Then came December 7, 1941 and the Japanese attack on Pearl Harbor. In one awful day, everything changed. Now, not only were the Japanese our enemies, but the Germans were no longer just "theirs" either. Older brothers of my friends began enlisting in a favored branch of the military or were called up in the draft.

Having the entire world in upheaval kept the family's noses in newspapers and ears cupped to the radio. Many of the expected goodies of everyday life simply disappeared. It was no longer OK to borrow the family car for a date, because, like most families, we had an A gas ration card — essential driving only. This meant I couldn't take a drive to the lake front with my best girl, which meant there was no making out in the back seat of the car.

Even the Lucky Strike cigarettes we secretly smoked now came in a white package, because the dye used in the good old green package was needed to make camouflage coloring or to paint army trucks. I mean, how far would this thing go?

By mid 1942, men were being called to service in ever increasing numbers, the draft age was moving down from 21 to 20. It was becoming apparent, even to an ostrich-like 17-year-old, that someday there would be a draft number with my name attached. Parental advice was to "wait until you are called." Then what — the infantry or a "swabbie" in the navy?

Now, when the guys got together the subject of conversation was "whatyagonnado?" How about the Air Corps, the elite of the services? Stories were appearing in the papers extolling the heroics of airmen in both theaters of war, and the Air Force song made flying in "the wild blue yonder" seem exciting and glamorous. Besides, the uniforms were snazzy. And so it was decided.

October 27, 1942

Dear Mom and Dad,

What a way to spend my 18th birthday. I got a bus out of the Illinois campus at 3 A.M., arrived in Rantoul about 5 A.M., then waited in line at Chanute field for my enlistment into the Army Air Corps.

For the past few weeks, I ran our discussion about waiting versus enlisting over and over in my mind. As you know, I really want the Air Corps and I don't want to be drafted into the regular Army or Navy. The thing that finally made up my mind was a promise made by an Air Corps colonel who spoke here on campus last week. He said any of us enlisting now would be deferred until next June, provided we took some courses, such as math, that will apply to our service.

The first thing this morning, a bunch of us took the mental exams. Most of it was pretty routine stuff, and I passed easily. In the afternoon came the physical. They went over every part of my body, and all seemed to be OK until I got on the scale. I weighed in at 129, which is three pounds under the required weight for my height. I guess I haven't been eating too well down here. The food at the dorm is pretty lousy, and when I get busy studying, I sometimes forget to eat. The sergeant in charge said I should go back to school and get my weight up, then complete the physical. On the way out, he told me to eat a bunch of bananas and drink a lot of water for a few days, and that should do it. I'll keep checking my weight and go back as soon as it's OK.

It's pretty tough to do, but I must keep my mind on my studies. I have been doing pretty well in everything except trigonometry. I better stop hating math if I want to be a flyboy. I like the people I have been meeting here. Despite the unsettling effects of the war (or maybe because of it), everyone seems to work at having a good time. At the moment, I find social life incidental, but maybe that will change once I know where I'm headed.

I hate to bug you, but everything here is expensive and I could sure use some money. Just going out on a date costs $1.50. I'm trying to make the $5 allowance do, but it's not easy. I'll get some good grades to make it worthwhile. Love to you!

November 1, 1942

Loading up on bananas and water did the trick. I weighed in at 133, and the docs at Chanute okayed me for enlistment. So, I'm in as an aviation cadet, but on hold until I complete another semester. That means I stay here until next June, if I keep up with my studies and take a couple of required navigation courses. The one thing I dare not do is flunk a course, so I intend to study hard. The English course and the one in Economics are no problem, but I had to spend two dollars for a tutor to help me with the trigonometry. Math is definitely not my best thing, but please don't let on to the Air Corps.

I had a letter from Louise. She may come down for the weekend. That sort of distraction I can stand. There are plenty of chicks here, but she's still my favorite.

What do you say about running away from Chicago in a couple of weeks, Dad, and coming here for the Notre Dame game? It promises to be a lulu, and it would be fun to be seeing a game with the old pro again. If you decide to do it, send me five bucks for the tickets. My finances won't stand anything like that.

I'm beginning to get a little lonesome for all of you. Tell Pooz she's my favorite sis. I'll write to her soon. Lots of love!

November 15, 1942

Thanks for the dough. I was flatter than the guy who jumped out of the twenty-story building. I used a bit of it getting sharpened up for the dance at the women's dorm. Roz, a gal in one of my classes, invited me, and it was really a dilly. They fixed the place up like a night club with colored branches, twinkling lights, and they had an eight piece orchestra. It was a night I'll never forget.

I'm sure you read that they are going to start drafting eighteen-year-olds. The rumor going around is that they need more men, and they may not honor deferments like mine. That puts everything up in the air. If I'm going to the Air Corps soon, then school doesn't make a lot of sense. Yet, I need to have decent grades, so I can come back after the war. It really makes everything go fuzzy.

I certainly will be glad to see you this weekend, Dad. I really need to talk things out with you. Your guidance makes such a difference. And, going to the game will be swell. I got some good seats for us, and we'll cheer for the Illini [U. of Illinois team]. Lots of love!

November 29, 1942

The weekend was wonderful, Dad. I sure hate to be a burden to you, but I don't know what to do with my life right now. After you left, things seemed to hit the fan in every way. Lots of guys are dropping out of school to get ready for the army. Classes are all up in the air and everything is just sort of nuts.

In talking to my ROTC instructor, he seems very clear that the Air Corps will be calling men up very fast. I imagine that means I can finish this semester, but not much beyond. My feeling now is that I should come home for Christmas, and not plan to return. I'll try to find something to make myself useful until I get inducted.

My head feels so screwy. I want to finish up here with good grades, but my last exam in Algebra was a D. The instructor says not to worry, but I can't seem to put schooling in perspective while I keep thinking about what's coming up. I really feel that doing a job for my country is more important than anything right now, but there's a little part of me that is dragging my feet. I was just getting into being a college student, and look what's happening.

Dad, I really appreciate your settling up my bills while you were here, but I will need some money for my train trip home. I'll try to make the ten bucks I have do until then. It'll sure be nice to be with all the family during the holiday. I love you all.

Chapter Two

A Buck Private in Miami

As it had been through every day of 1942, at the beginning of 1943, the attention of the nation was on news of the war and on winning it. Radio broadcasts of President Franklin D. Roosevelt's fireside chats kept the nation unified and focused on the war effort. One evening, he said:

"I have seen our men — and some of our American women — in North Africa. Because of the secrecy of my trip, the men of our armed forces in every place I visited were completely surprised. And the expression on their faces certainly proved that.

"In every battalion, and in every ship's crew, you will find every kind of American citizen representing every occupation, every section, every origin, every religion and every political viewpoint. Ask them what they are fighting for and every one of them will say, 'I am fighting for my country.' Ask them what they really mean by that, and you will get what on the surface may seem to be a wide variety of answers.

"One will say that he is fighting for the right to say what he pleases, and to read and listen to what he likes. Another will say he is fighting because he never wants to see the Nazi Swastika flying over the old First Baptist Church on Elm Street. Another soldier will say that he is fighting for the right to work and to earn three square meals a day for himself and his folks. And another will say that he is fighting so that his children and his grandchildren will not have to go back to Europe, or Africa, or Asia, or the Solomon Islands, to do this ugly job all over again. But all these answers really add up to the same thing: every American is fighting for freedom."

In early 1943, the outcome of the war was not so certain. The Germans controlled most of Europe and the Japanese controlled China, the Philippines, Korea, and the Malay Peninsula. However, American strength was growing as industries completed conversion to the output of war materials. Shortages of civilian items increased and the Office of Price Administration (OPA) both rationed goods and controlled prices. Tin went to war, restricting production of cans for food and toys. Watches vanished from stores, zippers from clothing. Binoculars and other optical goods were gone, the lenses used in weapons. Shortages of metal either eliminated many everyday objects or changed the way they were constructed — frames for handbags, office files, pins, sewing gadgets. Lawn mowers were discontinued for the duration. Automobile production had long ago ended because the huge production lines now made airplanes, tanks, and military vehicles.

For the good of all, some things remained unchanged: *Once Upon a Honeymoon*, with Ginger Rogers and Cary Grant, opened at the RKO theater in New York on New Year's day, and UCLA, with Bob Waterfield at quarterback, beat Georgia in the Rose Bowl 9–0. Baseball did see a change, as Joe DiMaggio enlisted in the army.

January 30, 1943

Dear Mom and Dad,

Your son is a soldier in the Army Air Corps. After the induction, we were marched off to Union Station and we are now on a troop train headed to Florida for a new type of schooling. All the naval aviation cadets are sent to pre-flight basic training before they go as cadets, but it has been the Army's policy to send the men straight to flight training. Now, in order to avoid so many washouts (or so we're told), we will be the first to go to Army Air Corps basic training.

We're to spend two months in Miami doing hard conditioning, as privates, and drawing fifty bucks a month pay. At the end of the basic period, we go to Cadet Centers. They say it will lower the failures and up the physical standards. I hope I can get through it. So, now we are on this Pullman train headed south.

January 31, 1943

It's noon and we're in Alabama. I slept well in my Pullman berth. Some luxury! We just left Tuscaloosa, where basket lunches were waiting for us with sandwiches, cookies, milk, and fruit. We have all the windows open and our coats off. It's quite warm, about 60 degrees I guess. Pretty soon we will take off our shirts. Whee! Wintering in Miami shouldn't be too bad a deal.

I'm glad I took that creative writing course at school last semester. If I had to do a paper for the professor now it would go like this:

Notes on A Journey

Three days on a troop train headed for Miami! No grumbling or grousing over leaving home; only laughter and anxiety to get into uniform. They are all here — tall ones, short ones, fat ones, thin ones. No one talks of the seriousness of war, we only share how great it will be to serve our country.

This morning, as we awakened, the sun was peeping over Florida, casting an orange tint on a world of make-believe, far removed from warring frontiers. For some it is the first train ride, for others the first view of oranges and palm trees, and for travelers from families like mine just hello to an old friend.

There are boys from all over the middle west, traveling the country at government expense, seeing with their own eyes just what we are going to fight for. Anyone viewing the vastness and diversity of our country, as I do now through my train window, would know that we must, and will, win this war, to keep all of this the land of the free.

It's about 6:30 P.M. We just had supper, and was it ever swell. Ham for lunch and roast beef tonight. This army life is great. Nothing to do but sit around and eat and sleep. We won't be in Miami for another day or so.

Irwin Nite is on the train. He was a major in the ROTC at Hyde Park High School when I was there. Also another boy from Hyde Park, Les Waren, and one of the guys I know from Illinois. I met some other boys, too, all nice.

The sergeant was saying that those boys who enlisted before us will go direct to cadet school. We are an experimental group. I thought there would be grumbling at the idea of being privates instead of cadets for a few months, but everybody seems to agree it's a good idea as it will get us all in shape.

February 1, 1943

It's Tuesday morning, and we're all plenty damn sick of train riding. However, we're in the Florida everglades approaching the coast. The scenery is beautiful. I had a swell night's sleep, about nine hours. The bumpy train only awakened me once.

We're expected to arrive in Miami about noon. We're all filthy dirty and hoping for clean clothes and a bath. Breakfast was eggs, sausage, toast, coffee, and orange juice. What an army! I'll mail this soon as we get in. Love to all of you.

February 2, 1943

Here I am in Miami Beach, housed in what was formerly the Milburn Hotel, on Ocean Drive, Suite 326, facing the sea. Only, things are slightly changed from the days when this was vacation heaven. Now, the beds are bunks and there are six men to a room. My clothes are really smelly, they're the same ones I had on when I left Chicago; no signs of uniforms yet.

We are privates in the army, but headed for aviation cadet training. We are to get about two months of basic training — KP, guard duty, and other good things. So far, we've stood in line for about fourteen hours and done nothing the rest of the time.

The weather is beautiful though and, since I have nothing planned for the rest of the winter, I think I'll stay.

The food is swell and plentiful. If you could have seen the plate of lamb I had last night, you'd know why you can't get all the meat you want back there at home. My address is on the envelope. Please write soon.

P.S. We get up at 5:15 A.M. How about that?

February 3, 1943

Well, we still have no uniforms or equipment. However, I imagine we'll have the stuff tomorrow or so. They started right off drilling the hell out of us. They say they've got to discipline us, so we'll make good soldiers, and get us ready for cadet school where they are very strict.

I feel fine. The sun is grand and the food still OK. We took a test on general intelligence. I hope I did well. They told us to guess at what we didn't know, so on the last fifteen questions I just picked an answer. I'm worried that they may mark on a curve, then I might be washed out. I guess there's no use worrying — if I'm out, that's it.

We get our first liberty on Sunday, but we're not allowed to go into Miami proper, just stay on Palm Island. I'll be happy to get away for awhile. I'm not used to being herded around like cattle, but I better get off my high horse and get used to it. They tell us there are enemy agents everywhere, so we shouldn't say anything about where we are. But, you know where the Milburn is — in thirty seconds I can be in the ocean.

At 5:30 in the morning, we march to chow (that's army for breakfast) singing the Air Corps song. I bet the tourists who are here aren't too happy. Not only do they get the noise, but any girl who walks down the street could get mobbed by a squadron of soldiers. We have to pay through the nose for everything, just like the tourists, which is not a friendly way to treat us.

Then there are aviation terms for everything. Instead of "fall out," we get "bail out." In place of "move on," it's "take off." Our company is called a flight and it's not organized with squads like the infantry, but rather by squadrons. We get time for absolutely nothing during the day, and after 5 P.M. we have so much time we don't know what to do with ourselves. Going to cadet school will be a pleasure after this.

Now that I've given you the dark side, I'll tell you the bright one: The boys are pretty nice. We sing as we march along the street and we look pretty good. If Benito and Adolph could see us, they'd know what they are up against.

I miss you all and wish I could see you, but that's war!

February 4, 1943

Today, we got our equipment and now I know why they say we are the best equipped army in the world. I got two sets of fatigues and two of suntans — the regulation summer uniforms they use down here. The shirt and pants are lightweight gabardine worn with a khaki tie. It's very neat looking, but very plain. As cadets-to-be, we wear no insignia at all.

We also get those damned high top shoes, but we also get a pair of oxfords, which no other army service has. If you could see me in the one piece army fatigue, you'd die laughing. It's really ugly, and so huge I get lost inside it. We also got a tropical helmet, five suits of underwear, handkerchiefs, toothbrushes, a comb, and stuff like that.

One rather disconcerting note: They issued us our dogtags, the army's metal identification things we must wear around our necks at all times. It has name, rank, serial number, blood type, and a symbol for religion. The Catholic men get a "C," Protestants a "P," and mine has an "H." I asked what the hell that was, and they told me Hebrew. I said it was my understanding that Hebrew was an ancient national designation and also an ancient language, but I am Jewish. Too bad, they say, all Jewish men are identified with an "H." I don't imagine they think they are fooling German soldiers, so I don't know what it's about, but in the army I am officially Hebrew.

February 5, 1943

Well, today I got shot — with needles, that is. We got injections for typhoid, small pox, yellow fever, and malaria. My left arm is a little stiff and I have a bad stomachache, which I guess is from the shots. It sure isn't from the food we eat. Here's what we had for dinner tonight: two large pork chops, a big helping of mashed potatoes and gravy, vegetable salad, peas, applesauce, and fudge cake. Not too bad for poor soldiers.

This evening, I have on my class A uniform, the tan one, and I really look like a soldier. As a matter of fact, I am lovely. These clothes really are super. As soon as I can, I will ship my civies home. The sergeant said we won't need them for a couple of years. I hope he's wrong.

We just had mail call and they gave me the letter from Pooz. Boy, is it swell to hear from her. She's not only my sister, she's my best friend. Thanks for all your great letters. Write often. The mail line is the treat of the day.

February 7, 1943

Today, we had the whole day off and I went for a swim in the ocean. Then we went to see a movie with Jack Benny. Tomorrow, we go to work in earnest.

I'm sorry that I can't tell you exactly where I am, everything is a military secret (Note for the censor: Bah! I saved you the trouble). But you know the general vicinity. No, there's no need for you to come here for a visit. I can be shipped out at any time without warning.

What comes next is a college training program, and as soon as it is started, I'll whiz out of here fast. If you do send some candy or cookies, that would be swell. I can't keep other kinds of food unless it's in metal containers, and that's too much trouble in our limited space.

I am quite OK here and have few complaints, except that at 5 A.M. the stupid bugle call is played over a loud speaker system. I keep thinking about Irving Berlin's World War I song that says about the bugler, "I will amputate his reveille and step upon it heavily and spend the rest of my life in bed."

I may go to a USO dance Tuesday night. We had a lecture and movies on sex hygiene and we were warned about the girls down here, so I'll stay away from most of the babes. I do think a USO dance will be OK.

There are so many soldiers here it is unbelievable. There are only a few civilians here and there. After hours, one can hardly get through the streets. It's almost impossible to get into a show, and the price is double on everything for servicemen. Some places even have a sign, "no one in uniform allowed." That's the attitude of the people towards the soldiers. All we do is lay down our lives for them, so what can we expect?

I took out a $10,000 government life insurance policy, naming you as beneficiaries and Pooz as contingent beneficiary. If it happens that you receive the benefits of this policy, I'd like to have the money used to send Pooz to a fine medical school. I really would like to see her have her M.D. I thought it wise to take out the maximum amount, as it's inexpensive for me at my age. I don't have to pay premiums on it while I am a cadet, the government takes care of that.

I also ordered an $18.75 war bond to be taken out of my pay each month. I named Dad as co-owner, so he can cash it or use it when he wants. They will mail it directly to you.

Gotta go now and get some rest. In the morning, I have to get up, shave, see that my shoes are shined, wash, get dressed, and be in formation in four minutes. They make me shave every day here. How about that!

February 11, 1943

Sorry I haven't written for a few days, but I was too busy. We're getting our hind ends worked off now. From your letters, you must think I'm playing in the sunshine. The only place I actually get the sun is on the back of my neck and it is red as a lobster. We just got back from the drill field, and I am on a noon break. We're only learning how to save life, so far, not how to take it. That comes soon. We're learning gas protection, first aid, and personal hygiene in addition to our five hours of marching each day. It's really tough, but interesting.

I went to that USO dance and I was never so disappointed. The place was filled with soldiers, just like everything else down here. I wouldn't have minded, but there wasn't a girl under twenty-two or so. A lady there told me that they won't let any young girls on the street at night on account of all the soldiers.

Convoys of ships go by here continually and airplanes buzz around about 100 feet above the beach. It's just like a combat zone.

Last night one fellow got yanked out of ranks for scratching his nose during retreat. So you see they're not kidding; they're strict and they mean business. Oh, well, I didn't intend to play, anyhow. After the war, we can go on a vacation somewhere (not Florida). I have to go to chow now, so I'll continue later.

It's 6:15 P.M. now. I just got back from supper. Was it ever swell! Our food is always good, though. We got paid $10 supplementary pay today. Nice, huh?

Yesterday, some guy came through the hall asking for three men to drive the colonel's car. My roommate told him where to shove it, thinking it was one of the kids. I chimed in, too. It turned out to be the sergeant looking for men to clean up the garbage. He was just waiting for a couple of wise asses like us to mouth off, so we got the job. I have now learned my lesson and I shall forever hold my peace.

We saw some fine movies today on chemical warfare. They told us that the Germans may be using it, so our guys are taking no chances. The masks we have are really excellent, not the usual training kind, as they call this a combat zone and they expect a gas attack here some day.

The drilling is boring because I know it so well from ROTC, but I let on like I'm interested and pay attention. We have this regular army drill sergeant who is a real jerk. He hates cadets, says we are a bunch of slobs ducking the real war on the ground. He was in Pearl Harbor when the Japs attacked, so that makes him a hero for staying alive, I guess. He never lets up on us, and my feet are killing me from hours of marching. I wonder if he thinks we are going to peddle those planes to Berlin and Tokyo.

There's the usual running to line up and then waiting in line for half an hour. I must spend two hours a day waiting in line for an order, but that's the army. I'm developing remarkable patience, quite a new thing for me.

February 13, 1943

They have had us on an 18-hour-a-day schedule for the past week. If this continues you may get letters less frequently. I'll try to keep brief notes of what's happening, then put them all in the mail as I am able.

Saturday night, after I talked with you, we had guard duty. I was on the ten to twelve shift as orderly for the sergeant of the guard. Then, Monday night, we had some classification tests that included physics, which I flunked flat, and math, on which I got 100 percent. We don't know what they were for, but we'll find out soon. Last night, we had a demonstration of the prevention or care of incendiary fires. They demonstrated with bombs of different sizes on the ground and, as a climax, three big bombers flew over and dropped incendiaries on a make-believe city they had built.

We've averaged six hours sleep a night since last Saturday, and I am just plain exhausted. We are learning infantry combat tactics. I am not permitted to give you details, but you will remember it, Dad, as the basic army stuff.

Thanks for all the goodies, but please don't send me any more food for awhile. I have several boxes, my roommates have some, and we're having a hard time putting it all away. I feel terrible that I can't write to everyone, but I am sure they will understand.

It really is grand to hear from all of you, and at bedtime my thoughts turn to home. I am sure we will all be together again. Maybe that's why I am working so hard, because if we all do that, we will beat those guys and then we can go home. I'm going to sign off now and go to sleep. Thanks loads for your regular letters. Keep it up.

February 19, 1943

I just got my fifth shot, all in the left arm. I don't know what they are for, so I hope they know what they are doing.

Now for something important: Some of our group just shipped out of here, and we are cautioned not to take our laundry out. That means we'll probably be leaving within a week. Don't know where we'll be headed, so if you don't hear from me for several days you'll know the reason. Of course, this is not information for publication. The men who left were issued regulation winter olive drab uniforms, so that probably means the north.

My nose is now so sunburned that it's cracked. It doesn't hurt, but it sure looks funny. We're still doing drills, getting lectures, learning commando tactics, etc. I have the usual rookie's sore feet and blisters.

It's surprising, but it does get cold down here. Our uniforms are thin khakis, and we get up at 5 A.M. when it's freezing. Then the sun comes out and it gets hot. We stand in formation and if you wiggle or talk you get assigned to Sunday School, which means you drill on Sunday and not get time off. I guess it's all part of the hardening process.

Your letters come in regularly, and they are really swell!

February 24, 1943

Incredible, but I am still here. They put us on shipment, confined us to quarters for three days, and then sent us back to the field to continue our basic training. We're still on shipment, however, and can leave on an hour's notice. I'm getting used to these nutty things. Everything is backwards in the army. It does seem a shame to waste days when we're trying to get this war over with as soon as possible.

I'm fed up with Florida now, and what I'd really like is a decent break and some fun. The girls here are strictly commercial, and that's not for me. I'll be very glad to get out of here, even though the next place could be lots tougher.

February 26, 1943

Maybe this time they really mean it. A group next to ours got shipped out at 10:30 last night. There aren't many of us left. They issued us winter uniforms, all except me. I got an overcoat, but they didn't have other things to fit me. So, I go out in suntans. If we go to a cold climate, I'll get outfitted there. Despite it all, I still am OK with the army, but I'd like to be somewhere in the fight instead of wasting time around here. That's a minority opinion, not many of the fellows agree with me. They want to stay away from the combat areas for as long as possible.

No one knows where we're headed. My guess is that it's to one of the universities. If you don't hear from me, you'll know I'm on my way, and I will write to you from the new base.

Chapter Three

Back to the University

Once inducted into the armed service, like other new soldiers or sailors, I relinquished all control over my life. I went where I was told and obeyed orders. In the Air Corps, the training aviation cadets received, the planes they flew, and the units to which they were assigned were all subject to the luck of the draw.

The training command in the U.S. was faced with the need for improved training due to the urgency to provide replacement crews for casualties and new crews to man the ever-increasing stream of bombers coming off the assembly lines. All men entering the Aviation Cadet Program went to similar basic training. Those on a fast track went directly to classification centers where testing results and specific needs divided them into candidates for pilot, bombardier, or navigation training. This group went to pre-flight school, then advanced flight training in their specialties, and on to combat crew assignment as rapidly as possible.

Using the combat experience of returning veterans, a more comprehensive program was devised for selected aircrew officer candidates that would enable them to perform better in combat conditions and prepare them to handle the newer technology being put into production. These men went from basic training to university programs, where they took courses in physics, meteorology, mathematics, and other academic subjects.

At the Classification Centers, those of us on the more comprehensive track who were selected for bombardier training were assigned, first to pre-flight ground school, then to aerial gunnery school. There we received the same training as the enlisted crew members in manning the various gun positions on the bombers. This was important, because the bombardiers were the gunnery officers and they often manned the nose turret guns.

Next came advanced Bombardier School and ground simulation training with the Norden bombsight, followed by practice bombing missions in AT-11 training planes. We also received an additional six weeks of navigation training in both dead reckoning and pilotage. The latter enabled guidance of the aircraft by visual sighting and reference to maps of the terrain, important in those lead planes where a bombardier was often utilized as a second navigator.

On graduation, those of us who survived the high wash-out rate were qualified as combination bombardier/navigators on medium or heavy bomber crews, were ranked as second lieutenants or flight officers and awarded the coveted wings that were a prominent part of our flight crew uniforms.

March 4, 1943

Dear Mom, Dad, and Pooz,

I am in Ohio at the University of Cincinnati. We're going to have courses in math, physics, geography, and current history. We took tests that will determine how long each of us will be here, ranging from one to five months. If our tests show we are proficient in any of the required courses we will be allowed to take a regular university elective. Whatever we take will get full university credit that we can apply towards a degree program later.

Despite being on campus, mixed in with the regular students, we are told to remember that we are soldiers, and regular army discipline prevails. That means we start at 5:15 A.M. and work until 9 P.M.

If the food continues like the first few meals, we are in real luck. We're having all the things you find hard to get at home — steaks, plenty of butter, and all the milk we want.

They have set up the post the same way they do at advanced cadet school. We have cadet officers and strict discipline. I have been appointed a cadet second lieutenant, based on my ROTC training.

It's a lot of responsibility as there are only ten officers in the 250 men contingent, and I have a platoon with fifty-seven of them. With the administrative duties on top of the school work, I will be plenty busy.

March 6, 1943

We started the day with a few lectures from some of the college profs and an hour of drill. We really looked good, and the regular officer in charge complimented me on the fine way I handle my men.

I hope things will settle in, so that in about three weeks you can come here for a visit. Be sure to bring sis, I really miss her. Now that you know my address you can tell others and maybe someone will send cookies and other goodies to this poor soldier.

March 13, 1943

We're really into it now. When we step outside the door, we have to start running — run to all formations, run to class, run back to the dorm. In addition to class work and study, each day includes an hour of drill and an hour of physical training. They're throwing the academic work at us so fast, it's almost impossible to grasp it all. As a cadet officer I can have lights on until 11 P.M., but that doesn't allow me enough sleep. Still, it's all very interesting and I like the routine a lot, although I'd sure like some time off for recreation.

The one new thing I don't like: They started a punishment routine called "gigs." If you do anything wrong at all, you get a demerit, or gig. Then, you have to work off ten demerits by walking a tour (back and forth on a measured path at 120 steps per minute, for an hour). The real bad part is that the cadet officers are responsible for giving gigs for misbehavior. If we fail to give gigs as required, we get gigged ourselves and have to do the tours. It is making us outcasts from the group. I guess we'll have to form an officer's club, so we can console each other.

Just as we will be in cadet school, we are addressed here as mister. Our rank is called aviation student, but we're still really privates with private's pay. As it stands now, I'll be through here in May, so I am already starting to think about advanced cadet work.

Don't worry about my smoking, Dad. I only smoke about four or five cigarettes a day, and I can quit any time. I know that it's harmful, but the small amount I am smoking should be OK.

With all the deductions from my pay, I only get 30 bucks for two months, so the 20 bucks you sent me was very welcome, indeed. Thanks a lot.

It was a beautiful spring day, the students were all sitting around on the grass sunning themselves, and it reminded me of my college days at Illinois. But, we can't join in — we're soldiers.

I had a sore throat, so I stopped by the medical officer after class. He gave me some sulfathiazole that knocked it right out. In our field packets, we have sulfanilamide powder to sprinkle on wounds and sulfa tablets to swallow. We hear great stories about sulfa's ability to eliminate infection.

March 26, 1943

Something not too pleasant happened yesterday. One of the cadets in my outfit made a few nasty cracks about my religion, and I had to cut him down a bit. I was very angry and I did a real job on him. Unfortunately, fighting in the ranks is a no-no, and, particularly, for a cadet officer to hit someone is not looked on kindly. Ordinarily, I could be court-marshaled, but a board of officers decided to just bust me down to the ranks (no more cadet officer) and confine me to quarters for a week. It's a tough thing to take, but I've still got my self-respect, and that helps a lot. It won't go on my service record, so it may not turn out to be any big deal. I can still be an officer again in pre-flight school. The regular officers privately say I did the right thing.

Otherwise things have been pretty good. My schoolwork goes well, and spring is in the air.

April 2, 1943

You asked me for details of how I got into that fight. Well, I have been having a slight sinus problem, so I was over at the dispensary getting a treatment. They put these sticks in my nose with some kind of medication, and I needed to sit there for awhile. This jerk was sitting next to me getting the same treatment and he starts talking about Nate Levine and how he was a no good Jew.

I told him I was Jewish, too, and I thought he should quit such remarks. Then, he said he never liked me and now he knows why. He kept up an anti-Semitic tirade that really pissed me off, so I told him to knock it off and shut up. He kept it up, so I took the medication out of my nose and went outside.

When he came out, I gave him a chance to put his books down, and then I let him have it with both barrels. He made a feeble attempt to fight back, but he was in pretty bad shape. A doctor came running out and caught him on the way down. They patched him up and, I was told, the doctor gave him a lecture about speak no evil.

Since he's forty pounds heavier than I am, I feel OK about what I did. I could have turned him in and kept my rank, but I'd rather hold my head up and take the consequences. Most of the guys are on my side. They all agree that there's no place for such things in the service.

Journal Entry

April 6, 1943 – The letters home keep me feeling in contact with the family and are a way of telling about my experiences, but there are many things going on that I need to get out of my head and on to paper. I've thought about a journal as a way to do this. This seems like a good time to start, because the events of the past few days have me pretty rattled.

*I never considered the possibilities — I just slugged the jerk.
Before the army nothing would have happened, except I might
have kicked him on the way down. Knowing the consequences
and given a second chance, would I do anything differently?*

*The army teaches me how to main and kill, then punishes me
for doing what is instinctively honorable. What is to be learned
from all this?*

April 10, 1943

I have been in solitary confinement for my punishment. I can't
go out of my room except for class and meals, and no one is
allowed in. It's really not too bad. I'm getting all my schoolwork
in good shape and my equipment is beautifully shined.

Just got back from chow. We had some steaks, about an inch
thick, with onions, french-fried potatoes, peas, soup, and ice
cream. Not bad for soldiers.

The men who were off the base this weekend rented cars.
They get five hours and seventy-five miles for six bucks at Hertz.
A couple of the guys will go in with me to do that next weekend.

The gym work is knocking me out. They're trying to make us
into some kind of supermen. We get some funny exercises, many
for coordination. There's some for neck and stomach, too, so that
we can stand the pressure on pull-outs from steep dives. The
neck exercises also help with the nervous fatigue that comes
from long flights.

They really mean for us to be tough guys. They have an obsta-
cle course in the drill field that's a lulu. There's a ten-foot wall to
climb, a ditch jump, rope swing, hurdles, and a few more tortures
for the body. They say it will be worthwhile in the end, although
sometimes I feel as if the end has arrived. Still, I weigh in at 138
pounds, a lot more than when I enlisted.

Dad, your letter read like you may come down this weekend. Not that I want to discourage you, but we're having a dance at the University in honor of the cadets, and I have a date with a cute little blonde. It would seem a shame to deny the lady the honor of my presence. But, don't let that discourage you — come right ahead! (You wouldn't do that, would you?) I hope I haven't hurt your feelings, but maybe you could wait until the next weekend and bring Mom and Pooz with you.

I'm glad to hear your business is good. Keep it up, I'll probably need money again before long.

April 15, 1943

Aside from being thoroughly pooped out, I'm feeling OK. They're really pouring the physical education on us now. The academic routine requires plenty of attention, too, but the only thing bothering me is physics. I have a buddy, a peach of a guy from the University of Michigan, who is a whiz at physics, and he's helping me.

We are going to have some flight training in small private planes that is due to begin in a week or so. We get ten hours of flying time before we move on.

I'm writing this from our Air Regulations class. It's pretty boring as usual. You'd really laugh if you could see this class. It's our first one of the day and, yet, about fifteen men are sound asleep. That happens in every class. We can't get too much out of these courses because we're all so exhausted. I often go to sleep myself. But, the subjects are really fascinating — like yesterday we had an hour and a half on the sex life of the mosquito, which was supposed to enlighten us on military sanitation.

It's been terribly cold for the past two days. It snowed like heck and we are all wearing heavy overcoats. Some spring! It looks like my flying time will be postponed because of the weather.

As I write this, Major Jones is discussing the relative merits of silk and nylon parachutes. He just finished telling us about his good friend who packed a parachute that forgot to open. So, we must always carry an auxiliary chute when we jump intentionally. Who does anything crazy like that anyhow? The only time I'll hit the silk is when one of those planes falls apart under me.

I need a number of things that I am going to buy when I get a pass, so I may go broke. I have some pay coming in about two weeks. Sorry I haven't been writing as I'd like to, but this is war!

April 27, 1943

Today was my big day. I got into the little Aeronca plane and off we went. I'm flying at a small local airport, but it has a control tower. We have a dual radio, and the operator in the tower gives the OK to take off. So, it's into the wild blue. The earth drops away and we climb to 2,000 feet. "Fly it," says the instructor.

Since I know all about airplanes from my previous ten minutes of ground instruction, I do what he says. It was fun all right. We did banks and turns and climbs — but, when it came to gliding, that didn't agree with my stomach, so I put my head out of the window and gave back my noodle soup. Although the day was clear, it was very bumpy. I wasn't afraid at all — it was just the bouncing around that got me sick. Tomorrow, I try again. It certainly is a wonderful feeling to look down and see all those insignificant things on the ground.

While I was at the airport they flew in a brand new B-17F Flying Fortress. I went and gave her the once over. Boy, is that a ship. I don't see how it's possible to shoot her down. She was fitted out with special bomb racks for block-busters, a total of fourteen machine guns, including ammunition. She had a crew of eight. It was really exciting to see such a huge plane roll in.

I fly afternoons now and have gym and drill in the morning. My only academic class is navigation, three times a week. So, I'm a veteran of forty-five minutes in the air. If I live through the next forty-five, I'll write again soon.

There is a possibility that we may get shipped out on short notice, so if you don't hear from me for awhile, you'll know what's happened. I'll try to call if possible.

Chapter Four

Getting Classified

Unlike other conflicts, such as Vietnam, Korea, or The Gulf War, World War II was a "declared war." Such a declaration committed all of the resources of the nation to the one goal of winning the war — everyone and everything was involved.

Early in 1943, with millions of men in the armed forces already, the Selective Service (draft board) announced that 4 million more men between the ages of 18 and 28 would be called up. With this many men in service, everyone had a family member, neighbor, or friend who had answered the call to arms, perhaps never to return.

The pain of separation and the longing for contact was expressed in the music of the time. The titles suggested the content: *I'll Never Smile Again, Tonight We Love, Sentimental Journey, My Reverie,* and *Heartaches* were among the hits. Four things were common to all tunes that made it to the top of the charts: the lyrics tugged at your heart, the music was a slow fox trot that made for easy dancing while holding your partner tight, a big band played it, and a big name singer did the vocal. The big band music of leaders Benny Goodman, Tommy Dorsey, Duke Ellington, Glenn Miller, and others has proved to be timeless and is still enjoyed today.

Top vocalists of the time — Frank Sinatra, Helen O'Connell, Helen Forrest, Peggy Lee, Bob Eberly, Dick Haymes — had voices that suggested snuggled-up-close love.

There were also war related songs, which were cried to by wives and sweethearts at home and by soldiers on bases around the globe. The Andrew Sisters sang, "Don't sit under the apple tree with anyone else but me, 'til I come marching home." Everyone sang the British WWI favorite, "There'll be bluebirds over the white cliffs of Dover, some day when the world is free." For the airmen and their loved ones the top stars sang, "Though there's one motor gone, we can still carry on — coming in on a wing and a prayer."

One of those who did not make it home was Capt. Glenn Miller. While serving his country on a tour entertaining our troops, the small plane he was flying in disappeared.

ARMY AIR FORCES CLASSIFICATION CENTER
SAN ANTONIO AVIATION CADET CENTER
SAN ANTONIO, TEXAS

May 15, 1943

Dear Mom and Dad,

I am sending this from the Army Air Force
Classification Center here at San Antonio,
Texas, where I arrived today. I am with the
rest of the future Army Air Crews.

I've been assigned to Squadron 106 where I
expect to remain until I am ready to enter a
Preflight School. During this time I will have
my physical examinations and tests which will
determine whether I become a Bombardier, Navigator or Pilot. If I am classified as one of
these, I will then be appointed an Aviation
Cadet and will receive free a $10,000 National
Service Life Insurance Policy. After being
classified and transferred to Preflight School
I will commence my actual preflight training,
which will last for about nine weeks.

You will, no doubt, think it strange receiving this type of form letter from me instead of
a personal one, but here is why: Our Commanding
Officer knows that during the process of getting settled during the next few days some of
us will be apt to forget to write the folks at
home. This is my way of letting you know where
I am and that I am well.

I know I'll have more interesting things to
tell you when I write a real letter. In the
meantime please let me hear from you.

May 16, 1943

Dear Mom and Dad,

I fell out laughing when they made me send the form letter to you yesterday. Can you imagine all those parents getting letters telling them that their sons now have a free life insurance policy. Isn't that reassuring? Hooray for the caring attitude of the commanding officer.

The classification exams start tomorrow, mental first. If I have to stay in this place very long, you'll get a form letter telling you I deserted. It's like Miami Beach, but with none of the living comforts. There are about 100 of us to a barracks, with six toilets and six washbowls. The food is scraped up from a dung heap, I believe. It's God-awful. No milk, just GI coffee or water. There is no talking allowed at meals. Doesn't it seem great? What a change from good old Cincinnati. I just want to finish classification and get out of here.

May 20, 1943

I'm over the crabbiness of the first few days. We're getting a sample here of what we'll be having in Preflight. The reason the food is so lousy is because we're on field rations. They're trying to break us of the luxury habits we developed at Cincinnati. All our personal effects are locked in a baggage room and we can only get to them on Wednesday and Saturday nights.

It's hotter than blue-blazes as the sun beats down unmercifully. And, it isn't even summer. The heat makes my beard grow fast, so now I have to shave every day.

We were just told that we can't sit on our beds, and since there is only one chair to four men, it should make for interesting experiences. I got another uniform at the PX last night — $3 for a shirt and $3.05 for pants. That's one place we get a break. I have heard all the stories about the rigors of Preflight. If true, and if I make it, the Nazis or Japs will never hurt me.

May 26, 1943

Still waiting for the classification tests. There is never a plausible explanation for the way the Army works. They keep us busy picking weeds. I had the fine job pitching the weeds onto a truck, then riding along to the dump. At least it was a nice ride to Kelley Field. I can take whatever they throw at me. I don't want to flunk out, as so many do.

The original deal for graduating cadets was that they were commissioned second lieutenants. Now they tell us that most graduates will have the rank of flight officer, with only a few exceptional ones getting commissions. Flight officer is a new rank that is the equivalent of warrant officer (j.g.) in the ground forces. This is an enlisted rank rather than an officer one, but everything else, pay and privileges, remains the same.

They eliminated the fancy cadet uniforms, too. We wear a cadet patch on our GI uniforms, a distinguishing pair of wings on one collar and a U.S. on the other, and a formal service hat with the big propeller on the front.

May 29, 1943

They said it doesn't rain this time of year in Texas. I don't know what they call that stuff that keeps falling from the sky, but it feels suspiciously like water, and there's a lot of it.

The stuff that fell from the sky cooled things off a bit and I got my first really good night's sleep. We had an orientation lecture today. The bombardier course is increased to twenty-seven weeks from twenty-one. The additional six weeks is dead-reckoning navigation. The additional schooling creates a combination bombardier/navigator rating for crews of the B-25 and B-26 medium bombers and the newer attack bombers. That's what I want, so I will put in for it and try my best to qualify for the program. Experiences from the various theaters of operation have demanded better trained, non-pilot officers, so the requirements are more rigid.

Again, they tell us the tests begin shortly, with the first of the series being a seven-hour mental on just about everything. Then comes a psychomotor test for reflexes and coordination. Finally a "64" physical, which is the toughest in the armed forces. Here's hoping I make out OK.

I got a peek at my flight log from Cincinnati. I got a grade of 84 percent in my final check with a notation that my flying is good, but to watch me because I might get cocky. What, me?

I had a short period of free time this afternoon, so I took a walk to the Service Men's Club. It's really a nifty place, with a huge dance floor, a nice library, and a restaurant. If I had someone to dance with, it would be swell, but the only women around here are a bunch of WAAC truck drivers.

We were told there will be absolutely no furloughs until after training is completed. There's not much to be said about that.

June 2, 1943

I just got back from the first part of my "64" physical. One session was with the psychiatrist. He asked me about my home life, school, and ambitions. He also asked about the writing I have done, if you approved of my being in the Air Corps, and if I wanted to stay in the army (NO!). At the end, he asked me what I wanted to be in the Air Force. "Bombardier," says I, and he asked me why. I said, "So I can kill more people faster." He

said, "Why do you want to go around killing people?" I
answered, "Mainly, so I can go home." He laughed and said,
"You're alright. Scram!" I guess I'm normal.

June 5, 1943

Still waiting for news of my classification. I got five gigs for
leaving my watch on my bed and four for talking in ranks. One
more and I walk a tour, so I gotta be good. Last night, I went
with one of the guys to the post theater and saw *Ox Bow Incident*
with Henry Fonda. Good stuff. It's funny how much pleasure
one can get from simple things when they are denied for so long.
I would give a lot just to be able to do as I please for a few days.
But, as the boys say, "That's life, Ace."

Yesterday, I drew a shit detail. I had to go over two square
miles of roads picking up everything that doesn't grow (those
were the instructions). There were three of us, and you would
have laughed like crazy if you could have seen us. I specialized in
chewing gum wrappers, Milt collected match boxes, and Rudy
took the rest. We would argue over whose turn it was to pick up
something and then just stand and laugh. We did that all day.
Then the trail led right into the PX, and suddenly we found ourselves with milk shakes in our hands. We couldn't figure out how
they got there. It beats last night when we had a GI party, doing
the whole barracks on hands and knees with scrub brushes.

There is a post newspaper that is quite good. The guy who
draws the syndicated cartoon *Terry and the Pirates* is a cadet and
he's on it. Also a few correspondents and reporters from the *New
York Times*, the *Chicago Sun*, and others. I asked for a job writing
features and editorials. It would be a nice way to kill some time
while I am waiting to ship out of this joint.

They are really very selective here. Many don't make it,
including a lot of my pals who are flunking out, and it makes me
sad. Nineteen men have been classified, sixteen as pilots and

three for ground duty only. They want thirty-five pilots to one bombardier, so there is a lot of pressure to go for pilot. If I qualify, they can talk their heads off — I'll stick for bombardier. A lot of wash-outs are for poor eyesight, many more from the psychiatrist. I am going to say good-bye to many friends, I fear, but I hope I'm not the one heading for the door.

The rest of the testing was X-rays, blood tests, and poking around. Tomorrow, I get eye tests, heart, and others. If I pass, I will be classified in about a week.

Journal Entry

June 10, 1943 – I keep pushing on the bombardier job, and asking myself why not navigator or even pilot? There's something I can't quite put my finger on that has me so insistent. The job of the others in the plane is to get the bomb load to the target, but the final responsibility for hitting the target is the bombardier's. I guess I want to be the one to pull the trigger.

June 19, 1943

I got a load of letters today. Boy, I'd rather get those letters than eat. The reason I haven't written to everyone is because there's nothing very interesting to tell. Nothing ever happens to me.

I thought I joined the Air Corps, but this must be the infantry. Today, I was digging trenches. They're setting up a regular battlefield out here, machine gun emplacements, fox holes, and all. They're going to teach the boys infantry tactics and maneuvers, because of the lessons they learned in Africa. Sometimes the enemy lines advanced so fast, American fliers had to get down in foxholes with rifles and fight. Maybe we ought to go to cooks and bakers school, in case they drop a bomb on the mess hall.

A load of bombardiers shipped out yesterday. They had been here two months. Maybe there's hope for me. If I get an open post, I will need some money, so how about sending me a fiver. I need some gym shoes, so I have to ask the CO for a ration stamp.

We had a swell meal yesterday, which makes me unhappy. Now I have nothing to bitch about.

June 28, 1943

Thanks for the *Gordo* cartoon. I really enjoy that comic strip. He's a funny character. It's 110 degrees today — I just love Texas. I get a pass to San Antonio tomorrow, because I am a good soldier. I think I'll go swimming in the municipal pool.

July 3, 1943

I was to get another pass to town. I had a date with a nice girl I met last time, but the army done me wrong. It seems that due to a torn sheet, issued me by supply, I was unable to make my bed yesterday. Lt. Giles, being a very unfeeling man, and not caring to hear about my problems with supply, gave me three tours for punishment. I wrote a letter to the squadron commander explaining the situation so, of course, he added three more tours, for a total of six, and revoked my pass. So, while I am on the ramp walking in the sun with a rifle, my friend Milt will be in town with my date. I hope, for Lt. Giles' sake, I never get to fly on his tail. Second Louies like him are expendable.

July 8, 1943

Oh, happy day! I am on shipment. Tomorrow, we finish details and pack up. In less than two days, yours truly will have achieved that pinnacle of success, an aviation cadet. I'll probably go to Ellington Field in Houston and I expect I will be there before Saturday. If there is a lapse in my letters, you'll know why.

In yesterday's letter you asked how I was fixed for money, and I was fixed with about twenty cents, so thanks for the dough you sent today.

In the next place we get aircraft recognition, naval recognition, morse code, aircraft and bombsight maintenance, and a number of other things in our nine week preflight. Then, gunnery school. Sounds exciting, doesn't it? Hold your mail for the next address.

Chapter Five

Ground Gremlin Training

As 1943 progressed, there were so many men in the armed services that the roles and what was expected of women underwent substantial change. The urgent need to increase production of armaments and war materials of all kinds brought more than six million American women into the workplace — many taking over manufacturing jobs that, formerly, were held only by men. In Great Britain, 40 percent of all production workers were women. In some aircraft manufacturing plants, they comprised 90 percent of the workforce.

Later, at the height of the manpower shortage, womanpower became so important there was even discussion in Congress about making it compulsory for all women between 18 and 50 to aid the war effort by holding down a critical job or joining one of the services. Rosie the Riveter became the poster girl of the war effort, but the women GIs carried into war in their dreams and footlockers were the pin-up girls of Alberto Vargas and Hollywood.

With the exception of nurses who served with distinction in combat theaters around the world, women were considered too fragile for the regular armed services. Despite this general perception, many did serve valiantly, often under dangerous conditions. There were 99,000 women in the Women's Army Corps (WAC) who drove trucks, performed clerical duties, and took over a variety of tasks that relieved men for the front lines. The women of the Navy, WAVEs, operated air traffic control centers, naval air navigation, and communications centers. The 1,000 Women's Airforce Service Pilots, WASPs, a civilian group under contract to the army, ferried new bombers and fighters and served as test pilots. Women in the Red Cross, serving right alongside the soldiers, provided social and medical services that were lauded by the men everywhere.

What was considered acceptable as feminine — roles, behavior, and dress — was being redefined. New jobs mandated a new look. Coveralls replaced dresses and long hair and nail polish were banned in some plants because of hazards to sensitive machinery. Many women became temporary, or permanent, single parents and sole breadwinners at home, while others became camp followers, setting up makeshift homes wherever their soldier husbands were stationed.

Although World War II held the promise of a continuation of the women's equality movement, the end of the war brought the men back to their old jobs and the return of many women to their traditional roles.

July 11, 1943

Dear Mom, Dad, and Pooz,

I am finally here. This is going to be really tough. You do everything perfect, or out you go. There is a Bombardier Wing, a Navigation Wing, and a large Twin-motor Advanced Flying School. It is funny to have planes landing on a runway practically outside the door of the barracks.

We are told we will have open post every weekend, if we qualify. However, they are very strict and there are cadet officers everywhere to enforce the rules.

They keep us hopping all the time. We run to formations, run to class, run, run, run. When taps plays, I just sink into the bunk exhausted. Classes are swell though. I got off to a good start with 100 percent on a map test. We have learned ten letters in code class already. A lot of guys quit and go back to the GI Army, because of the discipline and high performance standards, but I mean to stick it out no matter what.

To be a cadet is really something. The food is outstanding, a variety to choose from and plenty of it. We eat on tablecloths with cloth napkins and are served by enlisted men. There is a list of regulations a mile long, which includes no fraternizing with the ladies in the Women's Army Corps. Since we can't go to the enlisted men's club, we have one of our own. Yes, it's tough, but it's also pretty snazzy.

July 16, 1943

Dad, you wrote that it is hot in Chicago. You don't know what hot is. It's 105 degrees here in the shade, and there ain't none. Just for fun they drilled us today in gas masks. Mad dogs, Englishmen, and aviation cadets go out in the noonday sun. I may live through it, but with difficulty. I wonder how much Mexico paid us to take Texas.

Forget the idea of a furlough. They gave a cadet one in 1937, but they don't remember who he was. I'll be home when Hirohito and Adolph say "enough."

Our commandant of cadets is Roscoe Ates. Remember him from the movies? He's a captain and a decent old fart. Tough though — but who isn't around here? One guy cheated on a math exam and they gave him 25 hours of tours with a rifle in the sun. Violations of the cadet honor code get no mercy.

We have to wear these cadet hats all the time, even into town. The issue one I have doesn't fit too well or look good on me. A lot of the fellows have bought hats in town at a place where they make them to fit, but they cost $12.50. What do you think I should do?

July 17, 1943

My first week is completed and I must say that I am proud to be a cadet. These fellows are terrific. When they call us future officers they aren't kidding. The Corps itself is the nuts, the tactical officers are the best, the cadet officers are super, and each individual is the cream of the crop.

We just got back from Saturday parade. It was just like you see in the movies. We marched down the runway onto the big field. B-24 Liberator bombers were on both sides of us, their motors roaring. Squadrons of B-25s flew overhead in the sky — the real

McCoy. The drum and bugle corps is great and, in all, it was the most thrilling and beautiful thing I've been party to yet.

We're getting ready to go to town. They say Houston is a real soldier's place with lots of dances.

July 19, 1943

I got my open post pass and went into town. It's a really swell place, better than Cincy [Cincinnati]. A cadet is really something here. The GI soldiers don't stand a chance with the women. Army trucks took us half of the sixteen miles into town and then we got buses.

I spent until 9 P.M. just looking around the town, drinking sodas and what not with the guys. Then I left them and went to the USO. A lady in charge called a girl and made a date for me. I went out to her house, and we sat around and talked and drank coke and stuff. She was quite nice.

I had to go back to camp at night, but I got off again all day Sunday from 9 A.M. until midnight. I went into town and to another dance. Met a nice girl from U. of Texas. She was going swimming with her girlfriend and a date, so I declared myself in. The girlfriend lives in a mansion, the likes of which I have never seen before. Her parents are both doctors (very famous, I gather) and they have three cars — a Buick, a Chrysler, and a Cadillac — and three "C" gas ration cards, no less. Boy, oh boy!

So, with her family we piled into the Cadillac and went to their country club. The place was simply beautiful. I was swimming all afternoon. It was an afternoon worth remembering. Then we came back, dropped off the family, and took the dirty old Buick. The four of us went into town for supper. After that, we went to a juke joint out on the road and danced.

Now, this girl I was with was very cute and a real sweet kid, but the girlfriend was the nicest number I have laid eyes on in quite some time. So, during the afternoon I worked on her old lady and, sure enough, I'm invited up for dinner next Saturday. Of course, that creates a problem, because I'll probably have to take the beautiful young lady out after dinner and I just don't know what car to use. I think I'll take the Chrysler, it's nice.

So, I had the most wonderful weekend in a long, long time. I only got about nine hours sleep altogether and my ass is dragging, but it was worth it. I can get along fine with a weekend like that tucked under my belt.

Today, I am barracks guard. I just sit at this stupid desk and watch to see that nothing gets swiped. Tough detail. It's so hot the sweat is rolling off me and I'm trying to stay awake.

July 21, 1943

I have just finished with the toughest day I can remember. After classes we had physical training, then a full dress parade, then retreat formation, then this evening I had a two hour detail cleaning up the area around the barracks. I'm almost too tired to sleep. That happens here.

The good news — my test average for the first ten days is 100 percent! I have been put in as an applicant for West Point, although I'm not sure I'd like to go. I'm the only one in my squadron who can qualify and expresses any interest. They're sending 60 men from the 8th Corps area, which includes two million men. Some odds, huh?

I saw some of my friends from Cincinnati who came in with the new bunch. Fifteen washed out along the way.

Saturday night was just terrific. I went to Evelyn's (yes, she's the one from last week with all the cars) house for dinner. We ate outside on their porch, which is really a hot weather dining room. I had a swell meal and for dessert guess what? Yep! Watermelon — two big slices. After dinner, they told us to take the car, so off we went in the Buick to an amusement park called Playland. Then we went to a movie and saw *Hello Frisco, Hello!* It was a wonderful show. Then to a drive-in for hamburgers and milk shakes. It was just like old times at school. It seems like so long since I've been out like that.

I'm quite a big hit in Houston, in part because I am the youngest cadet they have ever seen. Evelyn's folks told me to come back anytime I am in town. All I have to do is call and say I'm coming. Isn't that nice?

I came back to the base from town plenty early. They gave one of the guys 35 hours of tours in the hot sun with a rifle for coming in ten minutes late, so I take no chances. The whole evening was a grand success. I enjoyed myself immensely. Evelyn will be out of town next weekend, but I am invited to her girlfriend's house for dinner, then we are going out. Her name is Bobette. She's very sweet, too.

I walked guard duty and, of course, it rained, I got soaked and my piece (that's a rifle, civilians) got soaked, too, so I had to stay up until 1 A.M. cleaning it. That didn't leave much time for sleep, but I still banged out a good grade in my maps and charts course.

They've now started physics on us, and that's a real beauty. It's a three week course. In it, we cover the entire background for everything we need to know in bombardiering. It goes so fast; if you drop your pencil, it's the equivalent of missing a year of college algebra.

We're also learning judo. That's a real honey; I'm going to be black and blue all over. They teach us all the dirty ways to maim and kill a man. Isn't that a nice thing for a kid like me to know?

They found out I used to play the drums, so I got roped into the cadet drum and bugle corps. I just have to play in parades and it's lots easier than marching with the squadron. I also get out two hours earlier on Saturday and I don't have to clean latrines with the rest of the guys. It's a lot of fun (the band, not the latrines).

July 26, 1943

I'm so tired tonight that it's just pitiful. On top of classes, we had two hours of physical training climbing over walls, an hour of drill, another parade, and now we're coming up on an evening formation for some idiocy like picking up garbage. I'm so pooped sometimes, I'd like to just quit. But no, I'll stick it out and die for my country, maybe right here. If they keep this up, none of us will live to go overseas. I guess I'll just grin and bear it. At least I have no gigs. I'm praying I can stay off that tour ramp.

I'm thinking of going to Galveston Sunday. It's right on the Gulf Coast with a beach. I understand the swimming is swell. I'll see if my date would like to go. All you get is a short letter today.

July 27, 1943

By the time you get this, you will have some idea of what we have been through here. I have read about hurricanes, but this is the first time I have been in the middle of one. Aside from a few minor bruises, a sprained wrist, and being exhausted, I am all right, but there are a lot of cadets who are not so fortunate. All day long, through the worst part of the gale, they had us out on the airstrip trying to hold down several hundred twin-motor training planes. There were long ropes attached to the engines, the wings, and the tails, and on each rope were about ten cadets hanging on for dear life. At times, we were in three feet of water. We were only partially successful, as some planes flipped over with many men injured and a few killed. It was one of the worst storms ever in this area, with winds hitting 140 miles per hour.

I imagine it will be some time before our training continues as the facility will have to be largely rebuilt. We have heard that Houston is a real mess, with telephone and power lines down. This was the most terrifying event of my life. It's one thing to fight an enemy country, and quite another to witness the destruction that nature can create.

It's now 24 hours since the storm subsided. The work of rehabilitation will soon begin. Part of the roof is gone from the barracks and most of my clothing and equipment is soaked, yet our
squadron fared better than most. Our officers were superb and
everyone acquitted himself gallantly.

There's one other thing I want to tell you. Although things
yesterday were the toughest I've ever encountered — some fellows passed out and couldn't take it and others got sick — I
stuck right in there and did my best. I kind of wondered if, when
the time came for me to meet a real tough problem, I could take
it and come back for more. Well, I'm pretty proud of myself. I'd
pit my ability against any Jap or German every time and never
have the slightest doubt about who would be the best man.
Good little men are often lots better than good big men. Ask my
buddies — they know!

July 29, 1943

We have had 20 inches of rain from the hurricane and everything is under water. The damage reported in the local papers
must be for enemy consumption, because it is far worse than
they say. You just can't imagine the material and personnel losses.
We still have no lights and no water, except what is boiled for us
at chow. But, mother nature is not allowed to interfere with pur-
suance of the war, so this morning we were back in classes, looking pretty funny with three day beards, all descriptions of uniforms, and smelling like goats.

Despite it all, I look forward to becoming a middle class
cadet in a few days, when some of the load will lighten. I added
a small arms course in place of drill. That will liven things up. I
have some pictures to send you, but I'm about out of postage.
It's difficult to get to the post office, so please send me some
three cent stamps.

July 30, 1943

I'm a baaaad boy. I accumulated a whole bunch of tours for really serious things like getting a drop of ink on the sign-up roster, and not having my chin tucked in, just so, while standing at attention during an inspection. So today, I was out on the ramp again with a rifle, marching up and down in the hot sun. They gave me an hour off for chow, then back out again. Tomorrow, I have one more to do, then I may get off to go into town and have a date with Bobby.

I had more aircraft identification yesterday. We learn about the plane, it's features and firepower, and we study the silhouette on the screen. Then they flash the silhouette on the screen for one second, then repeat it for a shorter time. Eventually, we have to identify the plane at 100th of a second. They say if you can't do it, you are potentially as dangerous as an enemy gunner. All it takes is one mistake to shoot down one of your own planes or assume an enemy plane is one of your own and get shot down yourself.

I'll be going into the pressure chamber, soon, where they will take us to 40,000 feet. They say that may be the new bombing level, and unless we learn how to handle ourselves, we can get into big trouble.

August 2, 1943

I walked off my last tour and went into town, blisters and all. Bobette and I went to a show, then to the Chicken Shack for dinner. They serve fried chicken with no forks or anything. Good, and great fun. So I got back to the base about midnight and today I was tired again, but it was worth it.

I passed my test on Morse Code and I started learning about the Thompson sub-machine gun. I have to be able to field strip it, clean it, and practice shoot with it on the range.

I haven't heard any more about being sent to West Point. One of the requirements was a score of 135 out of 150 in the General Classification Test I took at Miami. That's a lot, and I don't know if I made it. Even assuming I do get such an appointment, the next class is July '44. By that time, I'll (hopefully) be commissioned and flying overseas, and I would have to resign my commission to go to West Point. We'll see what happens.

I might have had a chance to become a cadet officer here, but the responsibility is terrific, and may be too much with the work load. As it is, I get the same privileges the cadet officers have for playing in the band. I get out early on Saturday and that's fine. I'll just continue as I am for awhile. I have my hands full, for sure.

I got the second of the ten bucks you sent. Thanks a lot. There's talk we are going to get overnight passes this weekend and, if so, I will put the money to good use. Imagine getting to sleep in a hotel with no bugler to awaken me in the morning.

Things are getting back to normal, with the electricity coming back on today. A lot of the guys got sick from the hurricane, but I am still OK.

August 9, 1943

We're expecting some Air Force Generals on the field, so everything is shined up. Last night, we had to scrub the barracks, when I should have been studying for an aircraft identification exam, so I flunked it. That's my first test with a grade below eighty. A few of the guys do OK with this course, but when they flash those planes on the screen, all I see is a blur. The guys who had an interest in planes before they came into the army really shine here. I never cared, so I don't have much to draw on.

The heat is terrific. I sweat off about two pounds per day, then put it back on by eating like a horse. If I ever get out of this state, I'll never come back. I'm about to head off for a parade in the hot sun, which should be a delightful experience.

Yesterday, I took a walk out on the ramp and had an opportunity to see a few of the ships first hand. A captain took me through a new B-17, my first time in one. I sat in the bombardier's nose for awhile. If I had stayed an hour, I couldn't have counted all the gadgets. It's inconceivable that they can teach us the complicated mechanisms of the Norden bombsight in the short amount of time for our training. The new version of the B-17 is armed with three machine guns in the nose. The navigator handles one and the bombardier the other two. They have already built up the tail firepower, so it's quite invulnerable to attack from the rear.

Now, the enemy aircraft are doing frontal attacks, so this new setup in the nose can put out 3,000 .50-caliber bullets a minute. I was in some of the new, more secret ships, which I cannot describe, but everyone knows about the B-17, now that *Life* magazine published all the details.

We have been restricted to the base, because of a scare about infantile paralysis in Houston. However, it's a real farce because there are civilian visitors all over the field, and the place looks like a church picnic. Of course, they can't go near the landing field, but it's stupid anyhow, having them here and keeping us out of town. I hear there's going to be an investigation of the whole matter. Maybe they'll bust Captain Ates, the old bastard.

August 16, 1943

A couple of my pals from Chicago are here in the Navigation Wing. They came over for a visit last night. It was good talking about home. A group of men who are ahead of us shipped out for gunnery school. I imagine that's where I'll go next. Some men from advanced training were here today and said the schooling is much tougher now, and longer, with navigation added. Almost 50 percent of the men wash out now because it's so tough. But, I'm not going to let anyone down. I'll make it all the way and come out with my officer appointment and wings, just as I planned.

If I could change just one thing in my life now, it would be the time for reveille — 5:15 A.M. is no time for a human being to get out of bed. I never imagined how much work one could be pushed to do in a single day. I am one pooped out soldier.

We did have one diversion — there was a USO show and it was swell, particularly after being stuck in this hole for two weeks without a pass. One more week and then freedom, I hope.

Now, everyone is flunking aircraft identification, so it's not only me. They'll have to make some adjustment in how they teach that course, or at least in their expectations.

Save the lineup for the baseball all-star game and send it to me, Dad, and let me know how it comes out. We don't have time to listen to the game on the radio.

August 20, 1943

I am an upperclassman now, and in two weeks I'll be through with my regular classes. I took my final exam in naval identification and came through with flying colors. That leaves physics (which I have down pretty well) and aircraft identification, which is still my nemesis.

I was out on the range this afternoon firing the .45-caliber automatic pistol. It is a terrific weapon, but what a kick it has. We shot at bulls-eyes and then moving silhouettes of men. In all, I fired 85 rounds. My ears are still ringing, but I qualified for a medal in pistol marksmanship. At first, I wasn't doing too well, but then I imagined the target was a Nazi and was surprised how many bullets I put through the heart.

I read about the bombing of Berlin by the RAF. We have just finished studying the planes they use. While they can't match the firepower, speed, or altitude of our Liberators and Fortresses, they carry much bigger loads. Our planes can't carry those four-ton block-busters they unload in their night missions.

Tomorrow, I go into the pressure chamber to take high altitude tests. We go to 15,000 feet without oxygen, to see what the effects are, then put on oxygen masks to go to 38,000 feet. The instructors watch to see how we react, so they can classify us for high altitude bombers or the new low altitude fighter-bombers. I prefer high altitude work, so I hope I'll react OK. Even the best enemy planes are sluggish at the higher altitudes, and the flack is less accurate. Flying over a target ten feet off the ground at 350 miles per hour doesn't appeal to me somehow.

August 22, 1943

Yesterday, we did the pressure chamber thing. They took us to 5,000 feet when a couple of the guys developed earaches, so they took us back down and let them out. Then, we all went to 18,000 feet without oxygen, to notice the effects of anoxia. We all turned a little blue and some took oxygen there. At 22,000 feet everyone except me took oxygen. They wanted someone to go on without it, to have the others notice the effects.

At 22,000 feet I could still match colors and seemed, at least to myself, normal. Then, I tried to write a few things. I remember writing "I am now at 29,000 feet," then I passed out. It seemed like I was only unconscious for a few seconds, but the fellows said I fell right down on the floor. They worked on me for about eight minutes. When I finally came to, I could hear the instructor's voice telling me to breathe deep. When I awakened I found he was shouting in my ear, even though his voice had sounded very far away. When I looked at my writing it was very funny, trailing off the page. That's what they wanted us to learn

about anoxia. While one feels perfectly normal, all sorts of
strange things are happening. The guys said I laughed like crazy
and thrashed my arms about. I remember only one negative
thing, and that was a slightly blurred vision.

There were no after-effects and, since that was the first time I
was "knocked out," it was quite interesting. Once I was on oxygen at 30,000 feet, I was just fine and noticed no difference from
my ordinary behavior. There were some men who had cramps
and earaches, but I seem to be able to handle the altitude with
oxygen OK. We were in there for an hour and a half, including
some time on new equipment used for bailing out. So, I am
approved for high altitude work.

While there are other possibilities, it looks like my next
assignment will be gunnery school. Some of the men skip this
and move on to bombardier school directly. On the one hand,
they need to replace crews that are either lost or have finished
tours of duty and, on the other, there seems to be a need for better, more complete training. I'll keep you posted.

August 28, 1943

They haven't lifted the ban yet, so we have another weekend
of restriction to the post. Thank goodness I graduate soon. This
afternoon I have three tours to walk. One I actually deserve, the
other two I got by mistake. But, if I go into the office to point
out the error, I could get 11 tours for arguing. It's not worth the
chance, so I'll put in my three hours in the sun. Here they give
you tours with a rifle. I heard that in advanced training you walk
tours with a back pack parachute. Our tactical officer is
absolutely inhuman. Yesterday, he had the entire squadron out in
the sun picking up butts and paper around the barracks. His
favorite expression is, "OK you men, pick them up. All I want to
see is asses and elbows."

I'd give anything to get out of here for awhile. I haven't laughed in so long I can't remember. I'd even love to hear your old jokes, Dad. But, there is no rest and no breaks for the weary. Boy, I am really tired. Maybe you could send me some vitamin B tablets, Mom. That might pep me up.

August 30, 1943

You seem to have forgotten that I am in Texas, for you put the stamps back to back, and they're all stuck together. I even have to keep my envelopes separated because the heat seals the glue in this humidity.

Since we're confined to the base, I spent the weekend practicing the art of bunk fatigue. Boy, did I sleep. I have passed all the major exams even, surprisingly, aircraft identification. So, pre-flight is now mostly under my belt. Shortly I'll be through and ready to move on — with one hitch.

I am having a reoccurrence of the skin rashes that I had at the other bases. They treat it and it goes away, then it comes back again. Now the flight surgeon is saying if they can't find a cure, they will have to wash me out of flying. They're proposing to hospitalize me for awhile to see if they can't find an answer. That's exactly what I don't need right now, but I can't see an option. I would sure hate to get booted out of the cadets after all I have been through. Do you have any helpful thoughts?

Journal Entry

September 1, 1943 – I am sweating the doctors out. I haven't written home or complained much, but having a rash on the skin under my arms is really painful. I have come through a lot in the past seven months and I sure want to go all the rest of the way. It's even more than duty and country — it's about what I need to prove, and who I want to be.

September 2, 1943

It's evening and I have been in the hospital all day. They took some blood tests this morning and have been giving me sulfadiazine regularly. If I wasn't here because I have a medical problem, this would be the life. I just lie around all day, except I can walk to chow, the toilet, and outside. The Red Cross came around and brought the newspaper and flowers. There are current magazines and a library.

This afternoon there was a traveling USO show here with Jack Teagarden's band and Mitzi Mayfair. There are also movies every afternoon for walking cases like me. There's a beautiful yard out back in which I can sunbathe or just hang out. What a life! This can't be the army. I could stay here for two weeks and not mind it at all. The rest will surely do me good, and they now feel they can cure me.

You should see my nurse! But, alas, she's a second lieutenant. If I try to make out with her, she'll probably gig me and get me lots of tours. There are also some nice WACs here, too. I think I'm going to like this ... no, I know it.

September 4, 1943

I'm so filled up with sulfa drugs, it's pitiful, but they are really doing the job because my skin is clearing up nicely. Since I am rested and getting better, I imagine I will be discharged in a couple of days and will be able to graduate with my class.

From here, I move on to advanced bombardment and gunnery. When that will be, I don't know, perhaps two or three weeks. But, this is the last of Ellington Field for me.

I have the medics to thank for saving my flying career. They say I probably won't have another episode. Thanks for the cookies, they help my morale and my stomach.

September 6, 1943

Out of the hospital and back to work feeling good. Yesterday, all the pilots were put on shipment, and we poor bombardiers had to do all the KP. A few of the guys got jobs as bosses (pushers, we call them). They didn't do any work, just told us what to do. I asked how I could get a deal like that. The result is I am now a KP boss until I leave. It is a real goof-off job. I work two days, then get open post the third day with a pass to town. I go to work at 8 A.M., while the others start at 4 A.M., and I don't have to meet any formations. I will be in charge of the trash disposal unit and all the men who work there. And, I can wear slacks and a tee shirt on the job, instead of a regular uniform. I'm happy for awhile.

I got 100 percent in my first aid course, which is pretty remarkable since I was only in one class. While we're waiting for shipment, they give us a course in the theory of bombardment. Bombardment needs a theory? What will these guys think of next? Imagine all the fabulous knowledge I will have to put to work in a career.

It will be sad to leave all the nice girls behind, but then, I leave so many of them. That's war, and the babes will have to put up with it.

The government is doing right by me now. I got 55 dollars in my last pay. So, I'm heading for town tonight to spend some.

September 12, 1943

We got the really big break — overnight passes and a graduation dance in town. There were no hotel rooms to be had, but Bobby's mother is friends with the owner of a real nice hotel, the William Penn. She got me a double room, so my buddy, Ed and I checked in. I took a shower and then called Bobby. We went out to dinner, then I took her home to get into her evening gown for the dance. The ball was really terrific, better than I ever expected. The whole room was fixed up with tables and candles and decorations. The orchestra was super, and all the most wonderful food and drinks were served to us free. There were professional entertainers for the floor show; even old Roscoe Ates did his number. Jack Dempsey was there, too, and talked to us. In all, it was a huge success. I met a bunch of the boys back at the hotel, and we sat and shot the bull until 3:30 A.M.

Sunday, I stayed in bed and read the papers until noon. In the afternoon Bobby and I went to a movie, then had dinner at her house. Her mom fixed fried chicken and it was swell. I took her a box of candy. It was a wonderful break.

September 24, 1943

I have a number of invitations for the Jewish holidays, one at Bobby's, one at Evelyn's, and the Rabbi asked me over, too, so I won't be lonely. They are saying all the Jewish men will get a three day pass for the holidays, and then we will take the guard duty and other post duties over Christmas. That's a really decent tradeoff.

Thanks for the ten bucks. I sort of outguessed myself on the money situation. Too much partying! I am really feeling well, and I have even gained a few pounds. The weather is cooler now — that's all I needed, to stop sweating and get some good food. There is persistent talk that they may turn this field into advanced training. It would be OK with me to stay here, as Houston is a good town and the field is well equipped. There are targets out in the gulf so all they need is some AT-11 aircraft, (these are the bombardier training planes). Whatever it may be or wherever it may be, I have no fears about going on. I know now, for a certainty, I have the background and ability to be a first rate bombardier. I also know that I can take the hard work and pressure better than most. Even though 25 percent of the men have washed out already, I am going all the way.

I was in an A-20 Douglas Havoc attack bomber on the field today. It's a beautiful ship. Although it mainly does low-level skip-bombing, I could be interested in working on one. The bombardier compartment is so small that only a guy like me could fit into it.

September 25, 1943

What a mess these last two days have been. They moved us to a new barracks that was formerly bachelor officer's quarters. In a room authorized for one man, we have three cadets squeezed in. Very homey! It has been raining and blowing since yesterday noon, and we have severe storm warnings again. They evacuated all the coastal camps and are preparing to abandon this one. It's predicted to be the worst storm of the year starting about noon tomorrow. This time they're a little smarter. All the planes flew off the field and everything else is tied down.

If I go to gunnery school, I'll make more money — $87 a month.

Chapter Six

Aerial Gunnery School

The surprise raid on Pearl Harbor left a dazed America wondering where and when the next attack might come. If the Japanese had the audacity and could bomb an American installation in the Pacific, might they not also go after the mainland? And, might not a German armada come steaming into New York Harbor and bombard America's largest city?

Such concerns led to a national dim-out — later, to black-outs in major coastal cities — intended to foil night raids. The upper half of auto headlights were covered, street lights turned off, and store lights dimmed. At home, shades were pulled down and blackout drapes installed. All of this was intended to make the cities less visible from the air.

Whether the dim-out would have succeeded in confusing enemy bombers was, thankfully, never tested, but it did transform the gaiety of coastal cities into caverns of darkness that matched the national mood.

The war produced little interference with most people's civil rights — the FBI was very successful in reducing sabotage by taking several genuine Axis agents into custody — but, the fears about enemy aliens became a national paranoia that engulfed Americans of Japanese descent. By executive order in March 1942, President Franklin D. Roosevelt established the War Relocation Authority which allowed the government to relocate persons, or classes of people, who supposedly represented a threat to national security.

There were 110,000 Japanese-Americans removed from their homes and businesses (primarily on the west coast) and taken to hastily constructed detention camps in California, Arizona, Washington, and Arkansas — there to remain until the end of the war. About 40,000 were aliens, called issei. Issei were ineligible for citizenship due to earlier legislation. But 70,000 nisei were American-born and therefore United States citizens.

From today's perspective, this was an intolerable violation of human rights. It takes a stretch of the imagination to understand this other America involved in a total war — it was a very fearful citizenry that allowed such things to happen to fellow Americans.

Another pervasive fear gripped America: No one ever wanted to receive a telegram. Families learned of the death or injury of their loved ones serving in the military in telegrams that began, "The War Department regrets to inform you …."

LAREDO ARMY AIR FIELD
LAREDO, TEXAS

September 29, 1943

Dear Mom, Dad, and Pooz,

The order sending me here to Laredo, Texas, for gunnery
school was no surprise. They marched us to the Cadet Club in
the Gunter Hotel, Houston, where they had set up the most
wonderful goodbye breakfast meal you can imagine, then to the
train, for an arrival in Laredo in the early afternoon.

My course here is six weeks long and, from all indications,
very tough. They arbitrarily wash out the lower five percent of
the class. They do that, in varying percentages in each location,
with the idea they will finally graduate only the best. The day
here starts with school at 7 A.M. and continues to 5 P.M., six days
a week. On two of the days, there are also evening classes. There
is no officer-type training, it's strictly technical. We are working
right alongside the enlisted men who will be the primary gunners
on the aircraft. There are no parades, no drill, no shined shoes or
brass — we can wear just about any uniform we please to class.

This is a GI field, with the cadets only incidental. The barracks are small and dirty, with outside latrines. The field is
rugged as hell, with clay streets. The food stinks, and there are
no more tablecloths and napkins. We have a bunch of corporals

bossing us around, which is funny because technically we out-
rank them by three grades. Laredo is a town of about 35,000 —
mostly Mexican-Americans because we are so close to the border. I'm really in the army now!

September 30, 1943

The unbelievable has happened: A few of the Jewish boys
went to the commanding officer and asked for passes to go to
services for the high holidays, and he wrote out overnight passes
for all the Jewish men on the base. So, we went in at 9 A.M. to a
small synagogue that serves a total Jewish population of 90.

After services, I met an older man and woman who took me
to their home for dinner. We were joined by their two sons, both
in the Navy. They were simply wonderful to me. After dinner a
few of us, including one of the sons and his charming Mexican
girlfriend, went to the family ranch about 16 miles from town.
It's right on the Rio Grande, which is just as beautiful as it
appears in the movies.

The town is quaint, complete with cowboys in high-heeled
boots. We walked to the river in the evening, and right across we
could see Nuevo Laredo, the real Mexico. I will have one pass to
go there in three weeks. I am told I can get such things as silk
stockings, without ration coupons. So, send in your order with
all the sizes you want, and I will fill it.

I have a nice air-conditioned room in the town's main hotel,
as I don't have to go back to the base until tomorrow. The temperature today was 96 degrees, but it's dry heat and not as bad as
Houston.

October 2, 1943

It's an open post night for all the cadets, but I volunteered to
take the guard duty. It's only fair because I was out on a pass just

yesterday. The Jewish men agreed that we would take all the duties at Christmas, too — wherever we are. That evens things out, as it should be.

I am anticipating the program here will be fun. The first three weeks are spent in learning all about the different guns and gun turrets on the current bombers, operating them and shooting skeet on the range. Skeet shooting is a rich man's sport, so I'll pretend like I am at some fine gun club. Also, we'll be both on the range firing live ammunition and on moving trucks using camera guns.

The final two weeks are firing in the air from trainer aircraft. We'll start with AT-6 single engine planes that have an open cockpit behind the pilot. We'll be using .30-caliber machine guns to shoot at targets that are towed by other planes. Then we move to twin-engine AT-18 planes that are converted Lockheed Lodestars. Finally we shoot from the waist positions and all the turrets of B-24 Liberator bombers.

They tell us we shoot up about $2,000 worth of ammunition apiece, so keep buying war bonds. We will be using the new Sperry computing gun sight that is reputed to be very accurate.

I hope you all had a swell holiday, as I did. It was a great way to start this program, so, tough or not, I will graduate from here and get my gunner's wings.

October 4, 1943

We started school today and, although it's very interesting, nine hours a day is rough. This morning we went into the nomenclature of the .50-caliber machine gun. It is standard equipment on the big planes. When taken apart, there are 200 pieces. We must learn to strip it down and put it back together again blindfolded, with winter flying gloves on. Some fun.

This afternoon was nifty. We went out on the range to shoot skeet. I got 17 hits in my first 25 rounds, to lead my class, even though I have never held a shotgun before. Maybe I am destined to be rich! It's a real first-class sport. If I can pick off Nazis like I did clay birds today, I will be a huge success as an airman. Then we went to another range where they have .25-caliber rifles on machine gun mounts and we fired at moving targets. I'm better at skeet, but this was fun also — somewhat like a carnival.

This is mainly a B-24 school, so tomorrow I start to learn about the Consolidated tail turret, which is an important defensive weapon for the plane. They started the day by showing us a film on the safeguarding of military secrets. A lot of the stuff we use here is quite secret, but, I know you won't aid the enemy, so I'll keep blabbering on.

Although it's pretty difficult for me to understand the mechanics of the various systems, I keep trying. I find the challenge enjoyable. I know this experience will also give me a good eye for bombardment. They spare no effort to make us first-class gunners, so I'm willing to put up with the lousy food, getting up at 4:50 A.M., and the other army privations. This is a lot more interesting than pre-flight, because it has hands-on action. Still, it's a crazy life.

If you care to, I would enjoy some cookies, particularly if they're homemade. Don't go to any trouble though.

October 5, 1943

This morning at chow I got aggravated because we only got half a glass of milk, so I liberated (that's army talk for stealing) a quart of milk and ran back to the barracks. But the mess sergeant caught me, really got mad, and gave me three tours. The punishment is so lenient, it's a big joke. I was afraid they'd get really tough and make me go back into town this weekend.

When they announce we have open post and can go into town, nobody budges; there's more to do on the post than in town. At least there's no brass to shine, because we wear fatigues all day.

How about sending me a salami and a loaf of rye bread, if it wouldn't take too many of your food ration points. I need a break from the GI food here.

I had a nice experience last night. At the PX, I ran into my old pal Sonny Kent. I'm sure you remember him — we ran around a lot together in high school and after. We sat around and talked over old times and laughed a lot. He's a corporal and radio operator with the Signal Corps, now on this base, so we can get together again.

I'm totally pooped out again. We've been in school from 7 A.M. until 11 P.M., with 45 minutes off for lunch and dinner. Far too much work. That's as much work in a day, as I did in a week at college.

October 7, 1943

As I expected, things are getting a little tough for me as we get more into the technical schooling. I'm OK with the guns, because of my experience in ROTC, but today, we worked on the Consolidated turret and its hydraulic unit. It is a maze of fluids and circuits — amazing they can get so much into such a small space. I need a lot of help to understand the mechanics. I probably won't bust the course, but I need to do more studying than most of the men.

Something big is coming off here at the base. We have new aircraft coming off production. Apparently, this is where they will be training men to crew them. They're flying the trainers off the field while they enlarge runways, so my gunnery flight training will probably be away from here, most probably Eagle Pass.

October 9, 1943

Some day! I shot .30-caliber bullets from the various turrets, then .50-calibers from more turrets, then the same from hand held mounts. From a moving truck, I shot 50 rounds of skeet at clay pigeons released from high towers.

Yesterday, I detail stripped the machine guns blindfolded, with no mistakes. Also, learned about mounting the guns in the Sperry turrets and aligning the computing sights with the guns.

I walked off my three tours in a pouring rain. Everything is red clay here so every time I step out of the barracks I am in mud up to my ankles. Marching at attention with a rifle in the rain in that stuff is some fun. I think I'll leave off liberating milk from the mess hall.

Your box of goodies arrived this evening. What a banquet we had. All the gang gathered around and we had a real first rate picnic. You always seem to know just what I love. Thanks a million. It was really swell!

The days are so long, it seems as if they never end. I fall asleep in class and standing up, even though I try hard to stay awake. This weekend, we get a break with passes to Mexico. I'll go with some of the guys and have a look around. I understand there's a bullfight, and I may get a chance to see it. Any kind of a diversion will do.

I found out that the class before me at pre-flight went straight to advanced bombardier training without any of this gunnery. They will graduate in December. Interesting the way they do things.

I hate to be a pig, but they haven't paid us and I'm pretty low on cash. In fact, I'm flat broke and I have this pass coming up, so if you'd like to contribute to the well-being of a member of the armed forces, it would be much appreciated.

Journal Entry

*October 12, 1943 – When I asked for bombardier training, I
had not expected gunnery training as well, but I am glad to be
doing this. There's something very comforting about the feel of
the guns in my hands, and being able to defend myself. At this
point, I can't imagine being a navigator or pilot when we are
under enemy fighter attack — they can't shoot back.*

October 18, 1943

We had our Mexico passes and off we went. When I said
Laredo was something different, that was nothing compared
with Nuevo Laredo. The parks and monuments are very nice,
but only the main streets are paved. The people are very poor
and live in shacks.

We started with a huge steak dinner, very good, and it cost
just 90 cents. Then we walked around the town and went to a
part called "Boystown." In Mexico, prostitution is legal. We had
all heard stories of this place, so, to satisfy our curiosity, we had a
look. If I described the section in detail, it would turn your
stomach, because it was pretty awful. I have never heard of any
of the fellows touching those girls, but it's OK to just look. After
we were thoroughly nauseated, we headed back to the U.S.

I met Sonny at the hotel in Laredo, and we had a talk at one
of the tables on the patio. We came back to the field to sleep,
then took off again in the morning to see Mexico in the daylight. I went shopping and bought a few trinkets for you, which
I am sending on. Then, we took a ride around the city in a horse
drawn carriage. Now, back at the base, I am tired but happy to
have had a break that was good fun.

You asked what I want for my birthday. Not much, really.
There's not a whole lot of daily needs that are not supplied by

Uncle Sam, and I don't want to accumulate "stuff" to carry
around and worry about. There is one thing: I could use some
Old Spice after shave lotion. I can't get it here.

October 20, 1943

Today, we were introduced to the Waller trainer. The gunners
back from combat claim its the best trainer possible, and we're
the first class to use it. Each unit costs $125,000. They spare no
expense to protect our lives and defeat the enemy. The gunner
sits in a metal swivel seat with the gun in front of him, and a
huge curved concrete wall ahead. On the wall, there flashes three
dimensional fighter attacks from the waist, top, bottom, and tail
positions. As the planes swoop in from all angles, they're so real
that it's actually terrifying at times. The gun jumps when fired,
just like a .50-caliber does, and the sound of the firing is like
real, too. The machine records hits only when the gunner has
taken into account the proper leads and ballistics. It shows the
number of bursts as well as hits. The whole trainer simulates a
gunner in a four engine bomber with a ground speed of 250
miles per hour. Quite something, eh?

Yesterday, we went to the malfunction range where they have
20 .50-caliber machine guns, each with something wrong. We
go from gun to gun, firing each and then trying to figure out
what is the problem. Even in prime shape, they make so much
noise and the concussion is so terrific it literally knocks you
around. I put the safety on my first gun, then charged it and as
soon as I let go of the charging handle it started firing — it was
a runaway gun. That's the most dangerous kind, because the only
thing you can do is turn your face away and throw up the cover
plate. There's one chance in ten that the gun will explode. They
minimize the danger by supplying a short belt with only five
bullets, but it still scared the hell out of me.

There are plenty of other problems we learn to deal with and they all teach a healthy respect for that weapon. I thought having gunner's wings was just a step on the way to the real thing, bombardier wings, but after the workout here, I will be proud to wear them.

October 25, 1943

Today, we were out on the ground range, a lot better than stuffy classrooms. It was so cold, early in the morning, we nearly froze, then it got so hot in the afternoon we nearly boiled. I have a sunburned nose, in October yet.

We started out on .30-caliber machine guns, then moved to the skeet range where we shot from moving trucks. In the afternoon, we went to a big range where dummy machine guns and sights were mounted on swivels. We had earphones that were tuned in to the radio frequency of the fighter plane flying around above us. He dived on us and simulated strafing us from about 20 feet off the ground, calling out his range as he closed in. This way we could see how much of the gunsight he filled at different yardage from us, and learn to judge distances. I've learned not to jump at the sound of a high powered weapon or to flinch when I fire it. I still blink a bit from the concussion, but I'm getting over that, too.

Soon we head for the AT-6 trainers and firing from the air. Those are the planes the advanced pilots fly just before they get a combat ship. They hit about 325 miles per hour. For the gunners, the canopy is taken off the rear cockpit and a Vickers ring installed for the machine gun swivel, the same as they do with the Navy dive- or torpedo-bombers. I'll be firing 2,000 rounds of ammunition from there during my aerial training.

Thanks much to you and everyone who wrote me with good wishes for my 19th birthday. It's a strange way and place to be spending it.

November 2, 1943

Early Sunday, we left for Eagle Pass, where I am now. It's about 140 miles from Laredo and we came here in big army trucks, starting out at 4 A.M. (Here we call it 0400. The army must figure using numbers like that makes it seem less bad than it really is.) Getting up at four in the morning appeals to me about half as much as five does. We're living in temporary barracks at this little postage stamp auxiliary airfield, with only tents to house the ammunition and guns.

I just came down from my first flight. It was quite a ride. I wore a helmet and goggles and a seat pack parachute and shot about 200 rounds at a target being towed by another plane. The target looks as big as a cigarette up there. I don't think I made a hit, but that's only the first try. I am here to learn, not to be an expert right away. We were in an open cockpit and, although they said the plane was going 175 miles per hour — it felt like 500 standing there in the slipstream holding on to a bouncing machine gun.

The pilot was a real wise ass. He overshot his landing and instead of climbing back into the pattern and coming in again, he did a chandelle (a 90-degree turn with a half loop) to get back into position. That left me (and my stomach) upside down, hanging by my seat belt. I got even, though — I barfed up my lunch all over the tail of his nice airplane. I think I aged two years with that experience.

It rained all night, and the field is one big oozing mud hole. I am the raunchiest looking cadet imaginable, as are all the others. I have been living in fatigues and they're full of paint from the bullets, grease, and Texas mud. I have bruises and bumps all over my body. The pilots are all officers, of course, and they are just as sorry looking a bunch as we are. They wear dirty old sweatshirts, fatigue pants, or just whatever is around. They wear no insignia of rank and no one plays soldier. Everyone is engrossed in training for war.

They said this course is a snap, but it's got me hanging on the ropes. When we're not flying, we sit around in the broiling sun. There's no shelter with a roof on it, and our meals are served from a field kitchen. It will almost be good to start being a cadet again — even with the chicken shit, such as formation marching — when we move on to advanced bombardier school.

Journal Entry

November 5, 1943 – This crummy day started with a shrill whistle from Sgt. Weinstein at 0415 (that's 4:15 A.M. civilian time). "Oh, blow it out your barracks bag," one cadet mumbles, while other remarks are not so kind.

In the movies, all the soldiers show up in nice shiny uniforms. This bunch looks like refugees from a prison camp, wearing greasy fatigues, with dirty fingernails, needing shaves, sun and wind burned, and visibly aching all over.

They march to chow under a blanket of stars, but they need something warmer, because it is very cold out. And, they don't sing, "Off we go into the wild blue yonder." After a gourmet (?) breakfast, they are escorted to the flying field in troop carriers, where they are unloaded into the darkness, stumbling over one another.

At the armorer's tent, they draw machine guns, then line up the sight with the line of the bore. This requires field stripping the gun in the dark. Since there's no place to put the parts, they drop to the ground, which results in some being lost, and that results in much cursing by the sergeant in charge. Then another giant sergeant checks the guns and puts his OK on them. After drawing his ammunition, each cadet gunner proceeds on foot to his assigned plane carrying his gun, which weighs 30 pounds, and the ammunition, which weighs 25 more. After a few steps, this load becomes two tons.

Now, he is in his plane and airborne. The plane peels off to approach the target. This maneuver consists of pulling up the nose of the ship, flipping it over nearly on its back, and then sliding it towards the earth at great speed. It always necessitates climbing back up a thousand feet, so the gunner can reclaim his stomach.

Back on the ground, following target practice, there's a chance at the latrine, which consists of an old board thrown across a deep hole. It is cold sitting there, and then it begins to rain. Naturally, there is no roof on this contrivance, so your aviation cadet gets very wet.

The rest of the day is cleaning guns and anything else in sight that might look like it should be cleaned. At six, our soldier staggers to dinner, but he's too tired to eat. It doesn't matter, because the food stinks. Another day, another $1.65.

November 8, 1943

Today, I was phase-checked on the .50-caliber machine gun, then fired them from the dorsal turret of a Lockheed Hudson bomber. That plane is obsolete for combat, but we have quite a few of them here for training.

Four of us and an instructor were aboard as we climbed to about 6,000 feet and headed out. I went back to the turret and watched while the other plane in our flight fired first. It's quite a sight watching tracer bullets whiz by. When my turn came, I charged my guns, and the pilot took me in to about 250 yards from the target. As I peppered away, I saw several of my tracers go right through the target. When we fired from the hand-held guns in the AT-6, I had to close one eye to line up the gun sight, but in the turret of the Hudson, we have an optical sight that superimposes the ring-sight on the target. That way, I can keep both eyes open and see the results of my shooting much better.

In all respects, I like to fly in the big planes rather than the AT-6s. The little jobs may be fun for the jocks who like to do loop-the-loops all over the skies, but I like to go up, fly straight and level, do my job, then go home.

After I finished firing, I went up to the co-pilot's seat and finished the flight from there. Even though the reason we are flying is to train us for killing in combat, there is something very special about being high in the sky, watching the poor earthworms below who must stick to the roads.

There is a feeling of ultra-aliveness, like being king of the mountain — no one can touch you. Maybe it is a little crazy to have that kind of experience in a war machine, but such exhilaration seems to be common to many of us cadets. Maybe that's why we signed on for this service, rather than others.

November 9, 1943

I returned from Eagle Pass yesterday. My scores there were just so-so, but enough to get by. This week, I fire from turrets in the Venturas here at the base and get phase checked on all the work we did during these weeks. Then, at the end of the week, we graduate and ship out to Advanced Bombardier School.

Today, we had passes. Since it was a nice cool day, Sonny and I rented horses and went for a ride along the Rio Grande. Then we had a big steak dinner in town followed by a movie. It was a nice break, and we enjoyed it.

Dad, will you please send me $25. I'm supposed to get paid this week, but I want to be sure to have some money when I ship out. If I do get paid on schedule, I will return it to you (but don't hold your breath).

November 10, 1943

I just came down from a camera mission on an AT-11, the plane we will be using at bombardier school. It's a slick little twin-engined job, and the ones here are fitted out with an upper turret that has a camera mounted on a non-firing gun. Each cadet has a roll of film (with his name recorded on it) that is used to "fire" at an AT-6 using pursuit tactics that simulate the enemy's. Tomorrow night, we'll have a session where they'll play back the films to see how we did. That is about the best training possible for gunners. I really enjoyed the entire experience. I know now I'll like the work in these ships at advanced school.

After the flight, we had time in the intelligence library. There, we can read up on the latest information from overseas. It's all confidential, of course, and we are not allowed to write anything down. Whatever we think important, we must commit to memory.

This has been a tough grind, but I have learned a lot. I hope I'll get to apply this knowledge soon, so I can dust off a few Nazis or Japs. When this war is over, maybe they'll melt down the B-17s and B-24s and make automobiles out of them. Make mine a Chrysler convertible with red leather seats and just let me tool down Michigan Avenue with a lovely blond at my side. Ah, dreams!

November 11, 1943

It's about 7 A.M. I am in the ready room waiting to fly. I'm in the first run of the morning. It is really cold outside, which is somewhat uncomfortable but makes for smooth flying. I need to get some good shots in today to bring my total up to standard.

There's always the threat of being washed out. A number of the guys have already been dropped along the way, and there'll be more eliminated here. I'll continue this letter from time-to-time during the day.

It's now 10 A.M., and I'm down from my ride. It was beautiful up there — smooth as silk. We turned on the cabin heat, so it was nice and warm. I shot last, then went up to the co-pilot's seat again. I got my radio working and joined into the babble that goes on between the planes. Everything must be pronounced clearly, usually with a letter to help such as, "A Able, this is C for Charley ... follow on my wing as I make another pass." We learned all this stuff in our radio course at pre-flight.

We got close to the target, it was full of holes. My tracers looked good as I fired, so I hope many of them were mine. Every time I go up, I love it more. This flying business sure grows on you. As long as I have to fight a war, the wild blue is the place to be.

I have your letter written Sunday about the gambling. Let me assure you, I have never once shot craps in the army. I have played cards about five times, but only penny-ante poker and only with my own group. I never sit down to a game with more than two bucks in my pocket, and I never play after pay day. So, please don't worry about me. The reason I have been broke is because I have been going out with Sonny, and he hasn't been paid in two months, so I loaned him some dough. If you can't do that for a pal, who then?

I got paid last night, about $87. I have to pay $25 for my food (can you believe that), so I have the rest. Your check for $25 came today. I am tearing it up because, as you can see, I am independently wealthy. I hope they issue me a leather jacket, because it is very cold. Sonny loaned me his GI mackinaw, and I could get away with wearing it around here. If they don't issue me a jacket, I will have to buy one, so I will need all that money.

As I told you, I leave here Saturday. I hope we go to Midland for the 12-week course of just bombardier training, with navigation training after I get commissioned. The other school is 18 weeks and includes navigation before graduation.

Bombardier School

Even in a country the size of America, the movement of 10 million young men out of their homes and into the armed forces made for severe upheaval in the social structure of the country. In many large and medium size cities that did not have a significant military presence, the graying of the male population emptied the dance halls and night clubs and changed the look of personnel in all types of businesses. In these places, the care and romancing of the young female population was left to the men who had not yet been called up or were exempted from or ineligible for military service.

The army sought out wide open spaces for its training camps, gunnery ranges, and battlefield simulations. Very often a small town was nearby where hardy residents, who had nurtured their peace and quiet off the beaten track, now found themselves inundated on weekends by thousands of soldiers turned loose from their GI captivity. Although the soldiers came from all walks of life, they seemed very much alike in their olive drab uniforms, short haircuts, and desperate need for diversion.

The women in these towns had the burden of dealing with far too many boyfriends (and husbands) of other women — the women left behind in the cities. The Saturday ritual disgorging of soldiers from huge army trucks had many local mothers secreting their daughters behind the gates. Others were allowed to attend only those USO dances where older adults supervised the activities and made sure the contacts that were established lasted only to the end of the dance.

For the GI lucky enough to get a real date with a girl, the army made sure that nothing much developed, by shipping him out in short order to another base or overseas. All over the country there were these abnormal, transitory relationships that began at a USO and only lasted for a few weeks or months. In the rare instance where momentary contact headed in the direction of something more permanent, there was the reality of the near-future with its specter of separation, combat, and death.

For the English, these problems were compounded. Not only was there an exodus of their men to battlefields in Africa, Italy, and elsewhere, but then they were invaded by thousands of American men, still in desperate need of diversion. After many months of having their women wooed the American way, the British began referring to U.S. airmen as "over paid, over fed, oversexed, and over here."

———◦———

Army Air Forces Bombardier School
Big Spring, Texas

November 14, 1943

Dear Mom, Dad, and Pooz,

Gunnery school is over and I have my first pair of wings. Now I am at Big Spring Army Air Force Bombardier School in Texas, near the border of New Mexico. It's the smallest of the bombardier schools with about 600 cadets, quite compact, but with a big flight line that can handle lots of planes. We will learn about the Norden and Sperry bombsights. If my letters about the training here are vague at times, it's because I'm learning about top-secret equipment and I am not permitted to give details of its use. As usual, I will stretch this as far as possible, so you will be up with my activities.

Until now this has been a 12-week program in bombardiering only. We will be the first to get an 18-week course that will include navigation. While I am anxious to move along, I suspect that the addition of the navigation expertise may serve me well.

I strut around here with my gunner's wings making my uniform look really nifty. So far the food is better than at Laredo and there's none of the baloney about standing at attention all the time and running to formation. We're supposed to be able to handle the job of being an officer by now, and we have a specialty to learn here.

November 16, 1943

This afternoon I took my second "64" physical and breezed right through it. That's the army's toughest and it always sets up a little pre-test panic. My height and weight are the same as six months ago, but I am a lot harder. Also, had our first class in the theory of bombing this morning. We will spend nine weeks with Norden sight, then six weeks of navigation that will include a 600-mile flight to assess what we have learned. The last three weeks is scheduled to be with the Sperry sight. I am aiming not to be in the 25 percent washout group.

I finally wore out the shoes I got before I left home. They gave us a shoe stamp, but I can't get another one when I graduate. I'll need a good pair of shoes when I get home on leave, to go with my dress uniform, so I wonder if you could save a shoe stamp for me. It's kind of nuts that the army has me in the position of putting the bite on you for a shoe stamp, but it's the way they do things. With over four months notice, maybe you can have one available. I also could use a couple of spiral notebooks for class. They're impossible to find down here.

This morning we took the bombardier's oath. It ends with, "I do solemnly swear to protect the secrets of the American bombsight, if need be with my life itself, so help me God." I am not anxious to have the wrath of God come down on me, so I will try to keep my big yapper shut.

November 18, 1943

I got your letters with your good wishes today. Thanks! I'll need a bit of good luck. I've been learning some of the preliminary steps with the Norden bombsight. What a hunk of machinery that is. They say it's the most complicated and the most valuable military hardware in the U.S. arsenal. It's going to be some job learning all that's necessary to perform well with such equipment.

Tomorrow, I start work on the bombardier trainer. It's a high platform-like affair that moves back and forth over the floor, where the terrain is mapped out just as you would see it from the air. It can simulate all the conditions of actual flight.

Last night they took our pictures for our officer's passes and graduation book. Pretty soon, I'll be ordering my officer's uniforms. Boy, do they put the cart before the horse. I still have three weeks of ground school before I even start flying.

Would you please send me my bathrobe. I need something warm to wear when I go outside to the toilet in the morning. It's really cold here early in the day and they don't issue us anything that would serve the purpose. We don't have leather jackets yet either, so we're cold for a good part of the day.

This is to be grinding hard work all the way through the program, but it's probably the most important thing I'll ever do in my life, so I'm going to really try and do it well.

November 20, 1943

Yesterday, I spent more time on the trainer. I'm getting a better idea of what the whole bombing problem is about. It's a lot more complicated than I imagined, but more interesting, as well.

They issued us two kits: the navigation one is a beautiful leather briefcase that holds computers, compasses, and all the necessary tables. The bombardier kit holds all the computers and spare parts I need for the bombsight. We also got two swell watches, one a stop-watch, the other an Elgin chronometer. The bombing and navigation tables are made so they glow under the fluorescent lights we use in the planes. Soon I'll be getting my winter sheepskin-lined flying outfit, including boots.

I had a few hours on the bomb release mechanisms and bomb racks this morning and then a couple of hours of drill. The army never stops having us march around. Today I completed my first week's training. I'm amazed at what I've learned — I'm also staggered by what is yet to come. When I get through with this, I'll be able to breeze through a college education with my eyes closed.

I have a pass for town and, when I'm done with this letter, I'm going to see if I can have a little fun. The town has only 13,000 people. They tell us there isn't much to do there, but I haven't had an open post for three weeks, so whatever it's like, it'll be a pleasure.

I am going to investigate the hotel room situation to see if it can be arranged for you, Mom and Pooz, to come down to see me. If you do decide to come, be aware that I can only get off weekends. However, guests can come on the field from 7 P.M. until 10 P.M.

Our class is scheduled to graduate March 18. That should bring me home right at springtime. Boy, will that ever be swell. But, that's a long way off.

I could use $10 to buy the pair of shoes I wrote you about. Thanks!

November 22, 1943

Saturday night I went into town to a dance they had at the cadet club. The town isn't much. Most of the fellows were discouraged and left the dance because there were only a few girls and lots of cadets. But, I was persistent, so I stayed and met a very nice girl, a graduate of Texas Tech who has just started teaching school. She's 21 years old, a blonde, and plenty cute, so I won't be choosy about the age difference. About 20 different guys tried to date her, but Byron got the nod. I picked her up

Sunday. Since the club is the only place to go, we went and had a lot of fun. Thursday night our class is having their incoming dance at the base and she will be here. Next Saturday she'll probably be going out with me, too, so I am assured of having a bit of fun on the weekends.

Man, am I a busy guy. Today I started classes on the C-1 automatic pilot. How in the world they ever invented such a device is beyond me. It's an incredible maze of wires, wheels, and junk, and we need to know all about it because it controls the aircraft through the bombsight on the bomb run.

I also spent about three hours on the trainer and I'm seeing some improvement in my handling of the sight. I am working with 120-second runs, but eventually I need to be able to make it all work within 20-second runs. If this all reads like gibberish to you, I'll explain after the war ends.

It is really cold here in Texas. We wore our overcoats to class this morning. In the barracks, the wind whistles up through the cracks in the floor, so when we awaken, the place is like ice. The food has turned lousy, but still, with it all, I feel quite good. I'll just have to put up with everything if I want to graduate from here, and that I do!

Dad, are we still betting that the war will be over by this Christmas? Say about 4 P.M.?

November 23, 1943

I got the bathrobe and it is more than welcome. I may not look GI in the morning, but I'll be warm. I have to stay alert and on the ball because Thursday I have my first phase exam. If I flunk two of those, I'm automatically washed out and it's back to being a foot soldier.

I got the new pair of shoes, really beauts. Now I want to buy a blouse. We can wear officer's blouses minus the insignia — most of the guys do. Officer's uniforms are not issued, so we must buy them. I have a chance to buy a blouse from a fellow that's graduating. It's a bit too small for him, but fits me and is in good condition. He paid $47.50 and wants to sell it for $25. I could buy it, wear it here and then, when I graduate, I'll have an extra blouse. Of course I need a little extra money to do it, if you could see your way clear.

November 25, 1943

I've been thinking about Mom and Pooz coming down here at Christmas and, although I have maintained so far that it's a bad idea, I've suddenly discovered that Christmas falls on a Saturday this year. That may allow me to be with you Friday night, Saturday, and Sunday.

Some months ago, we had agreed that the Jewish guys would take the duty posts, so that the Christian cadets could have the holidays. But, on this base the permanent personnel have all the duty, so the cadets can focus on training, which means all cadets get the holidays free, as well.

At the worst, I won't be able to leave the base, but you can come out here, I am sure. There are some decent places where we can be together. So, make your plans and come ahead. Let me know all about how and when you'll arrive. I really want to see both of you. I will enjoy it a lot. So, let's make it a date! I will even try to be a good soldier and not accumulate any tours.

November 26, 1943

Well, I'm doing OK. My instructor, a second lieutenant and a very nice guy, complimented me on the way I've picked up my procedure on the bombsight. I got my first "shack" (a direct hit) on the trainer. That was quite a thrill, but getting shacks from the air will be quite another matter.

You may be interested in just what a bombardier has to do in order to get a hit. It's not just 30 seconds of work as the public is lead to believe. For each bomb dropped there is about an hour put into calculating many variables. The altimeter reading (pressure altitude) must be converted to absolute altitude using the C-2 computer. Then the free air temperature reading must be converted to absolute temperature on the E-6B computer. Then the ground speed has to be figured from the air speed reading, wind readings, etc. again using the E-6B. All of these figures must be entered correctly into the bombsight. All the entries take place on the bombing run, which lasts a maximum of 120 seconds, down to 30 seconds in combat. They have just come out with a new computer, which we will be the first to use, that will do the job more accurately and faster, but it is a big headache to understand. Thank goodness I took trigonometry at U. of Illinois or I would be in trouble now.

In conjunction with the sight, there are a number of other devices to handle such as the bomb circuit switch, the bomb rack switch, the bomb release lever, the bomb bay lever, and a bunch of others. All must be handled correctly and in proper sequence on the bombing run in order to assure a hit. You can see why the bombardier is called the busiest guy in the army.

One little mistake anywhere along the line will cause enormous errors in the bombing. So, it's not very funny when a student bombardier drops a bomb five miles off the range and blows some poor farmer's barn to bits, but it happens.

I never thought that anything could take so much effort and concentration. Often I could use another pair of hands and I would still be busier than I'll probably ever be in my life again. I'm putting everything I've got into it, but at nine hours a day it has me punchy. Still, others have done it, so I'm sure I can.

Today is Thanksgiving. The schedule of training is like any other, except that we will have a big Thanksgiving dinner with all the trimmings. I am sure I will enjoy the fancy meal they are preparing, but I will miss being with all of you. I hope you are having a nice day at home. Our Thanksgiving meal together was always a special time for me, so I can't help feeling lonely today. However, we can all be thankful that our homes are not under attack like those in Europe.

November 28, 1943

I just got in from a date with Vera (she's the lovely blonde I wrote you about) and now I am listening to Jack Benny on the radio. Saturday night we had a grand time dancing at the club. I slept in until 10 A.M. today, then picked Vera up. We went to see *The Sky's the Limit* with Fred Astaire, then back out to the club.

I took Mac, the cadet club hostess, out to dinner with us. That woman is really a peach. She's about 36 years old and has four children, but her husband was killed recently. She's a second mother to all the boys, and we're nuts about her. She made all the arrangements for when you come down here, Mom and Pooz. I arranged for a room for you at the Settles Hotel and, as soon as you let me know the exact dates, I'll confirm it with them. Mac will take care of everything, arrange for you to get out to the base, and whatever else you need. I imagine she'll tell you what to wear as well.

Maybe you can bring her a hat from the store, if I can find out what she'd like. There's nothing to buy here. She has been just wonderful to me. The enjoyment I've been having on weekends is mostly due to her. By the time you arrive, she will be out at the new club they are opening on the base. She will take good care of you gals.

November 29, 1943

I have a problem of great importance to the future of the entire United States Army, and I would like you to draw on your worldly knowledge to advise me. You see, Christmas is only four weeks away and I have three women in various parts of Texas on the string (so to speak). Now, my problem is this. Should I: 1. buy inexpensive presents for all three and take a chance that one or more might be insulted; 2. buy them Air Corps jewelry and make certain to insult all of them; 3. buy presents for only one or two and take a chance on cutting down my stock of women; 4. pretend I didn't know there was a Christmas; 5. run away and join the Navy.

I would really appreciate your advice, but please bear in mind that Congress has appropriated only two billion dollars, instead of the 15 billion asked for by the president, for paying men in my position, leaving the possibility that my pay may be cut at any time.

December 1, 1943

I just received my slippers you sent. Now on Sunday mornings I can loaf around the barracks in my robe and slippers and pretend that I am at home. I also appreciate having my feet warm. It is really cold in Texas. The guys scheduled for flying today went in full winter gear and they said it was freezing upstairs.

Tomorrow, I am scheduled for a medium altitude flight, then Thursday, we go for our first high altitude mission. I drew my oxygen mask, earphones, and throat microphone from supply, so I am all ready. With all that stuff on, it complicates the work on the bombsight, but this is war, you know, so we must suffer in silence.

I had an exam on the causes of errors in bombing and I did well. My cumulative average is 92 percent, which puts me in the upper two percent of the class.

I just got good news: For the next two weeks we are going to fly extra missions so we can have three day passes over Christmas. That assures us time to be together off the base. Good deal!

December 2, 1943

I had aircraft recognition for the third time. You will recall what a tough time I had with it in pre-flight school. Well, now I can recognize planes in $1/50$th of a second.

Tomorrow is a big day. In the morning, we have a phase exam on the Norden bombsight and on the two computers we use. In the afternoon, I have a check ride on the trainer that will decide if I am ready for the air next week. I wonder how I will do up there; it's quite a bit different from "hanger flying."

Bobby wrote from Houston and said she may come to visit me on New Year weekend after you folks leave. That way I'll have plenty of company on the holidays. Because I have no demerits, I get an extra pass this weekend, so I will go into town and visit with Vera. I must not let my bombardiering interfere with my social life.

The class that graduates this week got ten-day passes to go home. I hope it happens to me. Everyone is writing me wonderful letters. That makes mail call the best time of the day. I get the most mail in the barracks.

Uncle Pete wrote from his South Pacific island. He said the flyboys stationed there pinned their wings on Aussie girls while they were in Australia, but the native girls on the island don't wear anything to pin them on. Tough luck!

December 5, 1943

After all the work learning how to handle the .45-caliber pistol, they now tell us they are going to issue .30-caliber carbines to bombardiers. Why? It's a nifty little weapon, but I wouldn't want to be caught dead with it — but I wouldn't really want to be caught dead with a .45-caliber pistol either.

In a few days I finally start flying. I've been in the Air Corps for over 10 months and I only have 24 hours of flying time. But now I will get in a minimum of 140 hours of bombing and 50 hours of navigation missions. That's more than most pilots have when they graduate.

The big news of the month is Gertrude (our squadron mascot) had seven cute little pups.

Last night Vera and I went out formal. I had on my new tuxedo for dinner at Del Monico's, then we went dancing at Mocambos, but the champagne at the Stork Club wasn't so hot. That's the dream, the reality is we went through our usual routine — Saturday night to the club, Sunday to the movies. We saw Coney Island with Betty Grable. Very nice (Betty, I mean).

I got your check, Dad, and it puts me in the clear. Thanks a lot, you're a pal. When I become an officer I'll be making enough money that I won't have to keep bothering you all the time.

December 7, 1943 (Pearl Harbor Day)

I celebrated by making four shacks in six runs on the trainer. We were simulating low level bombing, so it's easier. This week is a lulu. We start school at seven in the morning and go through until ten at night. We got all our flying equipment today — big fleece-lined jackets, pants and boots, leather jackets, and flying coveralls. Now I am all set to go up and blow this state to hell. What a pleasure!

December 11, 1943

The weather has been bad for bombing, but we put in two hours of flying yesterday, working on various problems. It's amazing how much training can be forgotten once in the air. I made my altitude calculations three times before I got it right. Up in the nose, I could watch the clouds below. They looked like a cotton quilt, a very thrilling sight. Then we went down below the clouds and flew over the targets at 150 feet to have a look at them. Back upstairs at 2,000 feet, we participated in a simulated dogfight, but my stomach was not made for loop-the-loops. As I have said before, I'm for the big bombers that can only do straight and level flight.

This morning we went up very early with ten bombs aboard for the instructor to drop — he has to do this at regular intervals to keep his rating. I was in the back over the open bomb-bay doors taking pictures.

The instructor is some peachy bombardier. I can learn a lot from him. After his drops we went to 7,000 feet and I made some dry runs.

It's quite difficult to synchronize the bombsight when the pilot is flying the plane manually, because his reaction time is slower than the AFCE (automatic flight control equipment) but I still did fairly well. We were up almost three hours, quite a long mission. Tomorrow, I'll drop five bombs by myself.

I ordered my officer's uniforms last night, spending $150 without batting an eyelash. It's a good thing we don't have to pay for them until we get our uniform allowance at graduation. Just ordering the uniforms guarantees nothing. If you wash out, they just cancel the order.

Dad, there's no truth to the article you read stating that a bunch of cadets were washed out to reduce the numbers. They're badly in need of aircrews, as you can tell by the huge bomber losses recently in Europe. Even though there is a shortage of bombardier/navigators, they still won't accept second raters, so the washout rate remains fairly constant.

The strategy in the 8th Air Force is still the same — to keep up the heavy bombing of industrial targets, thereby holding down future losses on the ground. Of course, the Air Corps casualties soar, but that's the price we pay. I'm still in favor of doing it that way, though.

December 16, 1943

Big news today! I went up this morning to 9,500 feet to drop five bombs. My first four were just fair, but the fifth one, ah! A perfect shack, right on the button. That's a fairly unusual occurrence. My average circular error (distance from the shack) was 84 feet for all five bombs.

The practice bombs we use are 250 pounders filled with sand and just a small explosive with smoke, so you can see where they hit. But, a regular 250-pound demolition bomb has a bursting radius of 150 feet. So, you can see that the Norden bombsight is quite good, even with an amateur like me at the controls.

The first call, "Bombs away," was quite a thrill. Hitting my first bomb just 115 feet away is pretty good when you consider what a ten-foot shack looks like from 9,500 feet in the air.

I had one good scare today. After I was through bombing, I started back to my seat in the rear and I slipped and fell against the door handle. Of course, I didn't realize it's impossible to fall out, because of the terrific air pressure against the door, but there was just enough play to let my arm slip out. Boy, did I turn green. We only wear parachute harnesses in the ship, and in case we have to bail out, we have chest packs that snap on. I think I swallowed my heart three times. The instructor had a big laugh. He told me to be more careful, because if I fall out, he gets court-marshaled. Very funny.

My bunkmate Hal fell asleep in class today and the instructor turned to me, "Quick," he shouted, "Wake that guy up before he falls off the seat and hurts himself. He's cost the army $30,000 for his training, so far, and I don't want him to break an arm or a leg." We had a good long laugh.

I slipped going to chow this morning and turned my ankle, so the flight surgeon excused me from Physical Training for three days. That's small compensation for the horrible (?) agony I'm going through. I was hoping for three weeks off. PT and I never did agree.

Only a few more days until Mom and Pooz arrive. Whee!

December 17, 1943

This will be my last letter to reach you before you arrive here. All the arrangements are complete. Mac will meet you at the hotel, bring you to the base for supper, then to the cadet day-room, where I will meet you when I am off duty.

Yesterday, I went to 13,000 feet to drop five bombs. I had a runny nose, which is some fun while wearing an oxygen mask. I had a lousy day, way off the mark, so I'm not a hotshot bombardier, yet. The instructor made me write out my procedure 15 times in the hope that I wouldn't screw up again.

Since we're flying all weekend and there will be no big time in Big Spring, I went to the dance that opened our new cadet club on the base. I was determined not to let my work interfere with my pleasure, so I stayed up until 1:30 A.M. having fun. With less than four hours sleep my hind end is dragging, but I am hanging in.

December 19, 1943

Even though the girls are on the way here, you're entitled to a letter, Pop. It's Sunday morning, and here I am down at the hangar waiting to fly. Jeez, do I hate to get up at 5 A.M. on a Sunday. While we wait for flight assignments, we're having a look at the D-8 bombsight. That's the hunk of junk they used on the Mitchells to bomb Tokyo. It's just a couple of rods and wires that enables the bombardier to set up his dropping angle; it's supposed to be very good for low level work at altitudes up to 1,500 feet. There's no auto-pilot, so the bombardier has to talk the pilot down the bomb run on the intercom.

The big news of the day: Yesterday I soloed! My instructor thought I was ready, so I went up in the ship with just the pilot and a cameraman. I dropped five bombs and didn't do badly. The first bomb I dropped 300 feet off, because I accidentally hit one of the knobs with my knee, but all the rest were good bombs. My instructor was very pleased and said, if I correct a few faults, I'll be a good bombardier.

The flight lasted five hours, all at 13,000 feet, and when I hit the ground, I was totally pooped out. Oxygen all the time is very tiring, it chaps my lips and makes my throat sore, but it's a necessary part of the work.

The opportunity to solo began with the early morning flight. The instructor was chewing my ass for some mistakes I made, whereupon I got flustered and made some more.

"Mr. Lane," he said, "Does it bother you when I yell at you?" I said, "Yes sir, it does." Then he said, "OK, you drop the next bomb by yourself and I'll just watch." So, I dropped a honey. He told me, "Hell, I'm not even going to talk to you anymore," and he went back up to the co-pilot's seat, while I dropped three perfectly placed bombs. That's when he decided to send me up solo. I'm sure he doesn't regret it.

I'm anxiously awaiting the arrival of Mom and Sis. I hope they won't be disappointed when they see me — I don't look anything like Capt. Clark Gable, even in my dress uniform.

The weather the last few days has been beautiful. It's zero degrees upstairs, but clear as a bell. Our flying suits are plenty comfortable. Sometimes the sun makes it so warm in the interior of the plane, I can work in just my coveralls. The bright sun also made the target hard to see, so I had to take two dry runs, which made the pilot pissed off, but he'll get over it.

Tomorrow, I'll be cameraman for one of the other guys who solos. I will also get in some pilot time. They want us all to have a bit of stick time before we get out of here. There are instances in combat where the pilot and co-pilot were both killed and the bombardier had to bring the plane home. I have also set up and flown the plane on the auto pilot. They really do give us the works. I will be one of the most highly trained men in any armed force, when I graduate.

December 23, 1943

Tuesday night, I went to the depot to meet the girls. Boy, was it ever good to see them. We were together out here at the cadet dayroom last night, and they will be out again tonight. Friday, I'll be off all day with them.

Yesterday, I pulled a lulu. The ship I was on had an instrument that allows the bombardier to drop a stick of bombs at regularly spaced intervals on the ground. I must have accidentally kicked the switch on with my knee because, after the first "bombs away," I looked out over the sight. It was like the fourth of July — five beautifully spaced bombs, all within 40 feet of the shack. Then I went ahead and dropped the other five bombs we had aboard. Back on the ground, the senior flight leader credited me with the first bomb in the train and threw the other four out. That left me with an average error for the day of 120 feet, not bad.

Saturday night, I get to stay at the hotel with the girls. Maybe I'll get a little extra sleep and even breakfast in bed.

December 26, 1943

Merry Christmas, Pop. There I was with both the women, and you home being a bachelor. Thanks for the loan, now I send them back to you.

We sure had fun. Pooz looks wonderful, and five guys thought Mom was my wife. She is beautiful and gets younger looking as the years pass. Pooz was a knockout at the cadet club, a very popular gal. She'll never have trouble getting guys. We sure do have a wonderful family! I stayed in town with them Friday and Saturday, then we had a super Christmas dinner at the base, one of the best army meals ever.

Mom gave me the Christmas money, and I am well fixed for the future. She went with me to the uniform store and sold me on a trench coat instead of a short coat. It's a good thing the government will pay for it; it cost $55.

Now that the wonderful break is over, it's back to the grind. We start flying at night until 3:30 A.M., then up at 8 A.M. to start over. But, I'm all hopped up from the visit, so it will be OK.

December 27, 1943

Now is the moment for the invasion to come. I can't see how the war will last more than two months after we land in France. I look for the war in Europe to be over in a maximum of seven months. Our Air Force in England is so powerful that there won't be a thing left standing to resist our ground forces when they land.

Today, I flew a simulated combat mission, solo. Man, I was really hot. The target is about 300 feet square and looks like docks and wharves. From 13,000 feet, I plunked four bombs out of five right in there. That's good bombing, and keeps me way ahead of the others.

We don't fly tonight. Tomorrow, we start our navigation work. We'll also work with the Sperry sight next week, although I understand we're the last class to learn Sperry. They are taking them off all the B-24s and B-17s in favor of the Norden. The Sperry isn't flexible enough and is not good for low altitude work.

Look for important news within three weeks. Our new B-29s are ready to go!

December 29, 1943

Mom and Pooz, I miss you already. All the fellows think I have a super family. Even my instructor asked if you had a nice visit. As we say down here in the South, "Ya all come back, ye hear!"

I am loaded up with holiday presents. I love the wallet you gave me, Sis. I got more boxes of candy today. That brings my stock on hand to 7,980,762 pieces of various goodies, or there-abouts. The boys roughly estimate that the whole barracks can now live entirely on candy for the twelve weeks or so remaining in our stay here. If you think that's not possible, you should see me wading through Martha Washington chocolates, Dutch Mill caramels, and other stuff to get to my underwear. It's awful (awful good).

Journal Entry

December 30, 1943 – It's the end of the calendar year, and near the end of one year in the army as well. So, where am I? Well, I'm a lot tougher and better able to handle discipline, discomfort, and duty. I have new skills and, while limited in application, they are mighty important right now. For the first time, I am committed to going all out to do a job right. I feel capable and good about myself. And yeah, I am still waving the flag!

December 31, 1943

Yesterday, I was on a low-altitude mission, 4,000 feet. The old shack looks like the Settles Hotel from there. I had one miss and the rest good hits.

Tomorrow, I start simulated combat bombing. Instead of a steady bomb run of three minutes, we are down to 25 seconds, bombing specific types of targets. Our target tomorrow is a power plant from 8,500 feet. You must get a direct hit — anything else is a miss, no matter how close. We do evasive action to avoid anti-aircraft fire, directed by the bombardier from the auto-pilot, since he can look down and see the flak that the pilot can't. Why they teach us to bomb from 8,500 feet is a mystery since the small-caliber AA [anti-aircraft artillery] is at its best at that altitude and the heavy stuff can be brought to bear also.

The men here who are back from combat said that over Freidrichshafen flying at 10,000 feet, the navigators got out of the ships, walked out on the flak, and stuck up their fingers to see which way the wind was blowing. It ain't funny! I'm for 30,000 feet.

Today, we saw the folders containing all the briefing information, maps, charts, etc. for the raid on the Ploesti oil fields. They knew everything about that place, the location of each refinery, each tank, every railroad, even every train. I can understand why the losses were so great — there were so many AA emplacements, a gnat couldn't get through unharmed.

I also saw some future objectives in Japan. Tokyo is so well laid out by our photographers that we can pinpoint individual buildings to hit. We even know what happens on each floor of the factories. Their day is coming soon.

It's New Year's eve, so I hope everyone's having fun. I will be, with Vera.

January 1, 1944

Happy New Year! Ike Eisenhower says we'll see the end of the war with the Huns in '44, and he's in a good position to know. Then, we'll roll the Japs up, and next New Year we'll all be together again. Let's hope so.

Although I was to be restricted to the post this weekend, they declared a holiday, so I got to take Vera to the gala at the club.

All the girls were in formal gowns and it was a fine time. I had to be in the barracks by 0200, so it wasn't like one of those hot New Year's eves at home, when I could come wandering in at 7 A.M.

Yesterday, I was on a solo combat-style mission and I really screwed it up. With only 30 seconds to set things up, I was a sorry sight. I did get two hits out of five bombs, but one was so far off that the pilot said he could do a better job toggling it out from his seat. I'd like to see the asshole actually do it.

I'm still better than even money to make it out of here with wings and bars.

January 2, 1944

Tonight, we were to spend all night on the trainer to get used to night vision and see how the sight works at night, but when we got there the chief said we should go home and hit the hay. We can sack in until 8 A.M. tomorrow, too. I think they're fattening us up for the kill.

It's a gorgeous Texas night, like spring, with the sky full of stars. Earlier, I went to a quick movie to see Carmen Miranda, Alice Faye, and Charlotte Greenwood in *The Gang's All Here*. Don't miss it.

January 4, 1944

Flying at night is awful. I have dropped 25 bombs in the past two days. Yesterday, I flew straight through from 3 P.M. until midnight with only half an hour off for supper. Night bombing is particularly difficult because of the glare caused by lights around the target. My second bomb was such a honey, the pilot couldn't believe it; I put out the light bulb in the center of the shack. Two more weeks of this grind before we go back to daytime bombing. I haven't had an instructor with me for 10 days, so I guess they feel I'm doing all right by myself.

January 8, 1944

It snowed last night, almost three inches. They'll probably make us go down and sweep the runway, so we can go flying. We didn't go up last night, of course, so we were able to sleep in.

It was clear during the day yesterday, so we bombed the outline of a battleship from 13,000 feet. I plunked one right down the smokestack.

Though we are off tonight, there will be no date with Vera. I got beat out by, of all things, a sailor. I must be slipping.

Pooz, many of the guys asked to be remembered to you. They thought you were real cute. I'm going to give you my gunners wings, as soon as I get the new bombardier ones, just like I promised, honest.

January 12, 1944

I've been flying two and three missions a night with my scores being just OK, not a hot rock, but not a dud either. That's OK with me, because I will go on to operational training as just another bombardier, with expectations that I'll do my job and not that I'll be an expert.

The other night one of the guys put out the lights on the north target with his first bomb. The Cosden oil refineries are right nearby and one of the wells looks like the target, as it is lighted similarly. No one knew the target lights were out and, before it was discovered, six cadets dropped bombs aimed at the oil well. The first few missed, but one guy made a direct hit on the damn thing.

The Cosden people had fits, calling up all night telling us to keep them out of the war. Very funny, and not much harm from practice bombs, so the oil will continue to flow.

Yesterday, I dropped bombs from 1,000 feet. I managed to drop them all on the range, no thanks to the Sperry sight. I also dropped my lunch, as it is mighty rough over Texas at that altitude. All the guys think it's funny when I get airsick. Flyboys are supposed to have cast iron stomachs, but not me. I'm just glad it happens when the instructors are not around or they might send me back to the foot soldiers.

We spent five hours in ground school doing pilotage navigation problems. Pilotage uses maps of the terrain to determine position and direction by reference to the ground you are flying over. It's an important skill, as bombardiers must often assist the primary navigators on lead crews.

Tomorrow, we're scheduled for a compass swing in the air. That's another vomit session for me. We rock the plane around 24 different headings to calibrate the deviation on each. I hope I never have to use the compass I calibrate, as it is sure to be snafued. The instructors have explained the process 100 times, and I still sit there and say, "Huh?"

The main topic of conversation around here is graduation. I'm waiting for word from you, Dad, about your driving down here to pin on my wings. If it's going to be too difficult, I will try to make airline reservations from Ft. Worth home. No train for me, thank you. I worry about jinxing myself by making plans for a leave to come home after graduation. There's still a chance to get the hook.

January 14, 1944

Last night, I was the first bombardier to fly in a brand new ship on a mission from 8,500 feet. I broke in the plane right with four hits out of five bombs on a railhead target. Right after we came down, the plane went back up with two more cadets and caught on fire. Thankfully, no one got hurt.

One of my pals, who has been with me all the way, got washed out yesterday and will go to armament school. I feel for him, and it's too close to me for comfort.

January 18, 1944

I had a sore throat, so I went on sick call. When they found I had a slight fever, they put me in the hospital. I hollered, but the flight surgeon said I needed a rest anyhow. So here I am, taking lots of little pink and white pills.

They're going to keep me here over the weekend, then I can go back to work. I have company from other members of my Squadron, all with cases of the flu. Perhaps we're all suffering from overwork.

Your package arrived. It was some treat. I put the chicken and olives in the ice box to let them chill, then we had a real supper. One of my instructors is here, too, so he joined in the party. The tangerines were nifty, as were the brownies. Thanks a million!

Don't tell a soul, but I'm enjoying this stay in the hospital. I'm feeling OK, thanks to a lot of sulfa pills, and the rest is much needed. Since the weekend is coming up, I won't miss much, and the guys keep me posted on what's happening.

The nurse here has taken to calling me "sonny, boy." She says she'll give me a kiss for good luck when I finish. It seems that I will be the youngest officer they ever graduated from this field.

January 21, 1944

They let me out of the hospital to go to a movie tonight. I have to go back there to sleep, but they will discharge me tomorrow. I feel fine now and quite rested. Breakfast in bed at 8 A.M. is not hard to take.

I got the cigarette case, Dad. It is just swell, especially since it was yours. I remember when you gave me your watch and how thrilled I was.

March 18 is projected for graduation, but it's not a definite date. My leave is not definite, either, so let's make any plans tentative. The talk is that I will probably get the blue bars of a flight officer, instead of being commissioned a second lieutenant. That's logical, as I am the youngest in the class.

January 26, 1944

I'm down at student operations, waiting out some rainy weather to see if we'll go on our scheduled mission using the Sperry sight. Monday, we fly to a 72-hour bivouac at a little auxiliary field about 50 miles from here. We will live in pup tents, eating out of field kitchens and simulating the conditions we are likely to find in a combat theater. We will be dropping real 100-pound demolition bombs from various altitudes, using different sights — sort of a review of all the bombing we have learned.

Let's reopen the discussion about your driving down here for graduation, Dad. It's almost impossible to get on the airlines and even the train is uncertain. If you do come, Ed and Matt will drive back with us to Chicago, then go on home from there. With four drivers, we could have two up front while two sleep in the back. That would get us home in about 35 hours, going straight through. The leave is so short, this would give us more time at home than any other way of travel. What do you say? I can get gas stamps, I believe.

If you still have that bit of parachute cloth I sent home, Mom, how about making it into a scarf for me as a graduation gift? A lot of the guys have liberated a bit of that fine silk cloth and wear it as a scarf with their trench coats. It's light weight and doesn't scratch.

January 29, 1944

Today rounds out one year of service for me. Little did any of us dream a few short years ago that so many American boys would be plunged into a struggle for the survival of the freedom that we had accepted as only natural. It seems like a dream — a

whole year — and yet, not a nightmare. There will be more
months of strife and struggle ahead, but soon the whole thing
will be over, and we who have been privileged to share in the
defense of our future happiness will return home, a bit sobered,
but enriched a thousandfold by our experiences in the army.

It's been a long, tough year, but one for which I would not
take all the gold in the universe. Among other things, I have
learned how to live and work with other men, to know the
meaning of close co-operation and the subjugation of the individual to the welfare of the masses. I've learned to take orders,
and perhaps to give them. I've learned under what circumstances to be kind and gentle and when to be firm. I've learned
when to work like a demon and when to sit back and relax as
the grind lets up. I've learned to make the best of an unpleasant
situation.

I've traveled around a bit and found that, fundamentally, all
our people are the same. A Texan says "you all," but fights with
the same patriotic fervor that carries the Americans to victory
after victory. I've seen the snobs of Floridian society open their
arms to a lonesome soldier boy, and those with little or no wealth
put themselves out to show this same soldier a good time.

I've seen good girls and bad ones and have learned to choose
carefully. I can differentiate between sincerity in an individual
and meaningless words. I've heard fellows say they would never
go overseas, others plead to go, yet both willing to die for that
elusive "freedom" when the chips are down. I know now that the
myth of the German "Superman" is false, for if anyone can claim
that title it is certainly the American boys.

Oh, yes, I've learned to goof off and hide when there's work
assigned that is unimportant, and can be done by the more eager
of the outfit. I've found out why they say its the prerogative of
the American soldier to bitch; it lets off steam and does no
harm. And, there's a million and one other things I have learned.

I've felt the inexpressible thrill of sitting in a plexiglass nose and watching the earth swim by below, and seeing the little insignificants who must stick to the roads in their travels over the tumultuous earth. Or, watching the sun peep over the horizon and knowing that I have discovered the magnificence of the day seconds before those below me. And there's always the thrill of the sportsman who watches his hundred pound missile hurtle through the air and strike a target dead center, two miles below.

Oh, it's a deadly game all right, but the bombardier doesn't think of that as he presses the release trigger. It's just a job — hit the target. That will always be my creed: hit the damn thing and get home to hit again.

A lot of rugged days lie ahead. It's almost a certainty now that I'll see combat duty. Be it in the Atlantic or the Pacific, I'll do my best to do the job right. I have the advantage of the finest training that any individual in any army can receive. I'll be provided with the finest of bombsights to perform my duty, the finest of guns with which to protect myself, and the finest airplane in the world to get me there and back.

Yup, it's a wonderful country — worth fighting for and worth dying for if need be. Thank God I didn't wait to be drafted into service. Should anything ever happen to me you will be happy in the knowledge that I was doing just what I wanted, of my own free will.

Barring unforeseen events, I'll have my wings in a few short weeks, and they'll always be a symbol of the right of a kid to fight for his home, his family, and his pursuit of happiness.

February 2, 1944

Bivouac has been moved up to next week. Then, we will be through with the main bombing training. We then start navigation hops. They will designate a railhead or a factory as a target. We will make a bombing run on it taking motion pictures designed to record accuracy through the bombsight. That effectively combines our navigation and bombardier training. Can't you just see the faces on the people in those towns as we fly over with the bomb-bay doors open.

I find pilotage navigation horribly confusing. I probably won't be able to find a town, let alone a specified objective. I can't even find my seat in the classroom yet.

February 8, 1944

We started navigation in earnest with a 250-mile flight using the pilotage method. We have sectioned aerial maps that identify features we can see on the ground. I sat in the nose giving course corrections to the pilot. With this method we have to keep changing the course, because we do not have a drift solution to compensate for the wind. Ed and I did OK going out, but coming back we blew way off course, and then gave the pilot a wrong heading. We finally followed a road back to the base. Some snafu!

Tomorrow, we are going to calibrate all the instruments in the ship and take a compass swing to figure out the deviation. If you know what this is all about, please tell me immediately, as I haven't the faintest idea of what's going on. I do know that my fanny gets very tired on these long missions, and I am beginning to bob when I walk, just like the ship does when we fly. We are to do 28 navigation missions in all.

Boy, I never realized what I was getting into when I joined the Air Force: gunner, bombardier, navigator. Next thing they'll send me up without a pilot.

February 13, 1944

We got back from bivouac yesterday. The first day it was so warm we were working in our shorts and nothing else. As usual, my nose took a terrific beating from the sun. I drew KP right off the bat, but got out of guard duty.

The second day, we flew off the dirt runways using auxiliary radios. I dropped 20 bombs with the Sperry sight, getting a shack with one of them. Then, we dropped 10 bombs with the D-8 sight from 500 feet on a long road with wooden trucks on it. That is, we were supposed to use the D-8. I used my big toe to take aim and got three hits.

Then, we went to 7,000 feet and flew in an eight ship formation with the lead bombardier using the bombsight, and the rest of us toggling ours out as his went away — just as they do in combat. We had real demolition bombs on board. It was some sight, as all those bombs went off at once. The concussion rocked us, even way up there.

You might like to know that those bombs cost $500 apiece, and I dropped $3,000 worth in 12 minutes, so you had better pay your taxes. It was a good field experience with the officers being chummy and less strict about regulations.

When I got back, I hopped into town for a date with Vera. Her dad gave us his car, and we took a ride to the top of the only hill around here.

In reply to your question, I don't know what's in store for me after graduation. There has been talk some of the guys will stay on here as instructors, but that won't include me — I am too young.

We got letters from the last class that graduated. They went to Westover Field in Chicopee, Massachusetts, for third stage operational training lasting six weeks, then overseas. Nobody really knows what comes next for us.

I wrote to Stephanie as you requested, and she has written back. But, she's just a kid, only 17. You don't want me to rob the cradle, do you?

I am going to the ration board within a few days, to see if I can get gas ration coupons for you to come down here for graduation, Dad.

February 15, 1944

We flew a two hour calibration mission yesterday. The compass swing worked out OK, but we snafued the calibration of the airspeed meter. We flew at an altitude of 500 feet. It was so rough I couldn't stay on the seat long enough to write anything. I must have banged my head on the plexiglass 20 times.

Some drippy new pilot flying a B-24 Liberator bomber crashed it into the ground here. He wasn't watching his altimeter, evidently. The biggest piece left was an engine, what a mess.

Thursday, we're scheduled for a long navigation trip. I am frankly worried, as I don't know a lot about navigation yet. We'll have an instructor along, though, so at least we won't get lost.

Tomorrow, I'm on the range firing the sub-machine gun. We must keep up our skills with small arms, too.

There's talk of a graduation hop for us of 1,000 miles. Navigation is new here, so they're still trying to standardize the program.

I have arranged for the gas coupons. Ed and Matt will be driving home with us, then they will fly immediately from Chicago to New York. Can you make reservations for them, please? It is wonderful to think about coming home. It has been so long since I walked the streets of our neighborhood.

Tomorrow, the field is being thrown open to the public in conjunction with a war bond drive. The commandant of cadets and his stooges came through here to see if the place was clean, and ordered us to scrub the floors. This is beneath the dignity of we who will become officers in a few weeks, but the major said "pretty please," so we did it. Part of the deal is to entertain the locals with a huge garrison parade. Man, do I hate parades!

Please put ten bucks in the mail to carry me through until pay day. I'm a little short.

February 17, 1944

Our class will not get dead reckoning navigation ratings — our course will not have been long enough. This means I will graduate with a bombardier rating only, not the dual rating. That's OK with me. I do not want to be assigned to being primary navigator, since I don't have that kind of confidence in my ability to perform. I am confident in my ability as a bombardier.

The finance officer talked to us about our pay situation as officers. At graduation, I'll get a $250 uniform allowance, plus my pay up to the 18th as a cadet, about $35. Then at my next base, I'll be given travel pay at the rate of eight cents per mile, probably $90. As an officer, my base pay will be $150 per month, plus 50 percent of my base, $75, for flight pay. I also get $21 subsistence pay. A total of $246 per month. Not bad!

I have decided I will not accept an instructor assignment, if asked. There are a lot of guys who are too big or over-age that can fill the bill as instructors. I can do the best job in combat.

Yesterday, we flew a four hour pilotage navigation mission. I surprised myself by doing very well. My log book procedure is a bit shoddy, but that's something that takes practice. We had two bombs on board that we were supposed to drop on one of the targets on the way home. As we passed over the range, I hit the salvo switch and dumped them. The instructor agreed that asking us to bomb after doing a mission like that was a little much. There's nothing like wasting the taxpayer's money.

February 24, 1944

I understand your wanting me to be an instructor, but, since you usually accept my judgment, you must believe me when I tell

you I can serve much better as a combat bombardier. I feel that
not only would I be doing more, but my heart would be in it,
while it would not be as an instructor. Besides, it's probably a
moot point, since they are unlikely to ask me to instruct.

I was on a dead-reckoning mission today and did acceptable
work. The navigation trips require terrific concentration. With
the drone of the engines and the pitch and roll of the ship, they
become quite tedious. I can understand, now, what they mean by
"flyer's fatigue." It is very necessary to completely let down after
a hard flight and just relax. I have frequently seen grown men cry
like babies from over-fatigue.

Today, they officially introduced "camera bombs." We have a
special attachment to the camera that fits right into the eyepiece
of the sight. We make a bombing run on a specific objective,
synchronize the sight, and, when the hairs in the sight cross, it
takes a picture. With some interpretation, it tells whether you
would have hit the target.

On our return from the navigation trip today, our objective
was the Settles Hotel from 6,000 feet. I'd like to try it from
about 200 feet and scare the hell out of the people living in the
penthouse. If you drop a pop bottle from up there, it makes a
horrible noise, like a bomb.

It seems that everything is ganging up these last few weeks,
the tension is rising and everyone is on edge. It's a project to
wind down each day.

February 29, 1944

Yesterday, I was on a solo-navigation trip to Amarillo at 4,500
feet, under a cloud cover. It was so rough, I had the safety belt on
the entire trip. The back end whipped around, papers, maps, and
computers flew everywhere. The wind kept shifting, making drift
readings really tough. It was quite an ordeal, but my estimated

time of arrival was only five minutes off and I hit Amarillo dead on. My pilot, Lt. Malo, did a great job of flying, and the navigation instructor was really pleased with the performance.

Even though the trip took almost four hours, they sent us right back up for a check of the auto pilot, another hour. I was the pilot most of the time on the second flight, and I was really glad to be on the ground after five hours.

In these final days, we fly every day and go to ground school at night. It's a killer pace, but they want to cover everything before we're out of here.

Next week, we have sessions with the classification officer to decide what type of plane we want, or should get, and what theater of operations. I'm interested in B-26 Marauders, but they have the final say over what I am to do.

March 5, 1944

We had an old fashioned Texas dust storm today. Everything in the barracks is under an inch of dirt, making for quite a housekeeping problem on top of everything else.

The Air Corps seems determined to have us appreciate our bars when we get them. I have flown 400 miles Friday, 500 miles Saturday, 500 miles this morning and, if it were not for the dust storm, I would still be wandering around in the wild blue yonder.

I did great with dead reckoning on all the trips, but continue to goof up the pilotage segments. That gives me a black mark, but not enough to offset my good ones.

To get all the work in, we have flown in every imaginable weather. Now, the instructors are maniacs. They are having us fly at 200 feet under a layer of clouds, through heavy rain, ground fog, and you name it. The pilots are really great, though, and have done a wonderful job. Of course, we're not second rate navigators, either.

The pressure is fierce, but thinking about coming home keeps me going.

March 9, 1944

The calendar says eight more days to go, which seems to make them work us even harder. I made a few mistakes on a dead-reckoning navigation mission, but got a big fat "satisfactory" on a pilotage mission. Tomorrow, we drop some bombs; I only need seven more to bring me up to the required 200. Then, we will do night navigation missions.

Our uniforms are in. I have to work on my hat to get it properly raunchy, as befits a flying officer. Getting us ready for our new status, they have stopped clipping our hair to half an inch, which means I may have all of three-quarters of an inch of hair when I get home.

We were just told that in a couple of days they are sending a group of us to Roswell, New Mexico, to participate in the Bombing Olympics. That's a competition between the various bombardier schools. It should be interesting.

March 14, 1944

I came in late last night, home from the bombing competition. They treated us like kings there, swell food, nice quarters, even command cars to drive us around.

Midland School gave us a real trimming. They have been dropping bombs consistently, while we have been focusing on navigation for six weeks. From 15,000 feet, my first bomb fell 145 feet short. I made some corrections, and my second bomb was only 90 feet off, which is very good. But, then I blew one out at 250 feet. My final bomb hit the edge of the shack and was scored at 20 feet. My average was 160 feet, which is what it has been all through school. Interestingly, that was also the team average and the average for the meet, so, you might say, I am just an average guy.

We finished fifth out of the nine schools, but we tried our best. In all, it was an interesting trip and a good experience.

I tried on all my officer's uniforms. I really look quite spiffy. A couple of more days of flying, then I'm done. I am looking forward to Dad's arrival for the graduation and, then, to coming home. The experience here has been demanding, far beyond my anticipation, but I am proud to have made it. Ten days with you, together, in our home will be just the thing to prepare me for whatever comes next.

The Crew Comes Together

T he B-24 Liberator bomber was built in greater numbers and flew a wider variety of missions in more combat arenas than any other American aircraft in World War II. An astounding 18,000 of these bombers were built by five different manufacturers. And, with so many men in the armed forces, much of the manufacturing work was done by women. At the peak of production in 1944, the Ford plant in Michigan rolled out one plane every 63 minutes, around the clock. Considering it took 140,000 person-hours to assemble the 30,000 parts, this was an incredible feat. Experience in combat suggested improvements to the plane and its armaments, yet, despite the constant design changes that resulted, there was no apparent slowdown in production.

The production of the B-24 is but one example of what the people of the United States were able to accomplish, when called upon to unite for the common purpose of winning the war.

The B-24 was 67 feet long with a wingspan of 110 feet and was powered by four 1,200 horsepower Pratt and Whitney engines. Fully loaded, it could carry 8,000 pounds of bombs and a crew of 10 as far as 2,000 miles at 290 miles per hour. The crew was made up of a pilot, co-pilot, bombardier, navigator, engineer, radio operator, and four gunners. Lead planes often carried, in addition, a pilotage navigator and a command officer. The plane's defensive armament consisted of ten .50 caliber machine guns — two each in the nose, top, tail, and belly turrets, and one in each waist position — and 5,200 rounds of ammunition.

With its slab-sided boxy look, the Liberator never received the reverence of it's counterpart, the B-17 Flying Fortress — often, B-17 crews disdainfully referred to the B-24 as "the crate ours came in." Though homely, as a war machine, the B-24 could fly farther, faster, and with a larger bomb load than the Fortress. During WWII, Eighth Air Force B-24s dropped 266,000 tons of bombs on the enemy. Although this was quite an accomplishment, it was costly — 2,100 B-24s and 26,000 airmen were lost.

April 6, 1944

Dear Family,

Being at home with all of you for a few weeks was just marvelous, but being at the Cornhusker Hotel in Lincoln, Nebraska, is just weird. Tomorrow, I will report out to the base, to wait there for my assignment. I can't get paid or assigned until all my papers arrive from Salt Lake City, so sitting around and doing nothing is all for now.

This used to be a clean little city, but with the influx of all the fliers, the mommas are keeping their daughters home at night. Still, I managed to meet a nice girl from the University of Nebraska, so I will have something to do this evening.

Journal Entry

April 7, 1944 – Now's a good time to get some memories from graduation down on paper, since there's nothing else to do.

After graduation Matt, Ed, Dad, and I piled into the car and headed for Chicago, planning to drive straight through, switching drivers. Around 2 A.M. the first night out, I was driving, with Ed in the front seat working the map; Dad and Matt were asleep in the back.

Somewhere outside Tulsa, Oklahoma, on a pitch black road, we must have taken a wrong turn. Finally, we discovered we had been going in the wrong direction for an hour. As Ed and I tried to figure out what to do, Dad awakened and overheard us. "Good God," he said, "I am up to my ass in navigators, and not one can find his way to Chicago." Well, we laughed until our sides ached. There we were with our shiny new wings and gold bars, feeling so sophisticated, when in reality we were just three kids who had lost our way.

During graduation exercises from bombardier school, the CO said that, because of the tremendous destructive capabilities we controlled, bombardiers are "the most dangerous men on earth." In one sense, as a soldier in the service of my country, I like that. Yet, in another, it scares the hell out of me. I certainly want to be effective, but I don't like to think of myself as some kind of monster who rains down death. I need to chew on this further.

April 8, 1944

I'm at the field now. The officer's mess is very good and it only costs 25 cents per meal. I completed my pay vouchers, so tomorrow I can collect. We get $70 for travel allowance and $79 for base pay and allowances. Not bad for the two hard(?) weeks I have put in so far as a second lieutenant.

We had a formation at 9 A.M., then nothing, so I went into town with a couple of officers who also are waiting assignment. We went to the University campus, met some students and made dates for the evening, then rented a car, picked up the girls, had a steak dinner, and went dancing. Since there isn't anything to do, I might as well store up some fun. I'll probably want to draw on it soon, as they say that operational training is very demanding.

Being an officer is a real kick. All we have to do is make our beds, if we want to, while enlisted men keep the place clean. They even have a guy who stays up all night in the barracks to keep the stove going, so all the nice new shavetails don't get cold. I have all my gear out at the base now. I called the motor pool and said to the sergeant, "Send a car around to the Cornhusker Hotel and pick up Lt. Lane's bags, please," and they did it. Terrific!

April 10, 1944

Some of our forms came today. Tomorrow, we get attached to a base squadron — a move that comes with such garbage as 7:30 A.M. formations, being allowed off base only until 1 A.M., a few classes, firing the .45-caliber pistol, and assorted lectures, most of which I have already had 40 times. The advantages of being an officer are somewhat limited, it seems.

Those in my group are the only bombardiers here who have training on the Sperry bombsight, so that probably means we'll go to B-24 Liberators.

The weather in Nebraska makes me long for Texas, so you can imagine what the cold, driving wind is like. I hope I get assigned to some place with a warm, dry climate.

April 12, 1944

They assigned a bunch of us bombardiers, pilots, and other specialists to crews and alerted us for shipment, tomorrow. I haven't met any of my crew yet, but I will on the train, tomorrow. The pilots are B-24 trained, so that looks like it.

Tonight, I am having my final fling in Lincoln with a lovely lady that I met at, believe this, the policeman's ball. What will I get into next?

Just so we don't get off easy, they will give us a last trip in the decompression chamber. We had a lecture on Malaria prevention. What do you suppose I will need that for?

OFFICERS' CLUB
DAVIS-MONTHAN FIELD
TUCSON, ARIZONA

April 18, 1944

Dear Mom, Dad, and Pooz,

After a nice train trip in a first class compartment, I am here at Davis-Monthan Air Base, Tucson, Arizona, in the BOQ (bachelor officer's quarters) with my first pilot Brad McFarland and the co-pilot Jim Walton. This is an old, established field with permanent buildings that are well constructed and comfortable. The crew is complete, with the exception of the navigator. We will start flying in a few days. Brad is a really great guy and he has had a good deal of flying time in B-24s.

It's really warm here. I am waiting on some laundry, to get into summer uniforms. We will take all ten weeks of our operational training in the new "J" model B-24s here.

I went into town last night. It's quite nice, not too metropolitan, with a desert feel and climate to go with it. I met a very nice redhead (don't I always), so things should be all right.

April 19, 1944

We finished all our processing today, which included several immunization shots, checking our flying equipment, and getting physicals. Tonight I attend my first dance at the Officer's Club, joined by Sally — the redhead. Tomorrow we start flying, a short hop for familiarization.

The entire crew got together for the first time today, and I am really impressed with them. They come from all sorts of backgrounds, some with college educations, and each one is intent on the job. I'll tell you more about them, as I work with and come to know them.

The weather is just grand. You know how I like it warm, the feel and look of the summer uniforms suits me. We have a swimming pool, where I am headed right now. The food is just fine, too, so, in the personal department, my cup floweth over.

April 24, 1944

I spent some time this morning learning the bomb release systems on the B-24. This evening the entire crew is flying from 9 P.M. until 1:30 A.M. We won't do any bombing, but I am responsible for checking the men and their guns. We are to be on a seven day schedule, so we need to take advantage of any time off. I started on that by picking up Sally and coming to the club where they had a Hawaiian orchestra, complete with hula dancer. That kind of duty, I like.

Yesterday, we had ground school and I learned about the Emerson nose turret that is standard equipment on our "J" model planes. Returned combat officers are instructors here, and they lectured us on the operational qualities of the B-24. Tomorrow, we're scheduled for formation flying. Doing that well is very important. The closer together we are, the more fire power we have as protection from fighter attacks.

April 30, 1944

Our schedule now is flying in the morning with ground school in the afternoon of one day, then alternating to ground school in the morning, flying in the afternoon, with night flying on the third day. Then we get off for 24 hours and begin again. I haven't dropped any bombs yet, but that's coming up.

It is quite a change from being an aviation cadet to being the bombardier officer on a heavy bomber crew. The responsibility keeps building as we get into more complex flying situations. I let go and relax completely while I am off duty; my latest relaxation was at the local half-mile race track. It was fun watching the horses run again. I got my money's worth, losing only $11.

I got paid this morning, and enclosed you'll find a money order for $100 of the $150 I owe you. If it looks like I can make it until next pay day, I will send on the other $50. This must be some kind of red letter day for you to get money back from me!

While I was in Lincoln, I bought a small .32-caliber revolver from a gun collector. I had a gun shop here make a holster for it. I bought a nice hunting knife, too. I hope I will never have to use them, but they are defense weapons in case I ever have to bail out. I am having a hard time getting .32-caliber ammunition around here. Air Force ordinance doesn't carry it, or I would get it there. Can you check Abercrombie and Fitch and see if they have some? Smith and Wesson or Remington types will work.

May 3, 1944

I know my last few letters have been rather sketchy, but I have been under a lot of pressure. Not infrequently, our work days are 17 hours long, so when I get some time off, I just want to relax or sleep. Since this is the final training I'll receive before combat, you can understand why my letters have been without their occasional funny stuff.

I know how to drop bombs. Now, I am learning how to hit the target and, at the same time, lessen the danger to the crew. The training is intended to keep us from flying a single suicide mission, but instead, to have us able to go back day after day and keep blasting them. So, I must learn evasive maneuvers to avoid flak, and to make short, level approaches to the target that expose us to enemy fire for the least amount of time.

My duties as armament officer on the ship are perhaps most trying of all. I'm directly responsible for every gun, bullet, and bomb on the ship — everything that has to do with offensive and defensive destruction. I must see that the gunners are always on the ball and know their jobs thoroughly.

Now, in a lighter vein: Yesterday, Mac, Jim, and I had a free afternoon, so we went to the El Conquistador Hotel for a swim. It was a beautiful day, just warm enough. I bumped into a girl from Chicago, that I have known for a long time, who is a student at the University here. She introduced me to a bunch of girls. Now, I have a long list of telephone numbers, so I am fixed for dates whenever I have the time and inclination.

I am getting a nice sun tan, the good food is putting on a few pounds, and the demanding physical aspects of the training and work has me totally in top shape. Now, if they would lighten up on the work load and give me some evenings off, everything would be grand.

Mac and Jim are both big guys physically. Jim was a professional football player, and Mac is one very bright guy who went to Williams College. The crew idolizes Mac since he is both a good leader and a remarkable pilot. Jim is a powerhouse who commands attention with whatever he does. I think I am beginning to earn respect for my work as a bombardier, although on a recent flight, I threw a bomb 500 feet off, because I made a stupid computation mistake. I sure felt silly. But, most of the time, I am a Class A bombardier.

Our crew chief is a good lad and knows his work. The armament man, Jack, is from New York. He's quiet and competent. He's also the ball-turret gunner. Another gunner, who works the waist and nose turrets, went to school at Oberlin in Ohio as an economics major. He backs me up, so I am teaching him how to release the bombs, in case I am injured. In turn, he coaches me on the Emerson nose turret.

The tail is handled by a happy-go-lucky guy who is a dead shot. The upper turret is manned by a shy, quiet lad from Tennessee. They're all good men and I am proud to work with them.

You would be amazed at what a sensation the comic strip *Gordo* creates around here. Jim howls when he reads it and he has developed a Mexican accent to read it aloud. El Señor Dog is everyone's favorite character. It would be nice if the cartoonist, Gustav Arillio, could know what he has given us.

You are probably wondering where we go from here. The training has been cut down from 13 to 10 weeks. There's a big demand for crews in all theaters of the war. So, it'll be around June when I leave. Then, we go to Lincoln or Topeka, Kansas, to pick up our plane. We get about a week of test flying it, checking for flaws, then we fly it overseas. There will probably be no leave to come home, so don't plan on it.

Please keep your letters rolling, but lower your expectations about letters from me. You are always in my thoughts and in my heart, even if my letters are not as regular as they have been in the past.

May 5, 1944

Yesterday, we flew an air-to-ground gunnery mission, firing 3,200 rounds of .50-caliber ammunition. It was really rough flying over the desert and, for a change, I was not the only one who got sick — everyone except the pilot did. It was a real laugh seeing everyone hanging over the side. I will remind them of that, the next time I am the lone one to heave.

We were shooting at a dummy airport from 400 feet, really no altitude for a B-24 to be, but we really blasted it. I got off some good shooting, but they expect it from me. The tail gunner, Bob, is a real hotshot, which I really appreciate, as I like my fanny well protected.

We have physical training this afternoon (yes, they still do that to us) and then a retreat parade this evening. After that I'm off and am invited to a party by some folks in town. We have a night mission Saturday, then I'm off again. I'll head back to the racetrack to see if I can get my $11 back.

I'm looking good in my summer uniform, have a healthy tan, feel fit, and all is well.

May 8, 1944

We flew for five hours last night, for five this afternoon, and we're scheduled for five hours at 6 A.M. tomorrow. This is a lot harder than flying at school. The missions are much longer, the pre-flight inspection is much more detailed, and pushing a B-24 bomber around on a bombing run takes real concentration.

Last night, we bombed from 16,000 feet and, I'm proud to say, we did an excellent job. I'm putting out a lot more effort than I needed to at school. My circular error for last night was 130 feet, which will destroy targets every time.

This afternoon, we did formation flying at 22,000 feet, the general altitude for bombing runs in Europe. This was my first time at this height and the ground looks quite different from there. Our navigator, Bill Harland, has joined us and was along on the flight. He's a small guy, so both of us could ride in the nose while he did star sighting with the astro-compass. Bill is 23, married, and has a six-month-old baby. He is a real right guy, and we should be a good team.

When we took off, it was a warm 95 degrees, but at our altitude it was 20 below zero. We had plenty of warm clothing, but it was still mighty cold.

We spent four hours, Saturday, on the ground, firing from the turrets. We got boiled like lobsters, so when I get some time off, I'm heading for the El Conquistador Hotel where I can relax and swim at the pool.

The other day, I was with a bunch of civilian students from the University of Arizona, all my age. They can't figure how or why I am a flying officer. Talking with them, it's quite amazing how we live in entirely different worlds. They can't relate to mine at all, and I can barely remember what theirs is like.

When I have free time, I continue to go out on dates, or with the guys, even though I know that the next day may mean getting up at 4 A.M., flying for hours, then going to ground school.

May 9, 1944

We went on a high altitude mission yesterday with a substitute co-pilot, while Jim was having some medical treatment. It was amazing to see how the teamwork fell apart. I dropped bombs every which way. Hitting the target is less important, now, than learning about teamwork. I will remember this.

I was having a little trouble with my vision at high altitudes from the sun-glare, so I went to the flight surgeon. He prescribed special sungoggles for me. They really take care of us, as they should. We're expensively trained soldiers, handling very expensive equipment.

At the ordinance range today, I learned the effect of different types of bombs and fuses. It was a spectacular, as well as informative, display. Tonight, I take the pilots over to the bomb trainer where they learn about the job and problems of the bombardier. By understanding what I am doing, they can respond to my commands better on the bomb run.

Tomorrow, we go on an 800-mile mission to camera-bomb a target in New Mexico.

May 16, 1944

I hope you got the flowers and my special delivery letter for
Mother's day, Mom. I really missed celebrating with you, but I
hope the day was an enjoyable one. In case you still consider
coming here to visit your son in the desert summer, I checked on
rates at the El Conquistador Hotel. It's the closest to the base,
it's very nice, and they have decent rates this time of year. It's six
dollars per day in the hotel and seven dollars in the cottages, and
that includes use of the pool. It's really lovely. I know it's quite
expensive, but ordinary hotels are five dollars per day, and this
one is special.

Yesterday, I went to ground school from 7 A.M. until midnight.
Today, we flew an air-to-ground gunnery mission and I fired out
of the Sperry ball turret and the tail turret. It was really an odd
feeling in the ball turret at the bottom of the plane. I never knew
in which direction the plane was going. Just as the pilots are
being familiarized with my work, it is important for me to understand what is going on with the men at each of the gun positions.

Tomorrow, we do formation flying at the inhuman hour of
4 A.M. Mac gets all the work. I don't have much to do on such
flights, so I can just sleep. Every day, I learn more about the ship,
try new methods of bombing, use 30-second approaches, and
generally grow on the job. All of our missions are at high altitudes now, as that's where we'll be in combat. Being tired now is
just an everyday thing, but I feel fine in other respects.

Our crew seems to improve with each flight, and we're round-
ing into shape quite nicely. The air inspector, a captain, flew with
us and complimented us on our teamwork. That's of prime
importance and we seem to have it down OK.

Thanks for the brownies and goodies, and to all the family
and friends who keep sending me stuff. I try to answer each person, but don't always make it.

May 17, 1944

I got a flock of mail today, which included the many issues of my favorite comic strip, *Gordo*. Mom, I think it highly inadvisable to come the final two weeks of my stay, as I will be very busy with last minute preparations for overseas duty. I have only Sunday off now, and an occasional evening or morning free, but I can spend that time with you wherever you will be staying. So, within the next three weeks would be best.

Today, we flew formation at high altitude for six hours. My face is all sore from the oxygen mask. I had nothing to do but ride, but I couldn't sleep because of the oxygen. And so it goes — flying, ground school, phys. ed., parades.

May 25, 1944

Hi Dad. Hi Pooz. Are you two behaving now that Mom is on her way here? I am on pins and needles waiting. I plan to meet Mom at the train, as I probably won't be flying Saturday. I am grounded with an ear block. It's not serious or uncommon. I went up with a slight cold, and that did it. It just takes a couple of days to return to normal.

I dropped bombs yesterday, and I wish I hadn't. I had a bum bombsight, and bombs went everywhere but on target. It's not me, it's the equipment, I told them. Even hot guys have bad days.

My gunners are doing very well, and I am proud of them. They are all being promoted with another stripe, which makes me very happy.

June 2, 1944

Sorry about the lapse in letters, but I have been running off every chance I get to be with Mom. You should see her, all sun tanned and looking beautiful. Last night, she got access to an apartment that one of the officers has and threw a party for the crew. What an affair! We had her famous chicken with stuffing and all the trimmings. Apart from the festive atmosphere and great food, it was a good thing to get the gang together like that. Off-duty comradery helps the morale.

We flew a 1,000-mile mission to Amarillo, Texas, on Wednesday. Bill got us there exactly on schedule. Staying on oxygen for six hours is a grind. Yesterday, we did combat type camera-bombing, going after dams and airports, with short approaches and evasive action. It was a good tuneup for me.

Mom is trying to get a reservation to come home. She will have first hand news for you.

June 9, 1944

The invasion is on. I thought for awhile they were waiting for our arrival. I wouldn't mind getting there just when the opposition is pooping out. I am dreaming of things like a three-minute bomb run, bombing the hell out of a target, and coming home having had no fighters and no flak.

We had a new "J" model B-24 on an air-to-ground run, and I worked various turrets. As usual, it was rough air. This time, Bill got sick and threw up in his hat. I have a buddy.

We have a flight on Saturday, but Sunday we're off. We have arranged to borrow a truck from the field, and all the crew will go on a picnic up in the mountains. We are getting food from the mess hall, and we have beer and pop. It should be a great time.

June 12, 1944

We flew a 1,000-mile night mission to Los Angeles. Bill did his celestial thing, and I did radio fixes. Between us, we came in right on the nose. I came home in the co-pilot's seat, flying and working the radio. It was almost seven hours on oxygen. I am getting used to it now.

We were out partying last night and got home at 1 A.M. only to find that we had to get up two hours later to fly. We took an assortment of gunners down to Almagordo for some air-to-air practice. I did some time in the tail turret, which gave me a real appreciation for Bob's job there. While the nose of the plane flies straight, the back end does lazy eights. When I finished, I went up to the flight deck and fell asleep. I awakened when we had trouble with the No. 3 engine. Mac feathered it, and we continued for 400 miles on three engines. It's nice to know we have that kind of reserve safety in our B-24.

This week we have our final administrative processing for overseas. They have frozen all state-side ratings for aircrews, so Mac will have to wait for his promised promotion to 1st lieutenant until we're out of here.

June 20, 1944

Yesterday, we flew over the Grand Canyon. It is incredible. We're just about done with our ground school work and close to being done with flying. The present plans call for us to leave here on June 30 for Topeka, Kansas, but I don't know what happens after that.

One of the guys had a birthday, so we went to celebrate at some joint out near the college. We drank beer until 1 A.M., then went outside, sat on a wall, and sang some songs. The bar owner asked us to move along, so nine of us piled in a cab and laughed all the way back to the base.

We have to fly at 4 A.M. tomorrow in a 54-plane formation as a last check in preparation for overseas. The rumors are running thick and fast about what's next, but, when one has been in the army as long as I have, you just take everything with a grain of salt.

I am sending my good watch home, along with a suitcase of odds and ends I don't need. We have a complete check of our equipment on Tuesday. All of mine seems to be in good order. I'm carrying a lot of stuff, because I don't know what I may need, wherever I'm going. It's not like packing for a vacation, when you know the destination.

June 26, 1944

We were supposed to get up at 3:30 A.M. to fly, but I was out with the guys, so we never did get to sleep. Imagine my chagrin when I walked into the briefing room to find that I was the lead bombardier in an 18-ship formation. They say I did a good job, but it was more from instinct than anything else.

For one dollar, I won a $25 war bond in a raffle at the club last night. That's the start of my good luck for the next year.

June 28, 1944

We're all set here. We had all our clothes checked, were issued field equipment — mess kit, canteen, cartridge belt, etc. — and we turned in all our flying equipment. We will draw all new equipment at the staging area.

Jim is pitching for the local baseball team, tonight, and we're all going to the game. He's a real athlete, and got a great write-up in the Tucson paper. We have a meeting tomorrow and then some sort of graduation.

I think our training here, on the whole, was quite good. I do know that we came here as individual fliers and now we're a smoothly functioning team. There is no question in my mind about our ability; this crew is prepared for any eventuality.

July 1, 1944

We're in New Mexico on the train headed for Topeka, Kansas. We should be there early tomorrow, then we'll find out what happens next. Naturally, with Jim along, we have two of the four compartments on the train. He's a procurement officer super-deluxe. I slept in the lower bunk last night and got ten hours sleep.

We got paid in cash just before we left and there's a lot of money floating around the train. The captain broke up the crap game at midnight.

Before we left, the commanding officer of our section told Mac that we had the best crew on the field. That's a nice comment to start us off. We really deserved it, as we all worked hard.

We had our farewell blow-out at the club the night before we left. They tried to hold things down by closing the bar at 10:30 P.M. and by having MPs all over the place, but it didn't do much good. Everyone got happily fried. It was a good windup to our training. We all seem to be in a good frame of mind and we're ready for come what may.

Chapter Nine

Flying the North Atlantic

W hen I flew across the North Atlantic recently, in a comfortable jetliner, sipping my drink and listening to music, my mind wandered back to more than 50 years ago when I made the same trip in a B-24 bomber. At the time, it was considered an immense plane, but it would easily fit under the wing of today's intercontinental jet.

Flying at 550 miles per hour, the huge airliner had radio beacons and sophisticated instruments to keep it on course for the six or seven hours it took to fly from the East Coast to London. Flying at 200 miles per hour, our B-24 bomber was allowed no radio contact and had only a few comparatively primitive instruments to plot our course by dead reckoning navigation on the four-day, four-stop trip to England via Labrador, Greenland, Iceland, and Ireland.

The air-conditioned comfort of the jetliner contrasts sharply with the cold, seatless, steel-floored austerity of a 1940s bomber.

Instead of the comfortable clothes worn on the airliner, we wore heavy-lined leather suits and big gloves to protect us against the freezing arctic air that whistled through the gunnery openings and cracks in the bomb bay doors, as we flew through inclement weather to an isolated airstrip in a frozen land.

Looking down from the airliner today, while flying at 35,000 feet, all looks peaceful and serene. But back then, at 8,000 feet, the movement of the waves in the black waters and the sharp edges of icebergs were ominous to the young men who were on their first trip over the ocean and away from the U.S.

In retrospect, it is simply amazing that thousands of bombers and thousands of fighter planes flew these North Atlantic routes to England more than 50 years ago. They were piloted by young men with only a few months training but with the daring and dauntless courage that they viewed as, simply, what one did as an American in wartime.

———❦———

Army Air Forces

July 3, 1944

Dear Mom, Dad, and Pooz,

I just came in from having dinner and a look at Topeka with
Mac. He's meeting his dad, so I came back out to the club on
the base. It's terribly hot and sticky. I'm waiting for it to cool off,
then I'll hit the sack.

This morning, we went out to the new plane assigned to us
and checked it out very carefully. It seems in good shape and,
except for a few minor things, ready to go.

They have given us 50 rounds of ammunition for each gun on
the ship, just in case (but of what, I don't know). We still have
not been told where we're going. My guess is it'll be ETO, as
everything points that way. Tomorrow, we'll be flying all day, cal-
ibrating our instruments in the morning and checking the auto-
pilot and bombsight in the afternoon.

We had our supply processing today. They gave us foot lockers
to load with the personal things they will send overseas for us,
but we won't see those for a month. We're allowed 55 pounds in
our B-4 bags that go with us, but I stuffed mine so full, it
weighed a lot more. Most of it they took out and put in the foot
locker, so I will start off with a few uniforms, a pair of shoes, and
underwear. However, being an inventive soldier, there was still
my aviator bag that goes with me, weight free, so I stuffed it
with all kinds of junk.

Our issue of flight gear includes a brand-new type of winter equipment. Instead of the heavy leather, sheepskin-lined suits, we have kapok jackets and pants, lined with felt and a layer of real fur inside that. It's a lot lighter and less cumbersome than the gear we have been using. We also have new type helmets with the earphones fitted right into them, so we don't have to wear headsets. They also installed microphones in our oxygen masks, which eliminates the throat mike. The boots are the same — sheepskin lined leather. The gloves are much better than before, too. For warmer weather, we have kidskin with nylon liners and, for winter, leather with wool liners. The goggles have no metal piece in the middle, so they afford better vision. What was glass is now shatterproof plastic, with interchangeable lenses of various colors that we can select for bright or hazy days. We also got gabardine coveralls and a really swell leather flight jacket for everyday use.

Our parachutes are the chest-pack type with a new harness that prevents an aviator's face from being cut by the shrouds when it opens. On the back of the harness, forming a back rest, is a ten-pound emergency bailout kit. It contains emergency rations, fish-lines and hooks, artificial bait, tablets for purifying water, atropine to prevent malaria, salt tablets, a two-foot folding machete, a complete medical kit with sulfa powder and sulfa tablets, mosquito netting, insect repellent, cigarettes, a frying pan, and 20 rounds of buckshot ammunition for our .45-caliber pistols. There's more stuff that I've forgotten, but it's all in a package just six inches deep.

There's also a small first aid kit strapped onto the shoulder of the harness, and there are ten first aid kits placed throughout the plane. Our ditching equipment is two, five-man rafts, a floating "Gibson girl" radio, signal equipment, and the "Mae West" life vests we each wear under our parachute harness. I would say we're well prepared for an overseas trip.

They gave me a new waterproof, shockproof, anti-magnetic bombardier's watch, so I sent my good one on home. I have saved up a lot of chocolate bars and gum, and they're going to sell us a carton of each before we leave. They will also sell us a couple of quarts of good booze at a real good price. What more could I ask for?

They have done all they could to make us safe and comfortable. Of course, it's pretty hard to be comfortable in the nose of a B-24; it's the only place in the plane with nowhere to sit.

So, as you can see, I'm all set. I'm going to get my chance to see the world from the air, and we'll have a fascinating trip, I know. I love you all very dearly and I will miss you a lot. Wish us God-speed, and we will be home before you know it. You're a wonderful family, and we are fighting for the greatest country in the world. If the Germans could only see the spirit with which we go to meet them, they would be plenty worried.

July 7, 1944

The first leg of our journey is over. It's hard to believe how efficient the army can be when they really want you to move. I'm at a "Port of Embarkation" somewhere in the East. Our ship weathered the first leg beautifully, and we're quite proud of her. Just before we left, we named the plane "El Dorty Treek" from *Gordo* and had a big picture of Gordo riding a bomb painted on the nose. Pepito and Señor Dog are painted down by the bombardier compartment. It's really humorous.

We're right in the heart of some of the most beautiful country I have ever seen (That's OK, censor, I won't say where. You can keep your lousy military secrets). This base looks like some of the summer camps in the north woods, with rolling hills and green grass, resembling anything but an army camp. Now that we're going into action, everyone has become sweet as sugar. The Red Cross gave us food and a bag full of goodies. When we landed, the base command had a station wagon waiting to take us to our final processing. They gave us terrific sunglasses, parkas, and arctic trousers. Pretty obviously, we're not headed south. Our ship is so jam packed with emergency equipment, Mac has to really gun it to get it off the ground.

I'm not worried about the trip at all. Harland is an aces-high navigator. He has proven it time and again. So, here's to the high seas! Don't worry about me!

Journal Entry

July 7, 1944 – This is a good opportunity to restart my journal. Now we are really under strict censorship and there are probably many changes in store for us. Coming in, we flew over Niagara Falls, some gorgeous sight. The next time we take off, it'll be goodbye to the U.S.A. It makes a lump in my throat when I think of it, but such emotional hurts go with the job.

July 9, 1944

Boy, am I having adventures. I still can't tell you where I am, but you would be amazed to know how far we have come in just two days. Our plane performs flawlessly. Old Bill is right in there, bringing us into each stop right on the button with only dead reckoning navigation — there is no radio contact allowed.

Yesterday, all I did was play blackjack back in the waist with the gunners. It's a bombardier's paradise, because all I have to do is eat and sleep. I swiped a pillow at the last stop, to make it more comfortable. The facilities at all the bases are miraculous. They have done everything to make our trip safe and pleasant.

We were held back a few hours from our scheduled departure, so I went to a Protestant church with Mac. It's probably advisable to be in good with all gods.

Journal Entry

July 10, 1944 – Here over the ocean where we're not part of the U.S. and yet not part of the fight, I look down on the endless ocean waves. They are doing just as we are, starting at North America and ending up on the shores of Europe. It's quite incredible to realize we started at Bangor, Maine, then went to Goose Bay, Labrador. Next was Bluie West 1 in Greenland. Now we're headed to Reykjavik, Iceland. From there, it's our last big leap to Ireland.

In earlier flights, the Germans put out false radio beams, leading ships off course to their destruction, so now we keep radio silence, relying on dead reckoning alone to reach the air-field in this vast permanent winterland. So, I am alone in the nose, and we are alone in the sky, surely for the last time.

Mac and Jim are responsible for this great machine that goes from ground to skies and ground again, carrying all of us to safety at the end of the day. Bill uses his navigational magic to guide us to our destination, the crew chief makes the engines hum, the radio operator, when allowed, keeps us connected to the world below, and the gunners scan the skies, ready to ward off enemies. I am the dealer of death, offensively, with my bomb load and, defensively, as the officer responsible for the guns and gunners.

There will be other times for reflection, but for now it is good to be lulled by the drone of the engines, and to dream of peace.

July 10, 1944

This is pretty amazing, I'll admit, but I am now "somewhere in Iceland." When we left the states, they gave us these big fur lined parkas and trousers, which we took as a joke. But, here inside the arctic circle, it is mighty cold. It is late in the evening, yet there is full daylight. They say it never gets dark this time of year. Everything here is built into the ground to withstand the weather, quite a departure from anything I have experienced before.

Our trip here was swell, over ocean all the way, but handled with no navigational difficulties. Tomorrow, weather permitting, we're off again. I can't tell you where to, but your guess will probably be right. We'll be seeing action soon. Write to me in care of my Army Post Office (APO), 16209-BJ-95, New York City, and I will look for your letters.

July 11, 1944

I have only a few minutes, for a short note. They won't let me tell you a thing other than I am now in Northern Ireland. The trip has been very enjoyable so far, and I am really getting my chance to see the world. I feel fine, and accepting of whatever lies ahead. The rush-rush is on and we're probably in for a lot of surprises. You'll get a better letter than this when I am settled.

July 13, 1944

Well, I'm finally here, "somewhere in England." Our crew will be replacements for some of our brethren of the skies who are no longer with us. We're in a temporary replacement pool and will probably not be here long.

England appears to be just as we were led to believe — it's been raining on and off since we have arrived, with no indication it will stop. The English people are much like Americans and, except for the shabby appearance caused by the war, the cities are similar, too. We got a good look at the countryside flying down here. It will be fun to examine it on the ground at my leisure, when I have some free time tomorrow.

We are less than a half hour by air from the fighting front and, of course, we are under strict blackout regulations. Guns and planes are in evidence everywhere and there's no doubt that there's a war going on here. Living conditions are not like those we had in the U.S. The food is rotten, the quarters are cramped, and every convenience is pretty minimal. Please understand that I am not complaining, just reporting. This is what we knew we would find and, in a theater of operations, we don't expect to be pampered.

I certainly am thankful that I am an officer. The enlisted men really get a going over, with KP assignments, latrine details, etc. It's a shame that aircrew members have to do things like that, but manpower seems to be scarce.

How about sending me some of Hattie's brownies. By the time they get here, I'll probably be desperate.

July 15, 1944

I'm learning how to write on this damned V-mail. I hope you can read my letters after they photograph them down. Let me know how they come through. I haven't received any mail from you, as yet. The way we have been hopping around, it's no wonder. I'm sure a flock of mail will catch up with me soon.

Our baggage hasn't arrived as yet and, after six days in the same clothes, I'm beginning to smell like a rotten herring. There's a traveling PX that sells officer's clothes, so I bought a few things to tide me over.

Last night, I got a pass, borrowed a blouse from one of the boys, and took off for town — a place of 70,000 about 18 miles from here. (No names, please.) I met some Limey, and we went to a pub for a wee drink. The national drink is ale, bitter or mild. It tastes somewhat like beer and, since there is no ice, it is served warm. I think I'll confine my drinking in the United Kingdom to water, thank you. After struggling for an hour to fathom the gentleman's cockney accent, I gave up and went for a walk around town. I saw some blokes (that's local for guys) coming out of a dance hall, so I sauntered in, just as pretty as you please. Being as how I'm an American officer, I created a mild stir, enough to attract the attention of a blond English lass who looked as if she had possibilities. We did a little dancing and then, by slipping her a few American cigarettes, with the prospect of more, we made a date for tonight. But, there's a catch: I am restricted to the post tonight, for reasons I am unable to mention — no, I haven't been naughty.

In my early contacts with the English, I have found them friendly and anxious to make the American boys feel at home. I am gradually getting used to the money system, though at first, I'll admit, I held out a roll of bills and said, "Here, take what you want." The stories about all the gum and candy going to the boys overseas is strictly bull. We get a ration stamp, which entitles us to purchase three candy bars, two razor blades, two packages of chicklets, one bar of soap, and seven packages of cigarettes a week, and that's all. However, cigarettes are threepence (a nickel) per package.

This morning, they put me to work censoring the enlisted men's mail (you will note that I am censoring my own). It was sometimes funny, sometimes sad, and makes me very aware how many varieties of Americans there are.

July 17, 1944

We spent Sunday in transit. Now we are at another of those bases "somewhere in England." We're waiting for something, but I don't know what, so we just eat, sleep, and repeat. I went into the nearby city, a place of some 100,000. The city is interesting, but the girls can't hold a candle to American women. I have a date tonight with an English lass who is about the best of the lot.

The sun is actually out, and it hasn't rained for two whole days now. They tell me it is only the fourth day the sun has shined this year. Some place, huh?

There are little shortages like writing paper, matches, and, of all things, cokes. No lighter fluid either. When I get back to our plane, I'll put a little gas in my lighter. There are no hotels or restaurants around, but the American Red Cross maintains an officer's club in town. For six shillings, nine pence (that's 70 cents) you can get a fairly decent meal.

July 18, 1944

And still I wait. In town last night with the lassie, we went to some boxing matches in the park. Billy Conn was there to put on an exhibition. He was fighting the Air Force champ and making him look silly. Then we went to the girl's home for some tea and chips (french fried potatoes). I am enjoying learning to be a tea drinker. Being in someone's home was really enjoyable, though these folks know what it is to feel the privations of war. They need coupons or permits for most everything. This girl is 18 and everyone in the family works, including her 15-year-old sister. They only go to school until 14. That's the way it is in all the families. Besides, most of them are caring for evacuees from London. So, you see, life for them is not very pleasant.

The blackout is still a strange thing for me. I have banged my head on lamp posts a dozen times. There are pipes running along the curbs carrying water to extinguish incendiary fires, and I always trip on those, too.

July 19, 1944

Now I am "somewhere in Northern Ireland." I can't tell you why, but it does not entail combat missions. We are here to work, but not for long. My clothes haven't caught up with me

yet, and I am beginning to feel like Robinson Crusoe. Facilities
are all overburdened, so we wait for showers, wait for chow, and
just wait.

Just about everyone I know from the army is at this base. We
had a reunion of my bombardier class — at least 60 percent of us
are here. Some of the guys came over on the Queen Elizabeth.
So, I sat around with my pals at the club talking over old times.
It seems that we are to fly 35 combat missions, then get thirty
days leave at home before returning. At least, that's the story
going around.

We have to unlearn some of the things we sweated over in the
states and learn some of the things that are peculiar to this theater. Time is very limited and there is much to do, but we will
make it. I'd like to be more clear, but I am censoring my own
mail and it is a matter of honor to tell only what is allowed.

I did get my first letter from you, since I have been here. I
can't tell you what a morale boost that was.

July 22, 1944

Food is fair here, but quite tasteless in the usual army style, so
Mac and I greased the cook's palm and got a freshly baked apple
pie. Then, I went to one of the many Irish farmhouses dotting
the countryside and got a woman to kill and roast a five-pound
chicken for me. We talked some store owner out of a bottle of
port he had hidden, and also managed to find half a dozen fresh
eggs (all the army ones are powdered). So, we have the chicken
and pie for tonight. The eggs are for breakfast tomorrow. As
long as we are amply supplied with money and American know-
how, we won't lack for some of the luxuries.

Sunday is no day of rest here. Germany must get its daily
pounding, and we must keep up with our preparations to join a
combat group. We are learning about some of the miraculous

achievements of the 8th Air Force, but we are also hearing that the Luftwaffe is far from dead.

The bombardiers take a good-natured beating around here. We're known as togglemasters and glorified nosegunners. That's because wing crews (those following the lead ship) drop their bombs when the lead-plane bombardier does, so the bombardiers back in the formation just flip a toggle switch. The guys suggest that in an emergency, when the load needs to be lightened, they should throw out the bombardier. I'm not going!

July 29, 1944

I hit the jackpot today, receiving twelve letters. That takes care of what's been ailing me.

I will be moving shortly to my permanent location, a B-24 bomb group airfield. Each group has its own field and operates out of there, rendezvousing in the air with other groups on a mission. I can't tell you where I will be, but if you find out where one B-24 group is in England, you will know we are within a few miles radius.

We will probably have a few practice missions, then combat. From the stories we hear, the Germans are on their way out. Losses in the 8th are very low. I'd like to tell you something that is just for you to know: If you ever get a notice that I am "missing in action" don't get too bothered. If I bail out, that's the way they must classify me. However, you would be amazed to know the high percentage of boys who make it back. I will be riding in the nose turret for the first few missions, and that is the most heavily armored part of the plane. It's not a particularly hard job, either. But, when I let you know they have made me a lead bombardier, then you will know I am earning my pay. Upon those chosen few, rests the success or failure of the 8th Air Force. Believe me, it's true.

Well, enough of that. Ireland has been an interesting inter-
lude. I learned a lot, got much wiser, and am better off for the
time spent here. I can't send you a picture of my ship because we
don't want the Huns looking for any particular one. There's a
story that one of the boys dug a 20 millimeter shell out of his
ship that had the pilot's name and serial number on it. This is
supposed to alert us to the war of nerves, but if you believe this
story, I have a bridge you might be interested in buying.

My APO will change shortly, so look for it. Your letters were
simply super. They have me in high spirits tonight.

Chapter Ten

And Now to War

One of the most often used acronyms during the war was SNAFU — situation normal, all fouled up. It applied to hurry-up-then-wait situations and to a myriad of small and large problems. But the grand SNAFU that affected everyone was V-mail. It was projected that V-mail would speed delivery and reduce the paper volume that took up valuable shipping space. In practice, however, V-mail presented a host of problems to users, and the promised speed never happened.

Letters destined for overseas were to be written on a government printed form, then mailed to a central Army Postal Service where it would be photographed and transported as a negative. Upon arrival, an enlargement would be printed — at only one-third the original size — and forwarded to the addressee.

The form severely limited the amount that could be written, so to compensate, folks would write very small and squeeze the most out of the space. The end result was a tiny thing that required a magnifying glass to read. Since not every location had photography services available, the original V-mail form was sometimes forwarded; however, without a special course in V-mail form-opening, all too often the message was torn or cut in the process.

The V-mail problem was compounded by censorship. One of the ubiquitous posters of the day proclaimed, "Loose Lips Sink Ships." This suggested that, if you talked about or wrote about troop movements, battles, casualties, or such, you might be giving aid and comfort to the enemy. To prevent loose pens that might lead to loose lips, every unit had designated censors who read outgoing mail and deleted questionable information. If the letter was on regular stationery, the censor scissored out the offending phrases, so arriving mail sometimes looked as if it had been written on a slice of swiss cheese. With V-mail the censor stamped black ink over the no-no words, so they would not reproduce when photographed.

Imagine pouring your heart out to someone you loved onto a V-mail form, then having it inspected by censors, scissored or black-stamped, photographed, then reproduced to one-third size before it reached the object of your passion. Some impact!

One good thing about army mail — soldiers were able to send their mail free of postage. This may not seem like a big deal at only three cents per letter, but to someone with my proclivity for wordiness, it meant saving a full month's pay during my army career.

UNITED STATES AIR FORCE

August 1, 1944

Dear Mom, Dad, and Pooz,

I am at my final destination, the 392nd Heavy Bombardment Group. Some of the boys who are here from my bombardier class at Big Spring have already flown two or three missions. I'm just a little bit scared, but I'll be OK after I get a few under my belt.

All the boys who don't fly all go down to the flight line when the Group is scheduled to come in after a mission. It feels strange to see a ship come in with one prop feathered, another with two engines out, and some with big holes in the wings or fuselage. But, most do come back — a real tribute to the builders back home, the ground crews here, and, of course, to our aircrews.

They have kept us busy today checking in around the field, meeting the squadron officers, and learning the ropes. The squadron bombardier is a captain, a great guy. They say he can really hit a target. We're on a school schedule again — one never stops learning in the army. We'll do that for a few days, then the crew will be operational (ready for combat).

I may not fly with the crew on the first few missions. They are talking about my taking an advanced dead-reckoning navigation course here at the field, enabling me to work in that slot when they need two or three navigators on certain crews. I'm not particularly crazy about the idea, but it's no worse than being a glorified nose gunner.

I was in the barracks yesterday when the other crews came back from their mission and finished debriefing. They talk about it just as we would rehash a football game. It seems that the guy who gets the most flak holes and still makes it home is the winner. They are certainly a marvelous bunch and I'm proud to be one of them.

This field is like the others I've seen in England, sort of thrown together. We live in Nissen huts — the beds sag, and it's a quarter of a mile to the latrine. The officers mess is about half a mile from the barracks, as are the showers and washing facilities, so everyone rides bikes. It's hilarious to see officers and men exchanging salutes from bikes. I have one ordered that I will pick up tomorrow night. If I don't get one, I'll likely wear my legs down to the knees.

The food is pretty decent and the equipment is marvelous. They do what they can to make the boys happy. There's even some good old American bourbon in the club. We are supposed to get a 48-hour pass every two weeks after we start flying. That's not a bad deal, as it is possible to get to London in that time. Of course, with the German buzz bombs flying around, I don't know if it will be such a good idea. I feel OK and ready for action. We'll be getting it soon.

August 3, 1944

We're not operational, yet. We have another day or so of orientation with the Group officers, then a few days with the squadron leaders. After that comes a practice mission or so. We stand around each night and wait for the ships to return. So far, we haven't done much sweating, because they seem to be doing all right.

The others may get a little ahead of me while I go to navigation school. They're short on navigators and long on bombardiers.

There's some marvelous new navigation equipment they want me to learn.

The weather around here is really lousy. How they keep flying is beyond me, but they do have many take off and landing aids and they do not seem to be losing planes because of the weather. I thought my personal flying equipment was great, but they have even better stuff here.

It's really quite amazing to be with these guys. I read in the papers, "1,000 heavy bombers were over Europe today," and the boys who flew in them are now sleeping next to me. Pretty soon we'll be making a little history ourselves.

You ought to hear the German radio broadcasts. At the end of them, they say, "American soldiers lay down your arms, you're only fighting to maintain Jewish power politics in Washington." Then they make up the weirdest stories of why they are losing. What a bunch of jerks.

The Russians are kicking a lung out of them. However, they're still not finished, and they are pulling a few new stunts in the air war. They are clever in some ways, those bastards.

I have a new bicycle. It gets me around the base pretty well. The food continues OK; we get ice cream three times a week. Every once in awhile, they feed us eggnogs and we get vitamin pills every day. I think they are protecting their investment. Today, we had cheese blintzes, no fooling!

Things don't seem as somber as I thought they would be. Yes, this is a serious business, but when the mission is over, everyone still jokes and laughs. I haven't seen any cases of the combat fatigue they write about. It may be something the magazines dreamed up.

If you have any old cookies laying around that you don't want, send them here to aid the war effort.

August 7, 1944

Mac and the squadron operations officer and I flew down to
Stone, our first station, to see about our baggage. They said they
had shipped it to us on the 3rd, however, so we're still sweating it
out. I hope it comes soon, I'm getting awfully dirty.

We landed at an RAF base. While we were waiting for
ground transportation, I got into a cricket game with some of
the British boys. It sure is a slow game compared to American
baseball.

We've still got to fly a practice mission before we go on a
combat mission, but we can't do either until our flying equipment arrives. So, here we sit. I got my parachute today, a back
pack. Most of the boys wear chest packs; it is only very thin fellows who can get into the turret with a back pack. I like the idea
of having my chute with me, not outside the turret, so being
small has some payoff. I have to wear a flak suit, too, so it is still
rather crowded.

I don't care much about little stuff anymore. I can remember
when I would moan bloody murder about trivial things, such as
uncomfortable quarters, long distances to latrines, etc., but now
what I want to do is get my mission finished and go home. I'm
sure we'll get started soon enough.

August 8, 1944

Today, I got a letter from you, written to my old APO on July
19. I hope our mail will settle down soon, to where it arrives in
seven days. It was so good to hear from home. I am chewing
nails over our luggage, which has still not arrived.

The squadron needs us, as a few crews are shot up and some
are on leave because they are a bit flak-happy. But, we haven't
any oxygen masks or other flying equipment, so here we sit.

Our crew is in good shape and we're getting kind of anxious to slip a little TNT to the Huns. The boys in this outfit are good, they hit everything they're assigned.

Please send me three or four Benzedrine inhalers. I use them to keep my nose and ears clear when I fly, and they are unobtainable in England.

August 10, 1944

Yesterday was Bill's anniversary, so I arranged a little party for him. Our work has been so confining for the past three weeks, we needed a break. The special services officer rounded up some booze, food, and a room for us, and we went at it. We all wrote a letter to Bill's wife. We signed it before the party, then after. We all got pretty fried, so the "after" signatures were a riot. We had a good time, and it was a welcome respite.

We flew a practice mission around England today, and now, we're awaiting our first combat assignment. They have decided, temporarily at least, that I'll fly with the crew as bombardier and that they're putting off any navigation training.

They're all well-satisfied with Mac's flying, we've rounded up our equipment, and we're ready for the word to go. We got flak helmets today, the only item we were lacking. We already had flak vests and extra armor for the ship.

They tell me the bookies in London are betting the war will be over by September 1, but that is only 20 days away. I hope they are right.

August 13, 1944

Well, we flew our first mission, and I sure was scared. I think I was in my flak helmet down to my waist. It comes down over my nose anyhow, and I just squeezed up into it. When we got near the target, I decided it was time for me to leave the turret, but Harland wouldn't let me out. He threatened to wire the doors shut on me. I guess he didn't want me to crowd him out of his hiding place. What a gremlin he is! I looked back and he had his flak suit up to his ears, a flak apron protecting the family jewels, another one on the floor, and he's all huddled up under his desk. I don't blame him, I would have liked a place to hide, too.

Fortunately, we saw no signs of the Luftwaffe. I did enjoy the sight of a flock of Liberators spilling their guts on a fuel dump and watching the flames and smoke come up nearly to where we were.

Remember how I used to complain about getting up at 5 A.M.? On mission day, some joker came into the barracks and said, "Lt. Lane, it's 0200. Briefing is at 0300. They're serving eggs and coffee at the officer's mess." They're totally nuts!

Yesterday, we had the day free, so I took off for town. Went to a show and a carnival. Pretty nice. I'm waiting on my 48-hour pass, so I can go to London.

Journal Entry

August 13 – No need for bravado in my own journal — man, was I ever scared. We have been lectured to about combat, read about it, had returnees tell us about it, and the veterans on the base tell us about it, so we knew just what to expect, right? Wrong! There's some huge difference between words and reality.

This was our first mission, so we were tail-end Charley, last in the formation. They say this is no place to be in a fighter attack, as they go after the last plane first. The target was Pacy-Sur-Armancon in Southern France. First, they called the mission, briefed us, then scrubbed it, then reinstated it. We finally got off at 0630. I was already a nervous wreck from the off-again, on-again bit.

Our target was one the B-17s missed the day before, but we hit it precisely. I toggled the bombs on the lead plane's drop, the right assignment for my first time. When the flak came up, my hand was shaking so badly, I could never have turned the knobs on the bombsight. The command knows what they are doing when they put a rookie bombardier in the nose turret of a plane farther back in the formation.

Well, that was number one. I hope I will learn how to handle my fear better, once I get some experience. The one thing I wish for is that my flak helmet could be the size of a bathtub.

Journal Entry

August 14, 1944 – Another mission to Southern France, with one small problem: A piece of spent flak came through the bombardier compartment and hit my oxygen mask over my mouth, breaking my front tooth. It was really no big deal, but if it had been a piece of flak at full velocity, it would have taken off my head. So, hopefully, that's my injury for the war.

The base dentist said, while they don't normally have any equipment for cosmetic work like that, he will get some plastic from somewhere, color it, and make a tooth for me that will work until I can either get to a better equipped base or home.

The CO said I should apply for a purple heart medal, but those are given to guys with serious wounds, or posthumously sent to families of those who are killed. It doesn't seem right for me to have a medal for such a small thing, so I will not go for it. I will let the memory of my close call be enough.

August 18, 1944

Today, when we got home, I read of the new landings in
Southern France. That made a little more sense of our last two
missions. I would like to tell you about the many things that run
through my mind, but I'm too tired. We're all tired because we
have been going full blast, but generally we're OK. We have run
into a little trouble, but nothing major, so we're thankful.

The maintenance of the planes is just great. When we get out
to the ship in the morning, it is always in perfect shape. Only
occasionally does something go wrong, as it did yesterday. My
turret got stuck midway into the raid, and I crapped 20 shades of
green before I got it going again. The boys all thought it was
funny and had a good laugh on me.

I had a dumb accident and broke a front tooth, which isn't
doing anything for my looks. They don't have facilities for handling cosmetic things like this, but the base dentist has assured
me he will figure out something and give me a tooth that will
work OK until I get home and have it fixed properly.

As we fly over France, we never know whose territory we're in.
The ground troops are moving so fast, the lines change between
our briefing and the time we get there. Our aircraft have managed to post-hole the terrain in advance of the troops. We haven't
had any of the usual trouble that visits the crews; in fact, things
have been almost oddly simple. I sure hope it continues that way.

We're having a big party on the base tonight for the combat
officers. The trucks go into town and bring back loads of local
women, and the liquor will flow. It should be a grand time. My
hope is that we won't have to fly tomorrow.

August 20, 1944

It's raining cats and dogs outside. Mac and I are alone in the
barracks. We've been hashing out some of the little problems

we meet daily and chit-chatting about our respective futures.
Every day with Mac is a revelation. I have come to respect his
friendship more and more. He has taught me a lot of things not
at all connected with the army and I've discovered that his tol-
erance towards individuals and organizations is gradually
becoming a part of me. Sure, like all of us, he has some faults,
but you know how high my standards are for friends, and he's
one in a million.

We had our big party the other night. I don't like to join in
these brawls as a rule, but sitting and watching the guys is a lot
of fun. I had a few drinks and danced a bit with some of the
local girls. The MPs are still trying to round up some of the
girls. They're hiding around the camp, and some slept in the barracks. Nothing like this could ever occur in the U.S. I think I
prefer nice American girls in a less wild setting.

Our pass is coming up in a few days, and we're anxiously
looking forward to it. We have decided to brave the buzz bombs
for a look at London. Mac, Bill, and I will head for Westminster
Abbey, St. Paul's Cathedral, Buckingham Palace, and other
places that are famous in English history. They say the changing
of the guard at Buckingham is quite a sight. I sure will have stories to tell. I am going to a ritzy hotel, sleep on nice clean sheets
over a thick mattress, and just luxuriate.

They have changed the pass time, giving us three days instead
of two, so that makes it a lot less hectic.

With the allies coming down from the north and up from the
south, it looks like our days of bombing in France are nearly
over. The papers say the Ruhr Valley is being built up by the
Jerrys, and I imagine we'll be going after it some day. The boys
affectionately call it "Happy Valley," after "flak-happy," so I
haven't got the tremendous hots to visit it. We are still flying out
on the wing and I'm just a "toggle boy," but I'm not complaining.

We have been living in separate places, but we were able to get the four officers together in one hut yesterday, so we're a bit more comfortable. The food continues to be quite good. We get fried chicken twice a week. It's OK, but not like yours, Mom. We get real ice cream, too, made with powdered milk, but still tasty.

On our last mission, they got us out in a hurry and we all missed breakfast. It was a real long flight. When we landed, we hadn't eaten for 27 hours. As usual, the Red Cross was there waiting for us with sandwiches (the only ones in the ETO), coffee, cake, and a shot of whiskey for all the boys. They are really grand. My admiration for the work they do is over-whelming.

August 25, 1944

Our pass was really a lot of fun. I visited Westminster Abbey, St. Paul's, and London Bridge. We stayed at a swell hotel, ate in some good places, and totally did up the town in grand fashion. I also saw what the buzz bombs can do and the ruins from the blitz. I bought some sheets in London. That should make my GI cot a bit more comfortable.

We got back pretty late last night and, as I expected, they put us on a raid early this morning. When we got home, late in the day, Glenn Miller was here with his orchestra, so we all stood around in our flying clothes and listened to him. I was almost too tired to enjoy it, but I'm glad I did summon up the energy. It was a really fine musical experience.

There was a flock of mail when I got back, including a box of brownies that were mailed to me in Tucson about the middle of June. They were still edible. By the way, I'm pretty far down the road to financial ruin. Any small contribution from the home front will help to keep the wolves away from the door.

Journal Entry

August 26, 1944 – Even though I was totally pooped out, seeing Glenn Miller and his orchestra made a mighty big impression on me. A couple of the ships were in the hangar for repairs and most of the men were sitting on the wings listening to the music.

I felt like I was mixing two different parts of my life: Glenn Miller from when I was home and Glenn Miller here, surrounded by the men and the machines of war. This strange picture keeps repeating in my mind and tugging at my heart.

August 26, 1944

The sun is out bright and warm — almost unheard of in England. I'm lying on the grass outside our shack absorbing some. We didn't fly today, so we're having rest and relaxation, which allows us to do a bit better on our correspondence.

I thought you might like to know more about how we live over here: Our officer's club is equipped with comfortable furniture, a radio, and a Victrola.

We get several dozen newspapers a day, so we can keep up with the English variety of the news. Unlike military posts in the states, for security purposes our huts are well scattered.

Our dwelling is a good old Nissen hut with eight officers (two crews) in each. We have the British version of GI cots, some shelving, a dresser shared by two men, clothes racks, and a couple of chairs that are furnished to us.

Through the ingenuity of crews before us and some of our own, we've made some nice additions that help our comfort. We've got a table and an iron to press our uniforms — no pressing services out here. From battered up airplanes, we have fashioned a cooking stove that burns cigarette lighter fluid.

We also have a two gallon water jug, so, with coffee, cream, and sugar obtained from the mess hall, we can cook up some fairly decent java. A little operating by Jim and me netted us a barrel of cookies. A couple of the other guys are obtaining fruit juice. All that, along with packages from home, keeps us pretty happy.

They're talking about making a first pilot out of Jim. He's really good, and now there are enough unassigned men around to form a crew. I may wind up with him as a combination bombardier/navigator. Some crews are carrying one less officer, and I can handle the navigation responsibilities on a wing crew.

August 27, 1944

Today, eight members of our crew were awarded the Air Medal. They tell you it's for doing something special, but I think it's given if you're still around to receive it after five missions. Still, we're all very proud to wear the ribbon.

With France out of the picture, our missions are getting longer, but we get a day or so of rest in between. Jim is still a waiting his check-out as first pilot, and I am being considered for a lead bombardier slot.

Yesterday was a big package day! The Coca-Cola, packed in a loaf of bread, was some of your genius thinking, Dad. I'm saving it (the coke, not the bread) for a special day. The cookies and nuts arrived in great shape, as did the salt water taffy. Thanks a million!

I sent you a cable today asking for 50 bucks. Although I'm getting paid in a few days, I'm still behind the eight ball. I have some bills from Tucson I must pay, I owe Mac five pounds (20 bucks), I have to pay mess fees, orderly fees, club dues, etc. I want to get myself in the clear.

I find that most of the boys haven't written their families that they are flying combat missions. You are much too aware to be kept in the dark, and I'm certain that you'd rather know what I'm doing than just be left guessing. I know that you read in the papers about a few planes being lost and hitting rough targets, but I have been on a few missions that were so easy they were hardly even mentioned in the papers. I can't tell you where I have been or other things that might put your mind at ease, but I will tell you something that will get my throat cut if the censor reads it, but it's absolutely the truth. Since I have been with the Group, we have not lost one ship and have only had two men injured.

I have learned to relax now. I must admit that I was pretty-well scared the first few missions, but now I take it in stride. I can even enjoy some of the scenery on the way over. My work has been fairly dull, but they're having us stand down for a few days for training purposes. I expect that they'll be making better use of my training shortly.

Here's an army funny: I was supposed to attend a class in target identification yesterday, but I slept through it. This morning, my name was up for writing a letter to explain myself to the colonel. In all my career in the army, I'd never heard of doing that. I wrote it, and the boys all laughed.

August 31, 1944

They are breaking up the old crew. Jim is now a first pilot and Walt is going to radar specialist school. I am going to a lead crew as pilotage navigator. This crew, piloted by Lt. Turner, has five officers and is a radar pathfinder lead (that's all I can say). I will get more rounded experience in preparation for the bad weather that usually comes up in the fall and winter. I did a practice mission with this crew, navigating from the nose turret. I hope I can do a good job for them.

September 2, 1944

I'm in town at a picture show waiting for the film to start. It's raining like crazy, and this is as good a place as any to try to save the crease in my uniform trousers. This should reach you for your birthday, Mom. I sure hope it's a good one for you, and that you liked the locket I sent. It's a Victorian silver piece.

I can stay in town all evening, but I'll head back to the base for a good night's sleep. I have been on the ground for awhile. I never know when they will have a lead mission assignment for the crew I'm with. The papers say the Canadians moved into Dieppe. We're thankful for that because it was a hotbed of flak guns, and we all hated it.

I spent three lovely hours in the dentist's chair while he worked on my front tooth. He'll have it all fixed up in a week or so. We're coming up for a three-day pass soon. Since I have been to London, I'm looking around for a nice quiet spot where I can do some fishing or hunting. I may have found such a place in a little town just north of The Wash. Besides, London is too expensive. I spent $100 last time. I figure I should cut that in half.

I've seen a New York paper where they are saying the war will be over in three to four weeks. I wish those guys were over here. Maybe the Hun is on the run, but there are good fights left in him. We sweat the Luftwaffe, too. They have some fight left to show us in the air. The weather has been so bad we haven't seen much action, but that will have to change.

September 4, 1944

I must be the best cared for flier in the ETO. I got three packages today with cookies, brownies, and other goodies. Everything arrived in marvelous shape. You're a great packer, Dad. All the boys just stand around pop-eyed when I open packages. They can't believe it, but they are happy to share in the contents.

The Nazis must have been very thankful these past few days. The weather has been horrible and all the Liberators have been grounded. I don't fly as much as the other fellows do on a regular basis, only going when they need us as a lead crew. With the bad weather, it's even less frequent. All of this is OK because now my work is a lot more important to the Group.

Even in the lead crew, we laugh as much as before and make jokes out of funny combat experiences. Yet, we mourn the loss of friends. The brutality of heavy bombardment is quite impersonal. We never see the people we kill, and that helps some. A hard part is the nervous tension, sweating out the weather, wondering if we'll fly, getting up early and going to briefing, seeing the target, and wondering about what awaits us there.

Then, when we get in the air, we start searching for the fighters, wondering if they will come and, if they do, how many. Near the target we wait for the flak to come up, then wonder if it will hit us, praying it won't. But always, when we're done, there's hot coffee and food waiting for us, and our own bed. That's something ground troops never know.

We went to work yesterday to fix up our hut. From old bomb boxes we made shelves, and from a salvaged plane we got a de-icer-fluid tank, hooked up some hydraulic lines, and converted our coke burning, pot-bellied stove to an oil burner. We managed to liberate some fuel, and now we have some pretty good heat. We even patched up the holes one of the guys made in the roof when shooting off his .45-caliber pistol. So, now we are in pretty good shape for the winter that is starting to set in. Still, I hope we leave before it gets too cold.

You might like to know, you are way off in your guess as to where I'm stationed. Pick up clues and try again.

September 6, 1944

The last time we were on our way to London, we met the wife of an English Lord on the train. During our lengthy conversation, it turns out that her home is near our base, and she invited us to come over for a visit. So, yesterday, through some very clever manipulating, I procured a command car, complete with driver, and Mac, Bill, and I headed out. Lady Beddingford's estate is about 15 miles from our base, on 3,000 acres, complete with a castle, moat, and drawbridge, all dating back to 1482.

We were greeted by a lady-in-waiting (I think that's what she is called), ushered into the study, and informed that, "Her Ladyship will be right down." I was thinking I would forget all my manners and spill the tea or something. Before tea, we had a tour of the castle, well, part of the castle, because a large section is sealed off where the ghosts of many of the ancestors live (honest, that's the story line). Since there are 80 rooms, we just needed to see a few to get the idea. I wondered how much it cost to heat the place. We learned that the drawbridge has been inoperative for several hundred years and just stays down. My funny fantasy is that something broke, and when they went to the store for a part, it was out of stock, so they never got the thing fixed. As it turned out, even with the fancy silver tea service, we were made to feel at home and we had a delightful experience.

The Lord is a colonel in His Majesty's Army, serving in France. Her Ladyship is a slick chick, about 27 years old and not bad to look at. She talked me into a ping-pong game in the play room. Her Ladyship beat my pants off, but good! We all had a great laugh out of that.

I took Her Ladyship a box of the salt water taffy you sent to me from Atlantic City. It paid off better that way than eating them. The whole day was one heck of a swell time.

For me, the 392nd is getting to be a big joke — all play and no work. I love it.

September 9, 1944

I gave up on the peaceful fishing idea and I am back here in London having a fine old time. The buzz bombs are gone for now, some of the boys are coming back from France, and, with thousands of American boys running around, the place looks like New York. I met an American Red Cross girl. We went out to a play, then to dinner at a little place where there's dancing. Then we went to another place where we sat until three in the morning having a few drinks, talking, and dancing.

It was very nice to be with an American girl, and we had a wonderful time. Today, I slept until noon, ate, then went to see Big Ben and to pay my respects to Lord Byron's grave in Westminster Abbey.

Tomorrow, it's back to the wars. I am due for another mission. This is a time of great anxiety all over England. Everyone is hoping that the Allies won't bog down and that we will be done with Jerry very soon. I'm enclosing a few snaps of London that I picked up near London Bridge. Things may appear very old to you, because London really is quite antiquated. If you could see the cabs, you would laugh.

September 11, 1944

Sometimes I wonder whether I am a damn fool or just a lucky kid. Jim stood down today, and I did not fly either. Mac and the crew went without us and ran into some fierce Luftwaffe fighter action. One of the gunners was killed and another nearly lost a leg. They brought a badly damaged ship home, God knows how.

I feel very mixed up. I should have been with the crew, I suppose, but the command here controls my destiny. Maybe I'll get a chance to do some good soon. I'm going to even the score for my pals, too. God help the Heinie who comes into my gunsight.

I can't write any more tonight. I'm OK and lucky, I guess.

September 12, 1944

You may have been reading the papers, so I wanted to write and let you know I am OK. Things have been a bit rough. I am fairly bewildered, but still hanging in. I flew today as bombardier and really think I did well, at least the results were good. I hope the folks back home don't think the war is over. I'll testify that it's not. Sorry about the quickie. I just wanted you to hear from me.

September 14, 1944

I was so pooped out yesterday, I fell into the sack at 7 P.M. and never got up until 9:30 A.M. I was beginning to get over the incidents of the last few days, saying to myself that this is war and horrible things happen. As I told you, I thought I did a good job a couple of days ago, then yesterday, I pulled a prize boner that nearly cost us dearly. They really ought to take back their air medal.

We were headed for Germany via the south of France when we ran into some terrible weather. Everyone split up and our squadron got separated from the group. We circled for awhile, a few more lost ships tagged on to us, and then the command pilot decided to have us head for home. So, we were leading 14 ships. But, after all the turns, we were fairly well lost. I finally figured out where we were, and we headed home.

The terrible part was that I tried to bring the Squadron out over Calais, the one city besides Dunkerque the Jerrys still hold on the French coast. For some reason, I forgot about that, and we came right over the city at 9,500 feet. We got the hell shot out of us, as did everyone in the formation. Thank God, no one was hurt, but the ships got a lot of battle damage. I was just getting out of the turret when the first burst blew me up onto the navigator's desk. The next one knocked out our number four engine. We were lucky we got out as easily as we did.

The major and colonel were really mad, and I heard about it
plenty. Of course, the first navigator is ultimately responsible, but
I should have warned him about the flak area. It was really
dumb, and I feel terrible about it. It's just lucky we all got back.
That's that, there's nothing that can be done about it now. The
guys just laughed and said it was a mistake.

Journal Entry

*September 14, 1944 – The last few days have been horrors. On
the 12th, we went to Hannover, only to find a smoke screen, so
we went to radar. Then we had a slight break in the coverage, so
I got over the sight and did a visual run with what looked like
good results. One ship in the squadron got jumped by FW-190s
and one ship went down from flak hits over Hannover. It's an
awful sight to see a B-24 heading down, streaming smoke.*

*While the Luftwaffe has been less active than in the past,
the flak is getting worse. I guess it's a lot easier to build anti-
aircraft weapons than planes, as the Germans are increasing
their AA power. The newer 88s are more accurate than the
older ones that have had the barrels used a lot. We are seeing
more accurate fire.*

*Then there was yesterday's fiasco when I let the whole
squadron go over Calais. We got a lot of battle damage. The only
thing that saved my ass was that no one was injured. I can't get
the picture out of my mind of us going through all that flak. I try
to tell myself that I am 19 years old, and if it weren't for the
war, I would be a sophomore in college, but here they put me in
charge of pilotage navigation for an entire squadron with millions of dollars worth of planes and 140 men. But then, I am
supposed to be trained for this work and to not make mistakes. I
also know that mistakes are made every day. Also, I am a damn*

good bombardier, but only a so-so pilotage navigator, so why don't the command officers wise up? So why don't I just stop kicking myself in the ass and get ready to go back to work. Planes can be repaired.

Journal Entry

September 15, 1944 – Sometimes I refer to members of my crew and other fliers on the base as "the boys." Even though many of us are under 21, I can't refer to any of them as boys. With all we are going through, there are no boys here anymore. We are forced to grow up fast or never to grow up at all.

September 16, 1944

Tonight there is a big dance to celebrate the Group's first year in the ETO. It is by invitation only and promises to be a nice affair. I am convoy officer for a few trucks going into town to pick up some of the girls who have been invited.

I seem to be out of dutch with the CO, as I am still flying in a lead crew. I flew with Lt. Turner today. It's a helluva good crew, and we did some bang up work — now, that's an apt description.

The dentist finished fixing up my tooth today. Once again, I can smile without covering my teeth and bite into the cookies and chocolate bars that arrived today in your package. What a wonderful sight (and taste) that was.

September 17, 1944

We had a heck of a party last night, with some nice girls and a good orchestra. Everyone had a good time.

I was going to go to Cambridge to join a family for the Jewish holidays, but transportation in England on Sunday is terrible.

There's a truck leaving here this evening for a nearby large town. I will hop on that, see if there's a synagogue there, or go on to Cambridge on Monday morning.

By order of General Eisenhower, all Jewish soldiers were to get three days leave for the holidays, but my CO asked me not to take it. Evidently, something is coming off where I am needed.

I will make it to services for one part of the holidays, for sure. You would be surprised at how religious I have become. They say there are no atheists in foxholes. I can assure you there are none in heavy bombers, either.

All is forgiven for my recent misadventure. They decided that it wasn't my fault. The maps were not clearly marked and I had not been warned about the flak danger. I also managed to get our collective asses out of a jam when I located us after all the twists and turns in the bad weather.

Your letters arrive regularly and they are a real joy.

September 19, 1944

I did use my pass to go to the large city, near here, where they had services for all the Jewish birdmen stationed in the area. The place was just a big hall, but there were a number of men I knew from training, and even several from my high school.

After services, I went over to the Red Cross Officer's Club and met more of the men I knew from Big Spring. In all, it was a good experience. I came back to the base feeling very satisfied and very religious.

I wish I could tell you about all that is happening here. There's a lot more than dropping bombs. You probably read about the airborne landings in Holland. The Group was in on it the day I was away. I wish I could tell you details but, of course, that is impossible.

We will have another pass coming up soon, but I am pretty
flat, so I think I will just hang out locally. Perhaps I can find that
place to go fishing. London is so expensive. It costs at least $80
to do anything. I should get a bit more money in this month's
pay, since I reduced the allotment, but that's two weeks off, so
maybe I am out of luck.

Chapter Eleven

Taking the Lead

When I was allowed my first pass from our airfield in East Anglia, I visited London, then later some of the industrial cities. England, in 1944, was a mass of wartime scars. There were physical scars that marked the bodies of people and transformed once handsome buildings and proud neighborhoods into piles of rubble and broken glass.

The emotional scars were not quite so visible, but laid just beneath the surface of conversations, glazed the eyes of the elderly, and made mini-soldiers of children at play.

First, there was the blitz — hundreds of Nazi planes bombing London and other industrial cities day after day. When it began, Reich Minister Hermann Goering, Commander of the Luftwaffe, said he would destroy the RAF in four days, but England stood proud.

The RAF still flew after 40 days, after four months, after four years. In one of his resounding speeches, Prime Minister

Winston Churchill spoke of the containment of the Luftwaffe by the RAF as "England's finest hour."

When I went to the suburban residential areas of London, I was struck by the eerie silence — there were no sounds of children. I learned that after the early attacks, many children were evacuated from London to relatives in the countryside or to hastily arranged foster families on the farms and in the cities of the north, leaving the nation's capital strangely bereft of these sounds — much like I imagine Hamlin after the Pied Piper played his tune.

When losses became too great for the German Air Force to keep up their attacks in piloted planes, pilotless buzz bombs made daily raids on London. I recall walking the streets when this strange new rocket aircraft, trailing a plume of fire, would appear over the city. Suddenly the flame would go out and the rocket engine stopped. Then, the craft would nose over, plummet to the ground, and a huge explosion would blow a neighborhood to bits. Londoners experienced no day without fear, nor night with peace.

Because England is an island nation, much if its daily needs are imported. But during the war, only ships carrying munitions braved the Nazi submarines to land there. This resulted in shortages of practically everything. Whatever one wanted, it seemed, had gone to war. My favorite pub dish, bangors and mash (sausage and mashed potatoes), was a casualty of the war. Meat needed for the sausages was going to the soldiers, so sawdust replaced the meat, first by 10 percent, then 20 percent, and later 50 percent. Even so, sawdust is somewhat nutritious, and the mixture became accepted fare.

⟹◆⟸

UNITED ✯ STATES

ARMY AIR FORCES

September 20, 1944

Dear Mom and Dad,

I am a grounded bird! They won't let me fly at all, except as squadron lead pilotage navigator, and that's it. I asked to fly now and then with Mac and the guys, but they won't take a chance on losing me out on the wing. It looks like it's going to be a long war for me. I am only flying once every ten or twelve days.

I have it fairly easy between missions. I study up on some navigation, use the intelligence library to learn where the flak areas are, and go on practice flights. I must be sure my turret is in perfect working order, because the attacks on lead ships from fighters are primarily head on. Still, I have too much time to sit and think. Whenever they want to, they can use me in the lead bombardier role. I know all the procedures and the pilotage work has sharpened my vision of the ground.

I wonder what will happen when the war is over, over here. Will we all go to the Pacific theater?

September 22, 1944

I am very tired after a long mission today. I am quite certain there is a German city that won't produce anything for a long time. Also, there are a bunch of dead Heinies laying around, which is OK because they are best that way. We got off pretty easy.

Your appraisal is quite right, Dad. Jerry is making a last ditch stand and we figure to see more of the Luftwaffe before this is over. They may get a few of us, but, we are now too powerful to have anything major go wrong.

Mac got a brand new ship, a real honey. I hope they make him a lead crew soon. Then I can get back with him as lead bombardier. Old Jim got an engine shot out the other day, so he brought the ship home on three. What a guy!

Jack Myrtle has been put in for the Silver Star for gallantry in action. When Piersall was wounded, Jack manned both waist guns and shot down an ME-109. The plane was in such bad shape Mac gave the command to bail out and the boys hooked on their chutes. Seeing that Piersall wasn't able to make it, Jack took off his chute and said if the plane crashed, they would go together. They did make it back to England with two engines, the hydraulic system shot out, and 500 holes of various types in the ship. And I was on the ground.

The next day, I went up with a lead crew, and we got the hell shot out of us by flak. I got knocked out of the turret and suffered a serious injury — a bruise on my heel. Am I lucky, or what?

September 24, 1944

We're having a real English rain, heavy and cold. I imagine that you visualize us in neat uniforms, but tonight I had on my parka, an old pair of OD trousers, a moldy, beat up, white shirt, and a pair of cowboy boots that Lt. McInerney gave me (he's from Montana).

Now we're in the hut. I'm sitting by the stove trying to dry off, Jim is making some tea, Bill is reading the paper, and Mac is writing. It's a good feeling when the four of us are together, whatever we are doing. I think this gruesome four is indestructible. Jim and I are too bad to die, and Mac and Bill are too good.

The wind is so strong now, we're going to have to throw out the anchor or this old hut will blow away. I go on pass tomorrow with Lt. Temple's crew. I'll have to borrow some money, then hope you'll send me some soon to get me out of hock.

September 27, 1944

I have been on pass since Monday. Letter writing from London is rather difficult. Yes, I know I wasn't coming back to London, but I was offered a deal that couldn't miss.

The navigator from the other crew living in my hut, Herman Vogler, has an aunt and uncle who live in London. They invited him down for Yom Kippur, and told him he could bring a friend. So, we left Monday noon, got in early in the evening, and went to their home. They put us up in a room that is very deluxe, with soft beds. Herm has a girlfriend who lives nearby, and she has a girlfriend, so we all went to this very cute girl's house and talked, danced, ate, and were just together. I had never imagined being with Jewish families in England. Some of the men on the base have talked about going into a church, either in one of the small towns or in London, and being invited to the homes of church members. They all say how comforting it is to be with people who share their religious beliefs.

Tuesday night, I went to Temple with the family. I didn't take part in the services very well because I was thinking of you and home all of the time. Then we went back with the girls and had another quiet, enjoyable evening. Tonight, we'll all have dinner out.

These folks have really been wonderful to me. They have corn flakes and milk for us in the morning, along with whatever goodies they can muster, and take care of us in ways we have almost forgotten. This is the nicest pass I have had since I've been in England.

September 29, 1944

I just got back from London and found your swell letter with all the news from the family in Philadelphia. I also got your check for 50 bucks, which comes in very handy.

The Group is keeping busy giving the ground forces support and giving the Hun's fuel supply sources hell. Strategic bombing has played a major part in this war, and I am awfully proud to be making my small contribution. We'll keep at it for awhile more and then one day the whole thing will crack wide open, although I don't think it will end as early as some are predicting. Then, we'll take care of the Japs. I keep dreaming about coming home.

October 3, 1944

For God's sake, stop sending money. No, I'm not flak happy, but I just got paid today, then I got your cable saying you had sent 100 bucks. So, now all my debts are paid and I'm ready for another big pass. Thanks a million. You sure keep me in good shape. I have plenty money, candy, cookies, nuts, etc. I even got my laundry back today.

I flew deputy lead with Lt. Turner. It was fairly easy, only rather long — eight hours. The dumb Jerries were way off with the flak, except for one lousy burst that popped a hunk into my turret. I just thumbed my nose at them.

The good news is that I am flying with Mac tomorrow, leading the dollar slot element. It will be great to be with my gang again. I feel out of place with anyone else, and Mac is still the best pilot in the Group. The guys are all happy that I am flying with them again, too.

October 4, 1944

The weather kept us grounded today. We got through a 3 A.M. briefing and were set to go when they scrubbed the mission. It's just as well because I didn't like the dangerous target. We'll probably go tomorrow.

I spent most of the day in a meeting for lead crews discussing our bombing record. The results throughout our combat wing are excellent, but our squadron has slipped a bit and we're trying to get things ironed out. We have suffered a few losses and the new men are not as good as they might be. (Listen to me, I'm a veteran.)

I need to get to bed early, so I can get enough sleep before we fly. When they wake us up at 2 A.M., it doesn't leave much sack time.

October 5, 1944

Damn, but it's cold. I flew with Mac today, and it was 38 degrees below zero. All the stuff dripped out of my oxygen mask and froze on my scarf, the plexiglass frosted over, my guns froze, the oxygen regulator froze, and I froze all over. We bombed an airfield in support of the ground troops and blasted it off the map. The flak was light. We didn't get any, but the Luftwaffe rose to the occasion. I guess they got mad because we blasted their field. We just turned around after bombing and high-tailed it out. They never caught up with us. That's the way to do it, hit them and run for home.

If I'm off tomorrow, I'll head for town to get a new scarf made out of a hunk of parachute cloth. The one I have now is all beat up. I got a new type of heated flying suit that's very good and I had my oxygen mask modified so it doesn't freeze up anymore. That's dangerous business to have oxygen trouble at 23,000 feet.

The enlisted men have been promoted regularly and they're now all tech, or staff sergeants. I wish Mac would at least get his promotion to first lieutenant. He really deserves to be a captain.

You can tell Uncle Stan that the prayer book with the metal cover he sent me is carried in my breast pocket whenever I fly.

October 6, 1944

They are definitely making Mac and the gang a lead crew, so he will stand down from missions for about ten days to get in some practice time, but they are giving him another bombardier. They all think I am a good pilotage navigator and a very good gunnery officer, but they're not sure about relying on me regularly as bombardier on a lead ship. I am still the youngest officer in the Group and some of them think I need more experience. Being young is problem enough, but they tell me I look like a 16-year-old kid, and that adds to their negative perception.

It appears now that I will fly in a variety of different assignments until they think I am ready for a big job. It makes me mad, because I always try to do a good job, but I can't do anything about my age. I will just go with things as they are, keep my mouth shut, and see what they do with me. I will probably sweat out some days waiting, but that's nothing new for me.

Journal Entry

October 6, 1944 – We lost the crew that shared our hut. They went to Hamburg, encountered heavy flak, and went down over the target. They were a wonderful bunch of guys, and being so close makes the loss hurt even more. I try to deal with things like this in some offhand way, like that's what we have to expect. I can do it on the outside, but acting tough doesn't help on the inside.

On my mission assignments, some of the same sort of thing is happening: When we get under attack from fighters or flak, my heart pounds and I am plenty scared. But, on the outside I remain cool and do my work methodically.

October 8, 1944

I am having several free days in a row and it's not the best thing for me. I need some assignments to keep in shape. These are trying times as I am moved from crew to crew. I don't feel like I belong anywhere, and there is little to keep me interested on off days.

An additional thing working against me: The weather has been very bad for visual bombing and my lead-crew work as both a pilotage navigator and a bombardier depends on being able to see the ground. When there is bad weather with a lot of cloud cover, the bombing is by radar.

Also, there are not many pin point targets we haven't hit, so the assignments are getting kind of nasty, like reducing all the cities to rubble. Eisenhower said he would need a lot of gravel when he got into Germany, so we're trying to help him out by reducing the buildings of Hamm, Kassel, and Cologne to big rubbish heaps. It's not a very decent thing to do, but the Germans are not very decent people; saturation bombing is what they did to London. I may get another pass this weekend and if so, I will go to London. I am assured of a good time there, as I now know a few people.

October 14, 1944

The army is teaching me more things — patience and ease of manner. The men who were here last winter warned us that there would be long days of waiting with nothing to do while missions were scrubbed or not even scheduled. That's what's happening, so the only thing to do is relax and let the time pass. The bad weather also means rain and cold and it is really miserable in these huts.

When we do fly, we are starting to meet the new German jet propelled fighters and they are really wicked. We spend a lot of time figuring out how to deal with them. The squadron bombardier likes me and wants me to fly in the lead bombardier slot, so he is going up with me tomorrow on a practice mission to see, personally, how I handle the bombsight.

We had a party last night and I had a very nice date, the first girl I have met over here that I liked a lot. During the dance, Father MacDonough, the Catholic chaplain, had a dance with Lynn. He's a great guy so I figured if he could borrow my girl, I could borrow his jeep. I did and Lynn and I had a brief, fun drive in the countryside.

October 19, 1944

Even with mature men fighting a war there's still some immature things that go on. I did a fine job practice bombing with the squadron bombardier watching me and he told the CO that I was real good and should be assigned as lead bombardier. The squadron navigator told the CO that I had goofed as a pilotage navigator on one trip, which is simply not true. He's mad at me because I monopolized his girl at one of our parties some time ago. It's all pretty sad, when I realize what's at stake.

The squadron needs a lead bombardier badly and I really am the best man available, but because some silly captain has a mad on, I may not be assigned. I feel that the CO knows what he is doing and if he wants to make me a lead bombardier, that's OK, and if not it's OK, too. I know I do a good job as pilotage navigator and that's what counts for me.

There's a party in the Red Cross Aero club for the staff tonight. Jim and I are going to be masters of ceremony. We have a lot of gags worked up, and when the two of us get going we are very funny.

The cigars were passed out last night, as Mac finally got promoted to first lieutenant. He has waited a long time.

October 20, 1944

They sent me up as bombardier on a practice mission with Mac and the crew that resulted in one of the most terrific examples of precision bombing known in the history of the 8th Air Force.

You will recall my telling you about our visit to the castle of Lady Beddingford. While we were there, we had asked her what she was missing that we might be able to supply. She told us that there was no ice cream available and she had not had any for years. We have been waiting for the opportunity to get some for her and it all came together today.

Last night we had ice cream with dinner and we asked the mess sergeant to save some for us. Before we left on this morn-ing's practice mission, we went by the mess hall and got a gallon of ice cream. Then we stopped by the parachute riggers and got a pilot chute (the small one that comes out first and pulls the main chute out). We wrapped up the ice cream and attached it to the chute. Then we went up on our practice mission over the North Sea where the temperature was 40 degrees below zero. You can imagine how hard the ice cream got.

After the practice mission, we hung the ice cream in the now empty bomb bay and dropped down to the area near the castle. We swung around a couple of miles away and buzzed the castle at tree top level. You have no idea how it sounds to have a B-24 pass just over your head; it was more than enough to cause everyone living in the castle to run out onto the grounds.

We executed a slightly climbing turn, lined up from several miles away, opened the bomb bay doors, and did a bomb run on the castle at fifty feet off the ground. With the greatest precision, I released the ice cream so that it floated to the ground right at their feet. We pulled up, returned to the base, and landed.

Later that evening we called Her Ladyship to see how the ice cream was. We were told they were still trying to thaw it out, but the bit they had tried was delicious. They really liked the special delivery, too.

Back in the hut, we were laughing about our adventure and decided to figure out how much the ice cream cost the U.S. government. We took the cost of educating our crew, amortized our life expectancy in combat, and applied the results. Then we figured the amount of gas our four-engined ship used on the drop, the amortized cost of the plane, and other factors, added them all together and came up with $360,000. We thought you, the family, and your friends might like to know about this as an incentive to buy war bonds and to continue to support the war effort.

October 22, 1944

Another Sunday raid today. Jerry doesn't get a day off. I flew as pilotage navigator with Mac and the crew in deputy lead. Jim was flying his ship in the dollar slot right behind us and Walt was radar man in the No. 3 ship. That's the first time since we have been here that the whole original crew (what's left of it) has been in the air at the same time. We went after some marshaling yards in support of the advancing infantry. We had some flak, but not too bad. We have never taken a serious hit when I have been with the crew. Mac says he wants me to fly with him every mission, just for luck.

I got an Oak Leaf Cluster for my Air Medal, the Red Cross is baking a cake for my birthday, and I am getting a lot of birthday cards.

I am sweating out mission No. 12b (we don't use No. 13). Only 17 more to go and I can come home.

October 24, 1944

I have received 25 birthday cards, so far, and it sure makes me feel good. We're going to have a crew party on my birthday. I got more of the money you sent. When I realize how much it has been, I am kind of ashamed. I will need to make an awful lot of money after the war to keep on living this way.

With me as bombardier, Mac and the crew were the squadron lead, today, in a radar ship. Being a "mickey" crew is reserved only for the best. We were supposed to do a radar drop, but I got a bit of clear sky and went for a visual one. It closed up immediately, so the results won't be known until we have a reconnaissance plane get some pictures. Since I made a decision to change the orders, I got an automatic ass chewing. If our bombs hit, I will be a hero, and if they missed, I will get hung from a telephone pole. They will probably hold this over my head for a few weeks until we know. It seems that in order for them to accept me in full faith, I will need to kill Hitler with my .45-caliber pistol from 20,000 feet.

I'm sorry that I can't give you any details of the Pathfinder bombing, as it is quite secret. After the war is over I will tell you all the wonderful details of how we kill thousands of helpless women and children on these raids. It's a real stinking thing and I have had several raids like that. We pick a big city and blast hell out of it. It's not a very fine way to wage war. The infantrymen need a lot of hate to do their job well, but it isn't necessary in the Air Force. We can see it as a dangerous game and still get the job done properly. All of us feel the same way — we'd rather have clear weather and pinpoint a factory or other military installation.

Aside from flying, I sit around getting grey hair waiting to fly again. The really interesting experiences occur on passes. I'm quite healthy and that's to the good. I hope some of your packages get here soon. I'm hungry for cookies and other such things.

October 28, 1944

After we got home from our mission, it was a very fine birthday. The club officer gave me an excellent bottle of Scotch, and six of the Red Cross girls threw a party for me, along with Mac, Jim, Bill, and a few other officers. The girls fixed food, baked a big cake with "Happy Birthday By" on it, provided a Victrola for music, and we sat around in front of an open fireplace and sang. The guys gave me a present of a pocket canteen that holds about a pint, so I can carry some water or juice with me on a mission. I was practically speechless, which is some rarity for me. Besides standard food, the Red Cross gals had toasted bread with caviar, sardines, and crab meat. Don't ask where they got it. I can't remember such a wonderful, mellow time. We broke up at 2:30 A.M. Since we were not flying, we sat around in the barracks and shot the bull for a few more hours. The ability to put a nasty day behind us and just party is quite an amazing thing.

October 29, 1944

I was assigned to check the bombsight, racks, and autopilot on one of the lead planes. So, Jim and an engineer and I went up for a few hours. I flew as co-pilot, navigated us to the range from the co-pilot's seat, then went down to the nose and dropped my practice bombs. Back in the co-pilot's seat, I flew the ship for awhile, the first time I had done so with only a first pilot. I made a few mistakes, such as putting the wheels down too early and forgetting to put the flaps up, but we made it OK. Flying around like that, without being shot at, can be fun.

One of the women at Red Cross, Mrs. Thetford, had her son on the base for the weekend. He's 12 years old and nuts about airplanes, so Jim and I showed him around the field and gave him a pair of goggles. Talk about an excited kid!

October 31, 1944

I am still being watched over. We were briefed early this morning for a priority target deep in Germany, one of the toughest there is. But, it was scrubbed because of bad weather.

We flew a couple of men going on leave to a base in southern
England. I did much of the piloting. I have accumulated quite a
few hours as a pilot, and I like it. I might go for pilot's school,
when I get back home.

Winter is setting in and the nights are cold, which makes
early briefings a real hardship. I cannot understand why they
have to fight the war so early in the morning. It will still be there
when the day warms up.

We're due for passes, but there is a shortage of lead crews, so
we may not get to go for awhile.

November 5, 1944

We had a bit of excitement today on a deep raid to another
tough target in Germany. My luck is still good, as the flak was
everywhere, except where we were.

Coming home, we ran into some hellish weather. Everyone
peeled off to find a place to land. We set the ship down on a B-17
base in southern England, had some supper, and flew on home.
We had 2,000-pound bombs again. One more raid and I am
halfway through, but who is counting?

I dashed off the short note above, then went out and had a
quick drink and some supper. Now I am back in the hut resting
and preparing for whatever tomorrow brings. I always tell you all
of the gory details, but now I have a funny one for you.

Early into today's mission, Bill had to take a pee. We were flying squadron lead, so he didn't want to leave his navigation work
and go back to the tube we usually use. His flak helmet was on
the floor, so he just peed into it. At 60 degrees below zero, the
stuff froze solid, and on the long flight, he just forgot about it.

Starting down the bomb run we all automatically put on flak
helmets. After the bombs were away and I gave the OK to get
out of there, I turned to give Bill a thumbs-up sign that we did a

good job. Between the heated suits and our anxiety, we get pretty warmed up. There must have been just enough heat at the top of Bill's head to start melting the pee around the edges.

When I saw him, it was starting to run down his face and into his glasses. We both started to laugh, which is pretty hard to do with an oxygen mask on, and in a minute we were doubled over with laughter, even with the flak bursting all around us.

Later, when we were safely on our way back to the base, I told the crew about it over the intercom, and everyone had a good laugh. You can imagine how this story will play out in the officer's club after a few beers.

November 6, 1944

They are really slipping it to us, for fair. We flew again today, and I have my eyes propped open with match sticks while I write this. They started this day at 3 A.M. which is an awful time to get a man out of bed.

We had 2,000 pounders on board again. They make a hell of an explosion. All the planes received flak holes, there were engines out, flat tires, and other assorted wounds, but we are OK. While it is ugly cold in the mornings, it is not too bad up in my greenhouse. The sun heats up the plexiglass and keeps it fairly warm. I still come down with icicles on my scarf from my oxygen mask dripping, then freezing.

We are coming up on a pass to London soon. It will be most welcome.

Journal Entry

November 7, 1944 – There is no such thing as getting used to flak. We have had it really heavy the last few missions. The wuff, wuff, wuff sound of the bursts and then the black puffs in the sky all around are fearsome. The real bad ones are those where I can see the orange flash in the center, because that means it's close. It's such a helpless feeling when we can't retaliate, and must fly on and take it.

When they get our range, planes are set on fire or just break apart in the sky. Sometimes, where there was a plane, suddenly there is nothing. Ten men disappear, as if they had never been there. Or, there are blood and body parts blowing around in the sky. Then, I fight down the terror, as I watch this scene from hell. I doubt the ability of anyone to comprehend this without going through it.

When we are out of the flak area and I see that my compartment is full of holes and yet nothing has hit me, I wonder how it is decided who dies in flames, who takes to a parachute, and who gets to make it home.

November 8, 1944

Tomorrow we go on pass. We will have the weekend in London, returning on Sunday, which means you won't get any letters for four days, unless I get to the Red Cross Club. But, you don't have to worry, because I will just be having fun. OK? I have a couple of dates and, now that I have many connections in London, I always manage to have a good time.

I went up today with the gang to drop some practice bombs. There is always concern that the lead plane be as accurate as possible, because when we miss, the entire squadron misses and no one is ever happy about risking lives on a failed mission. I had a good day and laid my bombs right where they should be. Being successful in practice doesn't necessarily mean a successful mission. We have smooth skies in practice, but over our targets the bursting flak often tosses the ship around. If a wing lifts or the nose tilts up at the moment of release, then the bombs go way off.

We have been doing a lot of roughhousing lately. About three times a week, the barracks looks like a cyclone went through it. It's good, clean fun, though, and relieves the monotony of long evenings, as well as pent up tensions and emotions.

That's the latest from here. I'll write again Sunday night at the very latest. I love you all very much and I guess I'm just about the proudest guy in the world to call you my family.

November 12, 1944

I'm on the train heading back to the base. I really was in tough shape when I came in to London, but I am all rested now and ready for work. We got in Thursday afternoon and I headed straight to the barbershop for a haircut and a shave. That night I took out Trudy Larkin, a nice girl I had met once before. We went to the Cumberland Hotel for dinner and dancing. When I took her home, it was rather late and her folks asked me to stay over. Friday, I did some window shopping, then took a Turkish bath that calmed me down considerably.

Friday night, I went out with Reba, a girl I have seen quite often before. A couple of the guys joined us for a special treat. One of the guys had given me two bottles of champagne that he brought back from Belgium — bottled in 1904, no less. So, that got things off to a great start.

Saturday, Reba and I went to a show, dinner, and dancing again. It was a wonderful three days, and now I am set to go to work. I hope they assign us often, so I can get finished and come home.

It's funny how things have worked out for me in London. Wherever I go, I meet nice people and they all treat me like a king. The barber is Mr. Kirsch. He gives me bagels when I come in. Reba's family is always happy to see me. I take them oranges and things they can't get, and they always have some goody for me. At night, taxis are very hard to find, but I just pick up the phone and call Harry Levy. He brings his cab around for me and charges me half price. I stay at the same boarding house and the lady who owns it brings me breakfast in bed. So you see, I am well cared for.

Journal Entry

November 13, 1944 – This is not exactly a war entry, but it is something to be remembered. When I stayed at Trudy's house in London, they put me up in their guest room. Fuel is scarce and the heating systems are lousy anyway, so getting into bed is a cold proposition.

I was trying to stop shaking from the cold when the door opens and in comes Trudy. She asks me if I'd like some warming and I say sure. So, she drops her bathrobe and there's nothing under it but this lovely body. In bed, she warns me to keep quiet, so her parents don't hear. There was this long, but quiet love-making. I wanted to get really into it, but I was afraid her parents would hear us and come in.

Between being cold, unprepared, forced into silence, and a relative neophyte at this sort of thing, it was not the greatest, but I am not complaining. I would very much like such an experience again, but under better circumstances.

November 14, 1944

I got four packages of food, when I returned to the base, which will take care of me for some time. I'll try to write thank you letters to everyone. I sent you the Oak Leaf Cluster for my Air Medal, which is no big deal. Jack Myrtle got the Distin-guished Flying Cross for what he did on that September 11 mission, that I missed. That is a big deal.

We have not flown in the past two days and with the bad weather, I'm not sure when we will. The temperature at bombing altitude is around 50 degrees below zero and that's not my favorite thing.

It's 8:45 in the evening and we have the Navy–Notre Dame football game on the radio. It's very weird to hear this so late and know that it's morning back home. One of the guys gave me Navy and seven points on a ten shilling bet (that's two bucks). I think I'm a winner.

We're on the battle order for tomorrow. With the exception of two times when I was on pass, I haven't missed a Sunday mission our Group has flown since I have been here. What a far cry that is from the Sundays we have at home — getting up at 10 A.M., reading the funnies in bed, then all of us fixing brunch in the kitchen. That was wonderful. The English don't have colored funny papers — I never would get to read them in bed, anyhow. Instead, I get up at 3 A.M. for a briefing. I hope we get off easy tomorrow. The Group got quite beat up on the mission today, while we were goofing off on the ground.

I got a pipe and, although it doesn't taste very good, it's swell to chew on. Don't laugh, I chew on this stupid pipe, then I don't smoke so much. Whoops, another touchdown for Navy. Final score: Navy 32, Notre Dame 13. I'll have to see where I can spend the two bucks.

November 18, 1944

I've had a bit of adventure for a change. Thursday we went on a troop support mission to pave the way for the advance of the 1st Army just north of Aachen. It's the kind of mission we like because, unlike strategic bombing, it shows immediate results. You probably read in the paper that the troop advance began in the Aachen area at 12:45 on the 15th of November. At 12:43, 1,150 planes of the 8th Air Force dropped fragmentation bombs

on the German troop concentrations just where our advance was
to take place. After the advance began, the RAF came with
1,200 planes and dropped some more fragmentations further in.

The target for our Group was a bunch of artillery emplacements with 88-millimeter guns. The Jerrys turned those damned
guns on us and had our squadron boxed in with flak. We picked
up a few holes and Jim had an engine shot out. Going home, the
weather got bad. Our base was so socked in they couldn't land a
gnat there, so they diverted us to an RAF base near London.
The ceiling was so low, we had to fly over London at minimum
altitude. The city was packed with people looking up at us. It
was quite a circus, as we had to pull up to go over church
steeples and other obstructions. The English base didn't know
what to expect as we peeled off and landed 40 Liberators.

The RAF suddenly found themselves with 400 hungry Yanks
on their hands. We proceeded to eat them out of house and
home. The payoff was that the weather stayed closed in and we
never did get off for 48 hours. The first night I slept there, but
the second night I decided it was too uncomfortable, so one of
the officers from another crew and I piled on the train and
headed for London. I had on the raunchy shirt and pants I wear
under my flying gear, just my flying boots, no shoes, an old green
jacket I carry in my flight bag, and my .45-caliber pistol hanging
from my waist. My buddy had on his heated flying suit. We both
had three day beards and were filthy dirty from the mission. We
didn't have any money either, but we didn't let that bother us.
Along the way, no less than 15 people offered us something to
eat and a place to stay.

At the London depot, we hopped in a cab and went out to
Reba's house. She gave me some money to pay the cab driver.
Then we were treated to a super supper of fish, fries, dill pickles,
and strudel. We sat around and talked for awhile, then got into
the great beds they provided.

We got up early and beat it back to the RAF base for lunch. The English fliers there were really nice to us. One of them took me up to his room for a shave and a bath. Their base was well equipped, but the food was not nearly as good as ours. In the afternoon, we flew home. Now, the jaunt to London is not exactly allowed, but I can't afford to worry. We had a lot of laughs. If I come home still a second lieutenant, don't be surprised. The major will probably hear about my escapade one way or another.

November 19, 1944

You will notice that my address has been changed to the 579th Bomb Squadron. While we were anticipating a nice restful day, we were awakened and told we would have to move to another part of the base. They took all the lead crews and put them in this one squadron, so we are here with all the big wheels of the outfit. Now, instead of each squadron putting up a lead when they need it, they will all draw from this pool.

Instead of the big Nissen hut we had, this one is divided. There are three of us in here — Mac, Deke Compton, who is our co-pilot, and me. We have one double bunk and one single, so, as you might expect, I drew the upper bunk. It's not as good a sack as in the other barracks, but we have one stove for just the three of us, so it's a lot warmer. We have the place fixed up swell, a thermos jug for water, the kerosene stove we took from the old place, a radio, and a goodly supply of food, so we're all set.

I'm not sure how this new arrangement will work out, but we are not small timers any more because only the hot crews are in this outfit. This also means our tour of duty is only 30 missions instead of 35, which is nice because a lot can happen in five missions. It will take us a lot longer than wing crews to complete a tour, but that's OK with me now. We left Jim and a lot of our friends behind, but we see them all the time, so it's OK, too.

They give us vitamin pills daily and sulfadiazine to prevent colds. It seems to be working because this is the worst possible weather and I have not had a trace of a cold.

November 20, 1944

Hi, Pooz! I'm sure getting a wonderful kick out of your letters, my little sister. I've heard from unimpeachable sources, and noted from your pictures, that you have become quite a peachy looker. Now, let's not let this get us into trouble.

You know, since I have been in the army I've seen a lot of good girls go wrong. Be watchful for some of the good time Charlies, especially a guy who is going overseas shortly. They like to have their last fling, and they don't care who suffers. I speak from experience, because I did.

There's another thing: You smoke, which is OK, I guess, but don't try drinking. I never touched the stuff until I was nineteen, and, if I hadn't been in unusual circumstances, I would not have then. I have a drink now and then with the boys, but always in moderation. And, I am in a position where no one could blame me if I got stinkin' now and then.

I'm not trying to set up an example for you, but drink is a funny thing. You lose your sense of reason and do things that you otherwise wouldn't think of doing. And, it is especially unbecoming a young lady. When the guys had our fling, we locked ourselves in the squash court, so all we could do was bang our heads against the concrete walls.

What I am trying to get to is this: You have always had most everything a young lady could ask for. We fellows are over here fighting to see that you and others like you can have the things you want, and so those who haven't had anything may some day have them. So, if you don't want to do things right for any other reason, just remember you have the most wonderful parents in the world. Never, ever, do anything to disgrace them or even bring them the slightest bit of unhappiness. Get it? That includes your schoolwork, too. That you owe to me.

I really haven't meant to lecture you, I just thought a little mental bracer might be good. Dad always used to hand them out to me when I needed them. Now, I'm supposed to be a man, but confidentially, I could still use a good boot in the seat of the pants now and then. I try to do things right, and for the most part succeed. The mere fact that, at my age, I'm able to carry on the way I have is the most wonderful tribute in the world to Mom and Dad. If I ever start to wander from the straight and narrow, I need only think of them.

But, anyhow, just keep on the way you have been. I think you are wonderful, and so does everyone else. It certainly pays off. I miss you, Pooz. I think about you often, and wish you the best of everything in the world. We have so much to talk about when I get home, and so many things to do together. Have a chocolate milk shake when you get this, and remember I love you!

November 21, 1944

It's just after supper and I am alone in the hut, there's a crackling fire going, and the radio is playing good music. I have the new pictures of all of you in front of me and, I am not ashamed to say, they almost make me want to cry. You all look so terrific. Pooz, you're pretty as a picture, and Mom and Dad, you haven't changed a bit. In fact, you're all just the way I imagine when I think of you. Gosh, but you look great! I wish I could give you each a big hug and kiss.

All of your letters are wonderful. No one except members of our family would understand that you write to me every day, Dad. In some way, your letters form a lifeline that brings me safely back to the base after each mission. Pooz, you keep me posted on your love affairs and your life at school, and Mom, you boost my ego and make me feel good all the time. We're the most wonderful family in the world. I feel that I am a lucky guy and I know I am going to come through this war OK. Then, we'll all be together again. We're much too great a gang to break up, so I will be winging home very soon now.

I want to bring you up to date on what I am doing. I have sixteen missions in — three over France, the rest to Germany. I am regularly part of Mac's crew, working sometimes as pilotage navigator, sometimes as bombardier, depending on the mission. I am also always gunnery officer. When I am pilotage navigator, I ride in the nose turret with a set of maps made up from aerial photographs. They are complete and marked with all flak areas circled in red. It is my responsibility to give the navigator pinpoint positions as we go along, to supplement his work. In that way, we make certain of following the briefed route and meeting our control points on time. I must also warn the navigator and pilot about approaching flak areas, so we can steer around them. My main job comes on the bomb run, however. The bombsight has only a limited range, so, at the IP, I take over the ship and "talk" the bombardier on to the target. That is, I make sure we come down the bomb run properly and tell him the location of the target through prearranged check points until he can see it. It's very important that this be done efficiently and accurately.

In addition, I am in charge of defense of the formation from nose-on fighter attacks. I must be very systematic, orderly, and know my equipment thoroughly because the turret is terribly crowded and is the coldest spot in the ship, with icing problems. I don't have this down to the degree that I do bombardiering, but I am getting better all the time. This is a job I didn't anticipate, but I am working very hard at learning it.

Even if I don't fly combat often, I will be busy with training and, if I only do a few missions this winter, it will be OK. It was 60 degrees below zero at bombing altitude today. When your breath starts freezing on your face, that's cold.

November 23, 1944

Today is Thanksgiving, my second one in the Air Force. We are having a big turkey feast on the base. I have a lot to be thankful for, as do we all.

I guess we're the luckiest people in the world to be citizens of the U.S., and I consider myself privileged to be able to fight for our country. There's not many places in the world where we can vote for our leaders, or where a soldier like me can protest to the higher-ups and be listened to instead of shot.

I can be thankful that I am still here to write this; there has been a time or two when it was a toss-up. Our family has been exceptionally favored, too. I'll be thinking of you when I sit down to my dinner. It won't be like Thanksgivings of the past, with 4,000 miles of ocean between us, but I'll imagine there's just the four of us sitting around our own table, and I'll smile.

November 24, 1944

We sure had a fine dinner yesterday — turkey, dressing, sweet potatoes, cranberries, and the rest of the trimmings. It's pretty amazing, when you think of where we are.

Today, we led a squadron on a practice mission. I finally found the solution to my cold weather problems and many of my navigation ones as well. We have a new heated suit that is made of a lightweight fabric with wires running through it. I put it on over my uniform, a pair of coveralls on top, and then my hooded parka. That eliminates a lot of the bulkiness, important in my job, and provides plenty of warmth.

I still don't have room to wear a flak suit when I am in the turret, but there is plenty of armor plate around me. I do sit on a sheet of flak armor and wear a flak helmet, so I am well protected.

The major flew with us again and he seemed very pleased with the way we did things. We have good cooperation between crew members, and we work as smoothly as a well-trained football team. Speaking of football, Jim is the leading player on our base team and Sunday we play another base for the championship of the 8th Air Force. Jim is such a pro he's practically the entire team.

The rest of the men went to a movie, but I wanted to write this and read a bit. It's quite comfortable here in the hut, so I'm pleased. I got a letter from you dated November 14, which is good service and keeps me happy.

November 25, 1944

I am rereading your latest letter and note, Dad, you say you feel in your bones that the crew will come through our missions OK. I don't want to drag out old ghosts, but the last thing you felt in your bones was that the war would be over by Christmas of '43. So, please don't feel things in your bones any more, as I would like to make it home.

Yes, the Oak Leaf Cluster I sent you is for my Air Medal; it designates a second award. Put it on the ribbon I sent home previously and when my child says, "Dad, what did you do in the great war?" I will show him or her my Air Medals and tell war stories.

Recent missions have been without fighter opposition, but there is still a lot of nervous tension waiting for them to come up. We expect them to give us a bad time one of these days. It won't make any difference to the eventual outcome, but it will to us in the bombers. We are ready for them, however.

November 28, 1944

I took some cleaning into town, saw a show, then went to a record shop for a few new hits to play on our Victrola. The records you sent were swell. I don't think it will ever stop raining here, everything I have is soggy.

With poor flying generally and us on this lead schedule, we will leave for pass on Friday, having flown only one mission since our last pass. I think it will be like that until the winter is over. At this rate, it will be seven months before I finish my tour.

The English papers came out with the complete story of the Air Force's greatest secret, the HRX or "Mickey" bombing, as we call it. It's our method of bombing through a three-mile cloud layer using a radar scope. That's what our crew is doing, so when they print the story in the U.S. papers, you'll understand how we look in the scope and get a complete picture of the ground below us. There are new developments that keep making our bombing more accurate, that are still secret.

I'd like to shoot the bastards who released this story. It makes lead planes with the HRX equipment perfect targets for the Luftwaffe. As it is, the Jerry planes knocked out nearly one complete group the other day.

There are things happening that I don't understand: In addition to a secret like this getting out, we do not have the types of bombs we need for certain targets and the ground troops are rationing shells on the front. So, instead of an artillery bombardment with no risk, they send us on a risky raid to drop a lot of odd size bombs on troops. We understand our job of strategic bombing, but when we have to supplement the artillery and get the hell shot out of us, we don't like it. Are the folks at home figuring the war is over, so they are laying down on the job? We have the Hun on the run, we can't give him time out to recoup. Now is the time to double our effort. Tell the folks back home that it is still a tough fight and to please work hard to keep us from dying unnecessarily.

December 5, 1944

Back from a wonderful pass in London. I stayed at my same boarding house. They always make me feel most welcome. Got in Friday night. On Saturday, Reba and I went to a show, then back to her house where her folks had steak, smothered in onions, and other goodies for dinner. That's my first steak in England; I cannot imagine what they had to go through to get it.

Sunday night, I took Reba to the Cumberland for dinner. She looked just beautiful. We had lobster (can you believe, in the middle of a war) and danced until the wee hours. I went shopping on Monday looking for a few gifts, but was unable to get anything I wanted. I'm sorry, but there will just be good wishes for now. Most things are rationed. Costume jewelry and the like are next to impossible to obtain — when they are available the prices are outrageous. I hate to receive the nice things from you and not send anything back, but I'm not able to do anything else.

We got some new records in London, then came back to find your package with two more. Unfortunately, the one with Swoonatra was cracked. I shed no tears, but the guys were disappointed. Still, the other was fine. Thanks a million. We now have a music library that would make anyone happy. The Victrola goes all the time.

We sat and listened to music until 1:30 A.M., then they awakened us at 6 A.M. to fly a practice mission. If practice makes perfect, we will be world-beaters. Back on the ground, I spent an hour on the bomb trainer, then got a typhus shot. I have had an inoculation for every disease known to man; my shot record looks like a medical library.

I received your package with cheese, sardines, and assorted other things. We have one big shelf just packed with food. One day soon, we will have a honey of a feast. I have received a lot of Christmas packages. I peek in to be sure it's not perishable food, then put it in a foot locker. I have a lot in there and I will open them on Christmas.

Friday we're having a big party to celebrate the Group's 200th mission over German occupied Europe. There will be women on the base from noon on. They will have an imported a leg show from London, tea dancing in the afternoon, and what not. I am beginning to believe we can have a party for almost anything.

Between passes and parties, you may be wondering what-in-the-hell I am doing here. This question occurs to me, too. I don't think it is to fight a war, because we haven't flown a combat mission for almost a month. Maybe they're saving us to lead the victory parade down the Champs Élysees. While we're waiting, we continue to party.

December 7, 1944

They got us up at 3:30 A.M. and briefed us for a mission they had concocted to celebrate Pearl Harbor day. Even though the Germans weren't in on the bombing at Pearl, they were scheduled to get a real load, just to remind them that their Axis partners were the ones that got us here. Just as we were leaving for the ship, they scrubbed the mission, so I went back to bed. I go when they tell me to, and I do the best job I can, and when they scrub lulus like that, it's OK with me. This one would have left us minus a couple of our lads, for sure. We're still lucky.

More packages today, more food for the shelf. We're going to go after it soon and we'll all get good and sick. Someone sent Bill a small Christmas tree with trimmings, so the place looks like holiday time. We're listening to Kay Kyser records and others from *The Hit Parade*.

December 9, 1944

Last night was our big party and, for a change, it was a grand affair. The Group was stood down for the next day, so everyone got drunk. The MPs were there, and when someone would get out of line, they would quietly haul him away to the jug. We got rid of 150 quarts of scotch in three hours, plus the gin and beer.

Late at night, we came back to our hut with a couple of the girls
and made toasted cheese sandwiches and cocoa on our stove.

Tomorrow, we are on the battle order again. I guess we will
really go, as the weather is good. The latest news is that I am
growing a moustache. Present estimates are that I'll have a good
one by 1948.

December 10, 1944

The weather is still haunting us. It has been raining, snowing,
sleeting, and hailing today, in turns and together. As Bob Hope
says, "The fog is so thick, the birds have to come in on instruments." We're on the battle order tomorrow, again. I'm beginning to feel like turkey on the menu at Lindy's: We don't ever get
off the damn thing, and we don't fly.

One of the pilots in the 578th, here on the base, is a good
friend. I have flown with him a few times, and he is going to
check me out as a co-pilot. As soon as I get in a couple of more
missions, I'm going to ask the colonel to get me a letter of recommendation from General Doolittle to take pilot training
when I get back to the states.

It's so cold here the icicles are coming indoors to thaw out.

December 11, 1944

There was a big mission today, but we were not on it. Why, I
don't know. Sometime between midnight and briefing time, they
took us off the battle order. I don't know what they have in mind
for us.

At 6 A.M. we were up to fly a practice mission. I dropped ten
practice bombs, then did some camera bombing before taking
over pilotage navigator duties. When I get in the nose turret, Bill
has to sort of pour me in, then slam the doors shut. This time we
ran into some bad weather. It started snowing. The nose turret is

like a sieve. They can never quite seal the gun ports so I get a blast of 50 degree-below-zero wind at 250 miles per hour blowing in my face. I collected enough snow to make a snowball, opened the turret door and let Bill have it. He was so surprised he couldn't imagine what happened. Gotta have some fun now and then.

December 14, 1944

We briefed for a mission again, but the weather socked in before we could get off the ground. I have never in my life seen fog like we had today. The forward visibility was in inches. I imagine we'll have a try again tomorrow, although the weather still looks bad this evening.

We haven't been on a mission for one month, exactly. We're scheduled for a pass again in a few days. I feel sort of guilty, but we have flown a lot of practice.

In the last few days, when the 8th Air Force did fly, we put up 1,600 bombers each time. That's a lot of equipment and men in the air at one time. What we are doing to the Nazi transportation system is incredible; there's not a marshaling yard east of Berlin that is fully operational.

December 15, 1944

Out of bed for a briefing, then a cancellation, again. It's really torturous doing all that preparation, then not going. This makes three in a row. So, this afternoon we had a practice mission. Bill was sick with a cold, so I flew as first navigator. We taxied to the end of the runway, I called Mac on the intercom and told him I was lost. You could hear everyone on the crew laughing.

Now, stretched out in my bed, my thoughts run in many different directions. You know, there is a strange thrill to the part of combat flying that has one plane against another, a fighter versus a bomber. I pit all my skills against those of another man, and the stakes are our lives. There's no other game in which you don't get a second chance. One mistake and you're through. The fellow in the other plane knows that, too.

My edge is to never stop learning about my guns. The other guys kid me because I am so thorough about my equipment. They say that Jerry won't bother us with me manning the nose turret. I never forget, however, that the guy in the other plane may not realize who I am.

One of the things I often wonder about is how anything in my life can be important again after this experience. I think of how hard it will be to just go back to civilian life. I'll have to go around shooting people every once in awhile for excitement.

I'm getting awfully damned tired of the army. I sure got more than I bargained for. Who would have thought that I would be in the army two years — it's almost that much, you know. I sure wish this war would end. I'm getting more lonesome by the week. It seems like so long since we have been together. I just ache to stretch out in the living room with all of you, just talking and being together. So, enough of my musings for tonight.

December 16, 1944

We had a lulu today! Got up again at the usual 3 A.M., briefed, went out to the ship (are you getting as tired of this stuff as I am), and actually took off. We climbed to assembly altitude and started to form up, with our ship as the Group lead. It started to snow, it got cold, we couldn't see ten feet in front. Can you imagine anything worse? They recalled the mission.

We headed out over the North Sea, jettisoned many thousands of dollars worth of bombs, and headed back to the base. When we got there, the base was weathered in, so we pulled up to clear a herd of cows and headed south. We landed at another base and had lunch. They sent down a bunch of trucks and picked up all the enlisted crew members. At 8:30 tonight, we were able to fly the ships back to the base. And, that was my day.

December 17, 1944

Tomorrow we go on pass, having completed four scrubbed missions and six practice missions since our last pass. I feel more in need of a pass now, than I do after flying combat. The scrubbed mission bit is really getting on my nerves.

You know the deal while I am in London — don't expect any letters for three days, unless I find myself with spare time.

Journal Entry

December 17, 1944 – There are some things that happen here but never, for obvious reasons, make the press: One of the statistics that never gets in the papers is the number of planes the division loses on takeoff and landing. The loads we carry are enormous and tax the ability of our engines. It is not uncommon to see a B-24 take off and disappear into the fog, then to hear the crash and explosion, as it fails to clear the runway.

Coming home, hydraulic lines are often shot out or ailerons and rudders damaged. The song about coming in on a wing and a prayer is quite accurate. My nervousness reaches a peak at takeoff time and, if we have any battle damage, peaks again on landing.

The other unprintable is the myth of our bombing accuracy. In school or in practice it is possible to put one down the proverbial pickle barrel, but combat is quite something else. Flak tosses the planes around, targets are obscured by camouflage or smoke, components of the system freeze up, and a lot of other things conspire to affect our accuracy. I just don't want them to pin a near miss solely on my ability. The great numbers of planes dropping in a cluster helps to make up for some of the inaccuracy.

December 19, 1944

Here I am in good old London, again. We were supposed to leave yesterday morning, but at 3 A.M. that little man came around and we were it, so we happily contemplated spending our first day of pass on a cook's tour of "Der Fatherland." We were briefed, got everything ready for our visit to Fortress Europe, and took off. The rest of the story you have heard before. We got as far as Ostende when the weather closed in. We did the usual about face and headed home.

It's now five times in a row and still no score. When we got back on the ground, I made haste to depart the 392nd for parts unknown — before they thought of something else for me to do. The other men decided to stay until this morning and leave early.

I hitchhiked to Norwich, then took the train to the big city. I got in near midnight and went right to the place where I always stay. The housekeeper welcomed me with open arms, as she always does. She fixed me some sandwiches and tea before I went to bed.

I slept late this morning, then got a haircut, and shopped for exciting things like socks and underwear. In an hour or so, I'm to meet Reba and we'll have supper and go dancing. The other guys will call me when they get in.

December 22, 1944

Got back from pass last night and found that the weather has kept the Group grounded, so we didn't miss anything. Now it's getting serious because the ground troops have had little air support while the Jerrys are mounting counter attacks.

Had a swell time, as usual, in London. Dinner and dancing Tuesday was great, then I went to Reba's for dinner on Wednesday. When I was ready to leave, the fog was so thick that the buses stopped running and I had to stay there over night.

With the blackout, nighttime in London in clear weather is really dark, but in the fog at night, it's positively eerie. If it's not altogether like pea soup, which cancels everything, the buses run in convoy. A conductor walks in front of the bus parade with a torch that shines down, so it can't easily be seen from the air. You can imagine how long it takes to go any distance.

Down in the center of town, where the nightlife happens, there are ropes to hold onto that follow the sidewalks, so you can get around by feel (if you know the ropes). From pitch dark outside, you can walk into a pub or other establishment, through a double door that allows no light to show outside, into the blazing light and noise of the inside.

Reba gave me a lovely ring as a holiday gift, and yesterday I headed back to the base, having enjoyed myself thoroughly.

With all the aircraft unable to get off the ground, the Jerrys are using the bad weather to their advantage. We figure if we could get three days of flying weather, we could stem their advance quite nicely.

The 8th heavies could cut communications and destroy the marshaling yards east of the Rhine that funnel their supplies; the mediums would area-bomb troop concentrations; and the fighter and attack bombers would destroy motor transportation on the roads. Three days would do the trick, and we can't get it. We need to get in the air. Things are in quite desperate straits.

One of our English friends sent yellow scarves for each of us on the crew, so we're wearing them to fly in now. That further enhances our reputation as a bunch of screwballs. Most of the guys hang around and stare at us, not understanding how we laugh so much and have fun while maintaining one of the best records on the base. But, we do it.

I volunteered to take over some of the duties on Christmas eve and day, so that the Christian men can be off. I will probably be duty bombardier. We're throwing a party on Christmas day for the local kids. We're putting in some of our rations and some of the food we have received from home. It's really pathetic — some of the kids are five years old and have never had ice cream, oranges, or nuts. We have these things to give them, and we can do without for a bit.

Noone here in England has any of the things taken for granted back home, yet whatever they have, they cheerfully share with the Americans. It increases my faith in the ultimate goodness of at least some of the people in our world.

December 24, 1944

It's Christmas eve, everything is decorated, and I just had a hot shower instead of the usual 50-50 shower (50 percent cold, 50 percent colder yet).

We paid a visit to Germany today that will make history, and I am mighty proud of the part our crew played. We mounted the largest air raid ever — 2,000 planes. We were the deputy 8th Air Force lead, which means we had all 2,000 planes carrying 20,000 men trailing behind us as we went over the target. The assault was so huge that, while we were hitting the target, the tail end of the column was still forming over England.

Our targets were tactical, in support of hard-pressed ground troops. We hit rail and road junctions, troop concentrations, and ammunition dumps. Needless to say, we caused havoc with the Huns. Tomorrow, if it's clear, we will give it to them again, Christmas or no.

Bill and Deke got promoted to first lieutenant. They passed out cigars and everyone is sitting around singing Christmas carols.

There are stories coming out of Germany about death camps where Jews are killed by the hundreds. Do you read of or know about this?

December 27, 1944

I didn't fly today, as we only put up two squadrons. We're kind of on edge here. I don't know what you read in the papers, but things are not what they should be. Even with our constant bombing of rail lines, road junctions, and bridges, the Germans are able to continue to advance. The place was littered with buildings we knocked down and areas we cratered, but they are still powerful enough to keep on coming. It's frustrating for us to know we are doing a good job, yet the ground forces are still taking a pasting.

German air defense is getting better, too. Flak is so bad in some areas, it's impossible to get through unscathed. Sometimes we can only put up part of a group, since many planes are down for repairs. This is not over yet; the Hun is well-trained, well-equipped, and fighting hard.

Air battles get bigger and bigger, but one day soon we're going to sack out the Luftwaffe, once and for all. If we could only get a maximum effort into the air for five or six days in a row, I'm sure we could turn things around, but the weather has not been cooperative. We can deal with clouds over the continent, but fog on the field is bad. We can take off in low visibility, but we can't land in it.

Well, I'm done expounding on the war for today. Personally, I am OK and have no kicks. It's very cold, but we're comfortable in the hut. Now, if you have some mixed nuts around and want to send them to me, that would be nice.

December 28, 1944

I flew as bombardier with another crew today. The weather was clear and my drop was right on target. We had a lot of heavy flak, took battle damage ourselves, and lost some planes. Not a nice experience. I am such a veteran now that I seem able to handle most of what comes along.

There was some mixup in reporting the planes we lost, and my buddies thought I had been shot down. When I got back to the hut, they were sitting around saying what a great guy I was. Talk about seeing ghosts, you should have seen their faces when I walked in with nary a scratch. It isn't everyone that gets to hear his own impromptu eulogy.

My really serious problem is this: We are having a New Year's eve party, and I don't have a date. How about making a quick trip over here, Pooz, and going with me. You would be the prettiest girl at the party.

Journal Entry

December 28, 1944 – Everywhere I go in England, I see memorials to troops and wars that have gone before, and I wonder if, some day, there will be a memorial here in East Anglia for us.

December 29, 1944

I said that with five days of good weather we could turn the tide. Well, we have had seven and we did. The Jerry transportation system is in tatters and the advance is stopped cold. Our bombing has been phenomenal. Tomorrow looks like more, and our crew is on the battle order.

I got some special commendation from the command for yesterday's mission. In addition to the bombardier job, I did some fancy pilotage work when the navigation equipment got knocked out by flak.

December 30, 1944

They only put up two leads today. We were scratched, leaving it almost certain that we will fly tomorrow. We went Christmas eve, so we might just as well go on New Year's eve. We're the

Sunday crew and, now, the holiday crew, too. I have flown over half my missions on Sunday. The RAF is doing round-the-clock bombing, and it is doing a lot of good.

No mail today, so I am going to read a book. Small consolation.

Journal Entry

December 31, 1944 – The Air Force defines casualties as those airmen who are missing, killed, or wounded in action. But, the horrors of this experience are such that, in reality, we are all casualties.

Chapter Twelve

New Year, Same War

T he story of the Eighth Air Force and strategic bombing is primarily of the men, but it is also about their machines, most notably, one piece of equipment — the Norden bombsight — that made daylight precision bombing possible.

The key to the entire concept of air power and strategic bombing was accuracy; it was essential that air strikes be massive and precise. The obstacles to achieving accuracy were formidable: to minimize anti-aircraft damage, missions had to be flown at high altitude; the bomber was a moving and unstable platform; winds were strong and unpredictable; targets were often obscured by clouds or smoke; enemy gunfire from both air and ground, destabilized the aircraft; and the sub-zero temperatures limited the performance of the crew.

Although, not nearly as accurate as the public was led to believe, the Norden bombsight was still good enough for the Air Force to commit thousands of costly aircraft and the lives of several thousand men to a strategy that depended on the bombsight for success.

Designed and developed by engineer Carl L. Norden, the bombsight was a complicated, 50-pound piece of machinery that consisted of a telescope with cross-hairs, a group of gyroscopes, motors, gears, levers, and mirrors. The bombardier entered necessary information, such as the size of the bombs, speed and direction of the wind, altitude and speed of the plane, and atmospheric conditions, into the bombsight. As the aircraft approached the target, the pilot turned the plane over to the bombardier and the bombsight. The bombsight worked in coordination with an automatic pilot to fly the aircraft down the bomb run and release the bombs over the target.

The way the Norden bombsight worked was one of the most carefully guarded secrets of the war. Bombardier trainees were required to swear an oath to protect the secret. Upon graduation, they had to repeat the oath before taking the secret overseas. The bombsight was removed from the aircraft and put under guard after every mission, and the bombardier always wore a sidearm when carrying it. Before bailing out of a doomed aircraft, or before a forced landing, the bombardier was under orders to destroy the bombsight.

UNITED STATES ARMY AIR FORCES

January 1, 1945

Dear Mom, Dad, and Pooz,

It's just shortly after midnight. My mind is so much on home
that I wanted to stop partying and write to you for a few minutes. I received the color pictures of all of you last night. I was so
elated the guys thought I would go through the roof. They are
marvelous and my proudest possession. I can't tell you how much
I love them, but you knew I would.

We toasted the New Year with a few drinks at the club. I
made my resolution to knock off as many Jerrys as possible and
get home to spend a peaceful New Year 1946 with you.

We actually celebrated New Year's Eve greeting Adolph in a
way he could not possibly like, by knocking down some bridges
and rail lines carrying supplies to their front. Although our
bombing was very accurate, I still have the DTs from this afternoon's (yesterday's) raid.

A bunch of Jerry fighters jumped us and made it hot for
awhile. Our tail gunner got a kill and I got enough hits on
another to get a probable. We took a lot of damage to the ship,
and Mac got a tooth busted from a hunk of flak, but we appreciate how very lucky we are. We came out of it fine, and that's
what counts.

Well, dearest ones, I'm tired, so New Year's eve or not, it's the
sack for me. I want to wish you the happiest of Happy New
Years. My prayers are that we will all be together again before
this year ends.

Journal Entry

January 1, 1945 – Although I seem finished with the early fears that had me visibly shaking, some horrors are regularly in my thoughts. The one I have most often is the fear of fire in the ship. I have watched men bail out of severely damaged ships with their chutes on fire and tumble out of the sky to their deaths. Another vision that recurs is bailing out successfully, then being machine-gunned in my chute by enemy fighters. It happens. Yesterday's mission really got to me. We had plenty of both flak and fighters, yet escaped such deaths, while others did not.

January 2, 1945

I spent an off afternoon in the plexiglass shop, where they repair battle damage, making a frame for the pictures you sent. I put them back to back with thin plexiglass on both sides, then flush riveted them together. It fits right into my shirt pocket. Now, all I have to do is slip the button open, and there you are right in the palm of my hand. You sure look pretty!

These are busy days for the 8th Air Force; the Group has been out ten days in a row. The division bombardier was over here today. He told us that our Group was head and shoulders above the rest of the Liberator groups in bombing accuracy. That's something to be proud of. I have been complimented by the CO on my own work recently. It's not too long ago that I was lightly regarded, but now they'll trust me with anything. The majority of the lead pilotage navigators are finishing tours, so I will probably be the senior officer in that group. I am generally seen as the best turret gunner in the outfit, and, on occasion, they have me instructing gunners. Considering the winter weather, the Group is getting in a remarkable number of missions. I flew three last week and we are on the battle order for tomorrow. At this rate, I may finish my tour in March. What a hallelujah day that will be.

January 3, 1945

Your pictures went with me on a good mission today. We had just 15 minutes over enemy territory, no sign of fighters, and only light flak. I hope they are running out of ammunition. They tried to get even with us, though. When we got home, they sent a buzz bomb at our base, but it fell short into the sea. Those guys have about shot their bolt now. We plastered the Luftwaffe but good in the past two days, shooting down 381 planes.

We got some statistics today that have been very secret in the past, but, now, no one seems to care if they become public. Last year, the 8th Air Force fighters and bombers shot down 7,000 Jerry aircraft while we lost 2,643 heavy bombers and 1,441 fighters.

We put another complete division into the air today. I imagine the Hun is getting mighty tired of this; perhaps they will quit soon. I have flown four missions in the past ten days. I am really a veteran now with 20 missions. Ten more to go, and then it's home.

Considering everything, we sure are a high morale bunch. In the midst of death and destruction, we manage to find time to play. Today, it took the form of a tag game on our bicycles. Mac got a pair of muddy pants when we ran him off the road.

Despite flying in 40 degree below zero weather, we're all fine. Your letters and packages keep me close to home.

Journal Entry

January 3, 1945 – When we returned from the mission today, General Johnson was waiting on the ramp for us. As I was coming out of the ship with no head cover and my jacket open, the general asked who was the lead bombardier. I said, "I was, sir." He looked me over, and all he said was, "Oh, My God!"

January 5, 1945

I received your letter in response to my questions about what's going on at home. I'm glad things are reasonably normal. I would be disappointed to come home on leave and find that things are not as I left them. I feel, as so many of you do, about the Germans. I'd never give the bastards a second chance. When a fighter makes a pass at me and breaks away, I shoot at the back of his head.

The reason I once expressed my dislike for using the center of a city for an aiming point on a bomb run is that it makes no military sense, not because I have any compunctions about killing Huns. The Germans learned the futility of civilian bombing in the London blitz.

It's very difficult to have any personal feelings about the enemy as the foot soldier does. I have talked with some of our infantry men who were in Belgium, and they are really bitter. Jerrys in American uniforms were shooting them in the back and killing prisoners. Now our men shoot first, then ask them if they'd like to surrender. It's a lousy business all around.

January 7, 1945

I got your letter about Cousin Ira being wounded. I found out where his hospital is located, got permission from the CO to take 24 hours off, and left to see him. I got about 50 miles from here and had to turn back, as I couldn't possibly make train connections to get there and back on time. He's about 200 miles from here.

I called the hospital and talked to the ward attendant, and was told that Ira is getting along fine. I left a message that I would be up to see him very soon, when I get a three-day pass. He is near Leeds in Yorkshire county, so I'll just spend my pass up there. Mac wanted to fly me up, but there is no field close by that can handle a B-24. If we can borrow the colonel's small plane, we may yet get to fly. I will definitely get there shortly and send you a cable about his condition. It seems that he is OK, so tell Uncle Charley not to worry.

This easy life with lots of sleep, plenty of good food, and nothing to worry about has me gaining weight. My clothes are all getting too tight. Figure that one out.

January 8, 1945

I bought a dozen eggs and a loaf of home-baked bread from a nearby farmer. Then, I brought out my mess kit and fried eggs over the fire. Mac and I had fried egg sandwiches for lunch. Good fun.

We have been going after tactical targets, so both the flak and fighter opposition are light. The real opposition comes from the weather — it is real mucky most of the time.

The combat mission for today was scrubbed, but we got out to the ship at 9 A.M. to go on a practice hop. It had snowed through the night and began snowing again when we got to the ship, so they scrubbed the practice mission, too. While we were waiting for the truck to pick us up, we got into a snowball fight with another crew. We got our flak helmets out of the planes and let fly from behind a bomb dump. We could have been a bunch of high school kids, except the background was B-24s and bombs.

We were dressed in our flying clothes, which we got all wet. That got the major all pissed off. We drive the command insane with our nutty doings, but they help to keep us sane.

It may be snowing and cold on the ground, but it's worse in the air. Yesterday, it was 54 degrees below zero. Our new equipment is pretty good, though. My heated flying suit is silk with wire running through it. On top, I wear a suit lined with alpaca that works well. If you take your glove off and touch anything metal, it fuses your hand to the metal instantly. That's why scarred hands are common among gunners.

January 12, 1945

I just got the mail with the *Varga Calendar*. Some cute girls. We get a London paper, *The Daily Mirror*, at the club. It has a comic strip called *Jane*. The girl is forever getting undressed. At lunch everyone grabs for the paper, not to see who's winning the war, but to see what state of undress Jane is in.

This is another typical English winter day. There is slush six inches deep; it's grey and miserable. I went to the traveling PX that is here today and bought a shortcoat. I wanted one when I graduated from bombardier school, but dear old Mom said, "Oh, those trench coats are so nice looking." So I got one. They're pretty, of course, except you can freeze in them. So, I finally got a shortcoat, and I will freeze no more. I may not look like the movie version of a flier, but I will be warm.

I'm still planning on going to see Ira on my next pass. It'll be a good idea for both of us. London is getting plastered with V-2 rocket bombs. Buzz bombs were bad enough — you could hear them coming. Then, the motor would quit and you knew in a few seconds there would be an explosion. The V-2s come through the upper atmosphere and there's no warning at all before they explode. I was standing at the corner of Hyde Park on my last pass to London, when out of nowhere there was this huge explosion in the park and lots of people were killed.

It's quiet in the hut tonight. The guys all went to a movie. I missed a class today, so I will go tonight. We have geography lessons. They give us certain sections of Germany that are under planned attack and we study maps, photos, and topography, memorizing outstanding features of the terrain.

My mind doesn't seem as sharp as when I was at Big Spring, but I am sure I can do better with education in peacetime. Education for killing is getting to be a little much.

Throughout this bad weather, our quarters have been reasonably comfortable. We manage to make a midnight raid on the coal pile, now and then, to supplement our rations and keep the place warm. I read a lot and there is always some good music from the radio or the Victrola. We have an orderly who makes our beds and cleans the place up, so there's not much to complain about.

My $40 bicycle is now worth about $2. The weather here ruins everything. I have spent a lot of money on things like boots to keep warm, but I can use them as a civilian, too — most happy thought.

We really bombed the Heinies out of the Ardennes salient and McArthur has landed on Lujon, so things are beginning to look bright again. Maybe soon now, eh?

January 18, 1945

I took the train to Harrogate to see Ira. He got hit by some glass but no shrapnel, and, in a few weeks, he will be good as new. I wrote a V-mail to his dad telling him not to worry. Ira is walking around, so we had chow together at the officer's mess.

After he went to bed, I went to town with his nurse. We had dinner, then went dancing, and had a swell time. It was nice to be out with an American girl again. She's cute and fun to be with.

In peacetime, Harrogate is a resort with mineral spas, but now it's an RAF center with a hospital. The countryside is beautiful, so I will have to go there again to visit Ira, and, of course, to see Norma, the nurse.

When we got back from pass, we found the place half deserted. The Group went on a raid to "Big B" (Berlin) and, although there were no battle casualties, they ran low on gas and the weather was bad, so they landed all over France and Belgium. Most of the guys took off for Paris or Brussels. The colonel is going nuts trying to round everyone up. Crazy war!

Our mission got scrubbed this morning, fortunately before I got out of the sack, so I slept until 11 A.M. At noon, I had to go to a meeting where the CO chewed out the bombardiers for hitting a wrong target. They were going for an oil dump and accidentally destroyed a huge aluminum plant in the Reich. For this you get chewed?

January 21, 1945

Today was a goofed up affair. We started out on a mission leading the high squadron. Three hours later over France, one of our engines failed, so we had to abort and come home. That's too bad because we get no mission credit and have to get up again at 3 A.M. tomorrow. I simply was not made for getting up to work at two or three in the morning.

January 22, 1945

After yesterday's aborted mission, we figured to fly again today, but the Group was stood down (that's Air Force lingo for not assigned to fly), so I amassed 16 hours of sleep. I'm going to a movie, then back to bed. Maybe I can sleep the rest of the war away.

Our aircrews have been having some fun lately. The missions have been quite long and everyone contrives to run out of gas at interesting places on the continent. Then, they get themselves weathered in for days at a time. We now have crews wandering around in Paris, Brussels, Liege, Metz, and other such places. I am perfecting a device to screw up the two port engines the next time we get near Paris — we want to be part of the fun, too.

We're having a party here Saturday night. Unfortunately, I find myself financially embarrassed, so I cabled you for some money, hoping it will get here in time. We're coming up on a seven-day leave in February, so I want to be well heeled.

How I manage to spend all the money I make and then need additional is more than I can understand. I really draw down a lot of pay, but I manage to get rid of it somehow. Each month, I tell myself that this will be the month I save some money. Then we get a pass and it's gone. I'm going to have one heck of a time learning the value of money again when I get home. How will I ever get a soft job like this again, where I work one day a week, sleep and party the rest, and get paid a bundle of money?

I'm going to try and get in touch with Ira's nurse tonight, to see if she can come to the dance here. She's a real nice girl. We're talking about her getting a pass and coming to London with me, the next time I get a pass.

This morning, I woke up early, got up, and built a fire while Mac and Deke were still in the sack. Then I made scrambled eggs and coffee. The guys had breakfast in bed. That's what you call a valuable crew member.

Tomorrow, we'll probably take to the wild blue, so we can earn our money. Recently, it has been down to 70 degrees below zero. I have read about temperatures like that in the books about Admiral Byrd in the Arctic, but I never believed it. That extreme cold is a worse hazard than the enemy right now.

January 26, 1945

Because of my early assignments to other lead crews, I am three missions behind the rest of my crew, so they are going to assign me as lead bombardier with other crews on some upcoming missions. I'll be glad to do them over the bombsight, instead of navigating.

Norma is going to meet me in London when we both get passes on February 4th. It will be her first time there, so it should be fun showing her around. Also, we are going to be sent to a rest home for seven days in about three weeks. It's part of the Air Force rest and rehabilitation plan, and costs us nothing. We have been told it is a very nice experience with breakfast in bed, horseback riding, sports, and good food. We're all for it.

January 28, 1945

We went on a mission today, that leaves eight to go. It wasn't too bad, but I am always glad when I see our home field. Tomorrow, I am scheduled to fly a practice mission, dropping bombs out over the North Sea. They want me to be sharp for the missions I will be leading as bombardier. If the weather stays good, I'll probably do double time, going with Mac and the gang on their assignments, and in between with other crews.

I got your package with the salami and other goodies, and as I write this, I am having a Dagwood sandwich. I am also tuned to the radio — they are telling about how the Russians are eating up Germany. We now must learn Russian aircraft identification, as they are patrolling many of our target regions. Come on Joe Stalin — let it rip! I am looking for a breakthrough in the west soon, then the war will be over.

The real good news is that Mac got promoted to captain. You should see him strutting around with the railroad tracks on his collar. We're all happy for him; he really deserves it.

January 29, 1945

Well, it's my anniversary again — two years in the army. I don't think any of us realized it would be that long when I enlisted. This is the time for me to reminisce, take stock of myself, and sort of pull myself up by the bootstraps. I remember writing to you after I had finished one year in service, telling you all the things I had learned, and how I had profited by my experiences. I thought I had learned just about all there was to be gained from the army. I didn't know I had only scratched the surface.

One year ago I was a cadet, striving to get my bars, those treasured bits of metal, symbolic of the toughest work of my life. I got them! Then there was my leave at home. Never was anything more appreciated. After that the meeting with the crew, training for combat at Tucson, and the eventful flight overseas. That consumed five months of the second year. And yet, that wasn't really significant. It was merely the marking of time until we got to England. Even when I first got here, I was still more or less "playing soldier." The gold bars were still relatively new — I was learning to be a good officer, assimilating knowledge that would make me a combat flyer. I had my wings, but I still hadn't earned them.

Then there was the first combat mission, so easy, but I hadn't yet seen the real combat. I'll never forget the first time we got hit by flak. Mean, ugly black puffs. They were shooting at us, yes, but "they" were 25,000 feet below us. There was no animosity for the gunners, rather the hatred was directed at the flak bursts. I watched with a fear I had never known, as they tracked us down, felt the ship lunge as a piece tore through the wing. There was nowhere to go, just sit and wait, hoping it wouldn't hit us again. I was sweating in the extreme cold, a sweat unlike the kind I associate with physical activity.

We made it through, but one ship didn't. It blew up — no 'chutes. I knew those men, talked with them the night before, sat with them through briefing. It hurt, it numbed. I wondered when we would get it. That was the first time. It happened again, many times. I never became hardened to it, merely accepted it as a fact of my life. It didn't hurt so much anymore and I began to believe in our own invincibility. I stopped being afraid of the flak, just sweated it out like I did the chow line. Then a good friend of mine got it. We had been on pass together many times and we shared many common likes and dislikes. I got drunk, really drunk, because I couldn't just sit and think of him. Then I began to hate for the first time. It was something completely new to me. I had disliked some people, but never hated. I wanted to kill Germans, lots of them. I began to get a peculiar thrill out of bombing troop concentrations and hitting big cities. I haven't gotten over that. I don't think I will. I want to exterminate the Hun, yet I know in my deepest heart that everything about killing is wrong.

Those are some of the things I have been through, and still there are more — like the first time I shot at an enemy plane. It was him or me. It was him! I could write for days about that. These are indelible memories, but I have learned something more — such experiences are but one part of the process of maturing.

I have lived with Mac and Bill constantly for eight months. Eat, sleep, fly, play together. I know what they are going to say almost before they open their mouths. I've learned a deep respect for Mac. He's a great flier, even greater officer, yet I wouldn't want to be like him. He's a deep thinker and he doesn't enjoy the everyday pleasures that are so much a part of my life. No, I'd rather be like Bill, in a way. He's tops in navigators — they don't come any finer. When he's not flying, he can play with enthusiasm. He's so very much in love with his wife that it hurts to watch him when he talks about her. I like Bill, I respect his judgment, and enjoy living with him. Deke and I work well together, but I have a hard time living with him. He's a good co-pilot, but there's nothing else there. We put up with each other because it's important to do so. Art is the designated bombardier, but all our missions together have been radar drops, so all he has ever done is pre-flight the bombsight. I have no way of knowing if he is competent or not. He's a nice enough guy,

The enlisted men are tops. I respect all of them and their abilities, but I don't have to live with them, so I don't have the same level of involvement that I do with the officers. For me, the intensity of the relationships is very tough. No matter how much mutual respect we have, or how much we like each other, we're bound to get on each other's nerves once in awhile. I make it a point to go off by myself when we go on pass. That helps.

I have realized, more than ever, my attachment to home and family. Yep, I've become sentimental. Some particular song will remind me of an incident at home, or I will look at your pictures and just be drawn into them. I long for the time when I will be a civilian again. Even though this place is totally devoid of the chicken shit I experienced in training it's still the army, and I am definitely a civilian on loan to this life.

Yes, combat has changed me and I never will be young again in the way that normal 20 year olds are young. Yet, this is the right — the only thing — to be doing. I hope by our achievements here we have really made the world a better place to live in. Many have given their lives to make it so. I know that if this is not a lasting peace, I will be an unhappy citizen.

You are very dear to me and I love you all very much. I am sure that I will return to you with new and better ideals, physically stronger and mentally more able to cope with the problems of this changing world.

Journal Entry

January 29, 1945 – They took away our .45-caliber pistols today. They told us that downed airmen with guns were being summarily executed, so they don't want us to put up a fight when being captured. They told us to try and escape after parachuting, but if caught, to surrender and be imprisoned. They also said, it is better to surrender to the military than to civilians, as there are many of the German populace quite bitter about the destruction the allied air forces have brought, and they want to retaliate.

I don't find this so easy to accept. I have these visions of my parachuting out, landing, and being surrounded. Then I see them looking at my dogtags, and learning that I am Jewish. After that, I envision many of the horrible things they might do to me. Now, before each mission, I strap my little .32-caliber pistol to my leg inside my flying boot. I am determined not to surrender peacefully. If I die, some of them will die with me.

January 30, 1945

I received the 75 bucks you sent by cable. Thanks a lot! We have a pass on Sunday, then a seven-day leave at the end of the month. Now I am well fixed for money.

I slept 14 hours after the raid on the 28th. Being on oxygen for a long time makes me very tired. Today is a quiet one in the ETO. It snowed, rained, and sleeted last night, and the roof is leaking. It's miserable enough in the air — who needs it on the ground.

I have a new problem. The girl I have been going out with in London is in love with me. Don't laugh, it ain't funny! I had a lot of fun with her, she's a nice girl, cute, and she's 21 years old — no chicken. She sends me packages, writes me letters telling how she misses me, etc. Well, I don't want anything like that. I haven't the vaguest intention of falling in love with anyone; I'm busy playing the field. I don't know what to do about her, so I told her I was assigned to Russia for a few months. I don't know if she'll swallow it, but by the time a couple of months is up, I may be on my way home. I have been trying not to contribute to the delinquency of the English girls, but it seems as though I have made an unintentional beginning.

I am scheduled as lead bombardier in the next day or so. I hope I can get in my three extra missions, so I can finish up with my gang.

February 3, 1945

It was beautiful weather and the 8th was out in strength
doing what we all wanted to do since the start of the Russian
offensive. We sent 1,000 bombers to the heart of Berlin! There
were no specific targets — just unload on the center of the city.
I'm really sorry I didn't go. All our ships are back safe. What the
news hasn't revealed is that many of our planes carried delay
action bombs with anti-withdraw fuses — some had as much as
12 hour delays. They dropped 2,500 tons of these bombs. That
should slow down some of the defenses against Joe Stalin and
his men.

Tomorrow, my crew goes on pass. I'm scheduled as lead bombardier with the other crew, so I won't be going until Monday.
The weather doesn't look too promising, though, so I may get to
go with the gang after all. I am meeting my little nurse, and
looking forward to a good time.

February 5, 1945

Back in London again, braving the V-2 rockets, for some fun,
and I am sure to have it. Right now, I am killing a few hours
until I meet Norma at the train. I came down yesterday with the
gang. They're over at the Red Cross, and I am here at my usual
spot, the boarding house. I'm the favorite son here now. They
greet me with open arms, and anything I want, I can have. When
I arrived yesterday, the housekeeper made me a swell dinner. It
was a beautiful evening, so I took a long walk, chatted with some
of the boys at the officer's club, and hit the sack at 10 P.M.

I got up early this morning and went to see my friends at the
barber shop, walked around window shopping, and just piddled
away the morning. I have great plans cooked up for the next few
days. Tonight, I have tickets for a very fine comedy, *Is Your
Honeymoon Really Necessary?* My pals got me good seats. Then
we'll have dinner and go dancing at one of the nicest places in

London, the Grosvenor House. Tomorrow, I'll let Norma do some shopping and whatever else female girls do with themselves. Then we'll do a tour of the town, including Westminster Abbey, one of my favorite places.

Tomorrow night, we're having dinner at the Mirabelle, a very special place. You know, at times like this, I feel like I never had it so good. When I can shut out the war, I am just a guy living it up in London.

February 8, 1945

I'm quite tired, so I will make this short and write you more about my adventures in London later. Got back from pass last night and sat around comparing notes with the guys until 1:15 A.M. At 2 A.M. they awakened me to fly a mission. I was lead bombardier. We got up to the assembly altitude and, while I was holding my eyelids apart, they recalled the mission. I came back to the sack and slept until five this evening. I'm assigned for tomorrow, but this time I will be rested.

I had so much fun on pass it will be hard to describe. I'll try in the next letter.

February 9, 1945

I got in a mission as bombardier today. It was a seven-hour run through some heavy flak to a difficult target. Our losses were moderate. Tomorrow, I am assigned with Mac and the crew.

Now, about the pass: I met Norma and we had a wonderful time. The play I wrote about was terrific, as was dinner at the Grosvenor House. The next day we did some shopping, looked over the town, saw a movie, and went to Mme. Toussad's Wax Museum. Tuesday night, we had dinner at the Mirabelle and drank champagne. The Mirabelle is a special place where many of the high ranking brass go. It's all glass chandeliers, fancy silver, and service that matches. On the street outside, the blackout is eerie, but once inside, there is gaiety, music, women in formal gowns, and fine food. Even though we are only lieutenants, we were treated in the same elegant manner as the generals. I felt like the glow from the chandeliers was inside me.

Wednesday, we took a tour of the city and, although I have done it before, it is always an amazing experience. It was truly wonderful, the best of all my passes. I came back quite happy.

Journal Entry

February 9, 1945 – I wish I had someone to talk to about the last few days, but there's no one here I want to confide in about this subject.

Since I have been in England, even when I am having the most fun, I am always a soldier at play. But, with Norma I can just be whoever I really am from moment to moment. Norma is 28 years old, with a lot more relationship experiences than I have, and a wonderful knack for being with me as a woman, while subtly teaching me in ways of loving. When the guys talk of sexual encounters, it is always about conquests. My few experiences have been stolen moments in the back of a car or hurriedly in a place unfamiliar to me. But these days together were something entirely different.

When we checked Norma into the boarding house, the housekeeper, bless her, treated our being together as everyday normal and gave us the only room with a big bed and a view of the park.

After our evening at the Mirabelle, with the champagne glow still upon us, we came back to our room. When we took off our uniforms and got into bed, it was like a magical transformation to a place far away from war, where there were no expectations and no passage of time — there was nothing happening except a man and a woman folding into each other and making love.

The army has taught me to be tough, impersonal, and professional. Being with Norma is teaching me to be soft and loving again.

February 12, 1945

We were only able to take 125 Liberators up for a mission yesterday — the weather was putrid. It was an important target and our crew led the whole division, bombing by instruments. I got a third Oak Leaf Cluster to my Air Medal. Each one tells me I'm getting closer to coming home. There are various conflicting rumors about where I will be assigned, but it's certain that I will have a 21-day leave.

You always tell me how wonderful I am in your letters. Now, let me tell you how wonderful I think you are. No one else gets daily letters like I do. Your attitude about the entire war and its consequences is marvelous; there's no moaning about what a rough time the civilians are having at home, like I hear from others. You tell nothing to make me worry — you only send good wishes and cheerful news. I think you are deserving of much credit.

February 13, 1945

This note is exclusively for you, Pooz. You are a wonderful writer, and do I ever love your letters and you! I always save your letters for last, the same as you used to save the best part of the meal for the end. And, the new color picture of you ... wow! If you were here, you could have a hundred dates with the finest fliers in the ETO. I'd be proud to take you stepping myself.

I would like to have been there for your big formal. Try and get me a picture of yourself at the ball. I'm getting along fine, but I sure miss you. We'll have fun when I get home. I love you very much!

February 15, 1945

Our leave to go to a flak (rest) home has been postponed. They can only send one crew from each base every two weeks, and there is no room for us now. So, we're going on pass for three days on the 24th, and should get the extended leave next month. On pass, I think I will go visit cousin Ira, who is still in the hospital, poor boy. Don't laugh!

In the next two months or so, if you get a cable from me saying, "Hope you feel better, I'm fine," you'll know that it means I have finished my tour. That won't necessarily mean I'll be coming right home, but at least you will know I am not flying any more combat. It will probably take from six weeks to two months for me to get home after I finish.

February 19, 1945

I know I haven't written for four days, but I have a wonderful excuse and a million stories. We flew a mission on the 16th, just a short haul of under five hours, but when we got back to the base it was fogged in, so they diverted us to France. That's where this great story begins.

We landed at a B-26 base. They split up crews all over the base, but as lead-crew officers we ended up in a French house taken over by the squadron CO and his higher ranking officers. We slept on cots, but they tried to make us comfortable.

Of course, Mac and I were eager to try out our high school French, so that evening, we went to a little pub to drink some cognac. We got into a discussion with an old guy about our Air Forces that taxed my French almost to the breaking point. Still, I was amazed at how much I remembered. He understood me quite well.

There were some French girls cooking and cleaning up for the officers in this billet. I talked with them a lot. We got pretty chummy. One of them took me in the kitchen and gave me fresh milk and real French bread, the first I have had since I left the states. The next day, England was still fogged in, so, we visited a small town that had been liberated from the Germans just a short time ago. When the Germans came, the French took their best wine and champagne, put it up against the wall, then built false walls to cover it all. After the allies came, they tore the false walls down and, *voila!* Champagne. So, we were treated to some. I also got a surprise for you ladies. *Vous désirez parfum?* I got!

We walked around and talked to some of the girls. My, are they lovely. Clean and neat, silk stockings, nice makeup, pretty hair-dos. *Oo la la!* One cutie invited me to sleep over, but I thought better of it. I'll probably be sorry some day. But, when we were getting ready to leave, she gave me a little Free French Emblem and a Tricolor. I gave her some stuff out of my escape kit. The kit also contained some French francs, which is where I got the money to buy various things. The army will probably put out charges against me for opening the escape kit, but what-the-hell.

The French are very friendly and they really like our boys. It's hard to believe they have been through a worse time than the English. They have all the luxuries the English don't have, yet they are desperately short of food. It's kind of ironic, *mais, c'est la guerre!* I saw huge bomb craters, the wreck of a bridge, and other devastation, but the French are very philosophical about the whole thing. *C'est nécessaire, n'est ce pas?*

I got some champagne to take home to the base, but most of it exploded in the transport plane that brought us back, when the pilot had to climb up high to get over some clouds. I did manage to save one bottle. When we landed, I was told that I had been promoted to first lieutenant, so the men ceremoniously pinned on my silver bars and we drank the champagne.

I could write all night, but I need some sleep.

February 21, 1945

I didn't sleep very well last night, wondering what I have become. Yesterday, we were group lead crew, with me as bombardier. During the morning briefing, S-2 pointed out that the primary target bordered on a huge park where many thousands of refugees from bombings of Berlin and other cities were living in a tent city. S-2 speculated that many soldiers may have sought cover with the civilians.

We have an unwritten rule that states, "Don't bring the bombs home." On occasion, when the primary target is obscured by weather, or we can't hit it for other reasons, we can go after a "target of opportunity." On an earlier mission, severe, unexpected weather kept us from our main target, so I picked out a railroad marshaling yard and dumped the bomb load there.

On yesterday's mission, our group was the last one in. The rest of the wing was in first. As we started down the run under heavy flak attack, I could see the target was hit so well that it was likely destroyed and dropping on the same area was probably a waste. I had options: I could drop on the primary target, and let it go at that; or I could order the group to make a full turn, giving me a minute or two to consult with Mac and Deke about seeking a secondary target; or make another run on the primary. Another option was to drop on the park.

I had about twenty seconds to make a decision. My immediate thought was that it was far too dangerous to consider taking the group over this target area a second time. With no further hesitation, I made a slight correction in the bombsight, lined up on the center of the park, and dropped the full load of the group, 500,000 pounds of bombs.

On the way home, I considered what would happen when I made my strike report. The colonel joined us in the briefing room and, after I explained my decision, he and the other officers congratulated me for making a sound choice.

But what kind of a choice was it, really? The victims were a lot of civilians, probably many of them women and children. One advantage of the Air Force is that we can never see the faces of those we kill. Still, I am a trained killer, in the service of my country. Would it make a difference if I could see faces, know them as human beings instead of "a target?" Is what I did any different than the German engineers who send the buzz bombs to London, not knowing exactly where they will land and indiscriminately hitting the civilian population? Or, am I any different than the German executioner of Jews?

This is one of countless such decisions made regularly by others in the Air Force, but this one is mine to live with. When I tried to sleep last night, the faces of children intruded. Are Nazi kids different from American kids? Do their deaths assure anything? In the eyes of the commanding staff, I did the right thing. But what other judgments are there? What about my own? I wonder, what have I become?

February 22, 1945

Remember this date, the 22nd, and if you read of the strange raid today, you will know I was on it. It was one for the books, and I hope I never have to go on another one like it. I am thoroughly pooped and I am going to bed. Tomorrow, I will try to tell you more.

Journal Entry

February 23, 1945 – They said it was an unusual mission yesterday, but I call it nutty. We were assigned to bomb the marshaling yards at Nordhausen, a very minor target for heavy bombers. So, they sent us in to bomb at 6,000 feet. We went over enemy lines at 10,000 feet, then let down to that ridiculous altitude. We were laughingly told by S-2 to enjoy the view, but the intense flak concentration made it very unfunny. It felt like they

could have a go at us with machine guns. B-24s were criss-
crossing all over the sky. And, we had to make a secondary run
on Northeim. It was a total nut house.

But, the worst part: Jim's plane was flying on our wing and
was hit hard. He feathered the No. 3 engine, then began to let
down. We got a report from him that he was low on fuel and
was going to go along the Dutch coast to try to make Belgium or
France. No further word has been heard from him.

I just don't know how to deal with this. We flew on the same
crew, lived in the same quarters, went on pass together. He's a
wild guy and a dear friend. He's also a fine pilot, so he can find a
place to put his ship safely down in Holland. I hope he can. I
know he can. He will.

February 23, 1945

We are scheduled for pass tomorrow, but rumor has it that we
will do a mission instead. With this heavy offensive going on,
they are giving the lead crews a terrific workout. One crew flew
two in a row, very unusual for leads. If we don't fly, I am going
to take off early in the morning for Harrogate. It's not jammed
with American soldiers, I can visit with Ira, and there's Norma,
of course. Mac just came in and said we won't fly tomorrow, so
off I go.

The news is good and our men seem to be hammering the
Hun hard. The clipping I am enclosing is about our raid of yesterday. It was repeated by the Group today. The Huns never
dreamed we would come in so low over Germany proper — nei-
ther did we. I imagine there are a lot of dead Huns around central Germany now. It was something to see from that altitude,
but some of the sights were not too pretty.

I have really had about enough of this war. I will certainly be
glad to finish my tour and come home. I hope they put me to

instructing, with no more combat. I am getting the first signs of combat fatigue. I have seen it in others, and I don't like it a bit. I jump at any loud noise, and I'm much more nervous than I have experienced before. I am sending my summer uniforms home. Will you have them washed for me? Just put the other things away and forget them, OK?

Journal Entry

February 27, 1945 – Scarborough is a summer resort, primarily, but the two days there with Norma, and practically no one else around, seemed like they were taken from another life and plunked down on the wild, cold English coast.

If we had been able to get rid of our uniforms, we would have been like lovers from ordinary times, walking along the water-front, stopping in for a coffee or a half and half, taking dinner at the hotel restaurant, and then making love under a big comforter while the wind made whistling noises outside the window. It is a powerful experience to completely shut out the world at war and be two people just being.

Chapter Thirteen

Countdown to Home

Toward the end of 1944, the Allies had penetrated deep into Germany. Many were saying that soon the war would be over. But, on December 16th the Germans began a major counteroffensive in Belgium that came to be known as the Battle of the Bulge. Weary American ground forces suffered heavy losses as they tried to overcome the final efforts of a doomed Germany. The Luftwaffe had been conserving its strength. To cover the ground offensive, hundreds of German planes resumed their attacks on U.S. bomber forces, causing heavy losses in the skies, as well.

Instead of the conflict winding down, the turn-of-the-year offensive began some of the most savage battles of the air war. In the final five days of December, 5,500 sorties by bombers of the Eighth Air Force struck rail centers, communication centers, marshaling yards, and bridges. In those five days, more than 100 of the big planes with their crews were shot down.

By the end of January, American ground forces had turned the tide and were back in positions they had occupied before the Germans launched their Ardennes offensive. For the Germans, it had been a terribly costly venture, both in manpower and material, and the Eighth Air Force had played a significant role in defeating them.

In February 1945, the retreating Germans began transferring troops from the western front, where they faced the Americans and British, to their crumbling eastern front against the Russians. The full strength of the allied heavy-bomber fleet was turned on the movement of German troops. Almost daily, the Eighth sent off "thousand-bomber" raids against targets throughout the Reich, despite unfavorable weather conditions. Thousands of tons of bombs were dropped on heavily fortified Berlin. On many of these raids, more than half the bombers suffered battle damage.

In a last, desperate attempt to blow the American bombers from the skies, German conventional and jet fighters began making frenzied suicide attacks. Urged on by a woman's voice broadcasting slogans like, *"Deutschland über alles"* and "Remember our dead women and children," German planes deliberately rammed the bombers, destroying many.

The fierce fighting continued until there were few strategic targets left in Germany. Then, the heavy bombers were reassigned to tactical support. During the final days of the war, the bombers of the Eighth dropped food to the starving population of western Holland.

UNITED STATES AIR FORCES

March 1, 1945

Dear Mom, Dad, and Pooz,

Sorry I haven't written in a few days, but things have been happening fast. Last Saturday I went on a three-day pass up to Harrogate to visit Ira. He's doing fine and we had good visits in the Officer's Club there. I also spent some time in Scarborough with Norma. It's primarily a summer resort town and simply beautiful. The weather was pretty good and we were able to walk along the beach. We even found an open ice cream parlor.

I got back on Tuesday to find that we were assigned to a rest home the next day. Rough war! So, we took off yesterday, spent last night in London, and came here this morning. We traveled on orders, transportation and expenses all paid by Uncle Sam. This is an old estate in southern England, leased to the U.S. Air Force. There are about 40 flak-happy officers here, including those from our crew. We are to have four terrific meals a day, including orange juice served in bed by the butler. We are wearing civilian clothes — simple pants, shirts, and sweaters. The only army touch is dressing in uniform for dinner. Everyone is called by his first name, regardless of rank.

This afternoon, the sun was shining, so we had a touch football game out on the lawn. It was really great sport, and just what the doctor ordered. In the next few days, we're going horseback riding. The countryside is beginning to show spring blooms, so being outdoors on horseback should be a real treat.

Our quarters are very plush and comfortable and the lounge is terrific, in true English country style. I am very happy about the whole thing. We are here for seven days, plus one travel day back to the base. This is a much needed rest. We should be in good shape to finish our tour of duty.

March 2, 1945

It's the second day of our week of kingly leisure at the rest home. It is really great. We played ball last evening until dinner time, with a break for tea at 4:30, then dinner at 7:30. The food is simply terrific, mostly fresh things, the best by far that I have had overseas. After dinner they had a horse-racing game — a clever affair, moving wooden horses by rolling dice. I won ten bucks. The rest of the evening we sat around a big fire and read, just perfect.

This morning, we got up to breakfast at ten, then played football in a sunshiny day. In the afternoon, I had loads of fun as first baseman in a softball game. I am hoarse from yelling and, I must confess, a wee bit stiff. But, it's gratifying to know I can still enjoy playing ball, even doing a decent job of it. We just had tea (complete with crumpets and jam, you know) and soon it will be time to clean up for dinner.

I also shot a bit of skeet this morning, not like in gunnery school, but rather like an English gentleman. There is an archery court here, too. I will have a go at that one day. Tomorrow, we will have the promised horseback riding. At another time, we can take bicycles for a ride through the countryside. There's lots to do, the beds are great, and I could not ask for anything more. The weather is even on our side.

This evening we can go into town for a movie or just luxuriate here. You should see me in baggy civilian clothes. I feel out of place, somehow, but I am trying to relax and make like a civilian again.

March 4, 1945

This place is truly a paradise. Yesterday, we all went horseback riding, and again today. It's been a long time since I have been on a horse, but I remembered well enough to go tearing through the woodland trails. It was just fine, except for one small incident when the horse stopped and I didn't. Even so, there is no apparent damage to other than my ego. I have played football, baseball, and badminton with gusto until every joint hurts, but it is pure fun. There's a sun lamp available and, along with the real sun, we are all taking on a ruddy look.

March 6, 1945

This morning I went horseback riding again, this time by myself. I found a winding trail way back in the woods and just lost myself in the peace and quiet. This afternoon was another of the tremendous baseball games and tonight there are movies in the lounge. Last night they brought in a group of WRENs (Women of the Royal Navy). We had a super dance in the ballroom.

This has been the most wonderful, healing time imaginable. For a few days, the world has seemed almost normal. Tomorrow, we leave for London, stay there overnight, and then the next day it's back to the base and the war. I feel just great and I am all set to have the last few goes at Jerry.

March 8, 1945

I returned from our leave this evening and found a whole bunch of letters from you, all of which were enjoyed immensely. While we were away, the Luftwaffe attacked our base, but did little damage. My bigger worry is that the orderly forgot to take my clothes to the laundry. You can see the extent of my problems.

I am starting to dream of home and such things as steaks, real milk, hamburgers, and white bread. Last night, I dreamed I was driving down the outer drive in your car, Dad. After driving on the left side of the street over here, I will need to be checked out, though. I don't think it will be more than four or five weeks before I finish the last missions, then I will be heading your way. The latest story I get is that, once I'm finished flying combat and having my leave at home, I will go to a rehabilitation center for a few weeks, then to Midland, Texas, as an instructor. Maybe I can get a car and drive to the various places. I will need to do something to keep from getting bored stiff after the experiences here.

In London, on the way back to the base, I went out with a WAC who was the runner up in the contest for the prettiest WAC in the ETO. We went to the movie and saw Judy Garland in *Meet Me in St. Louis*. Both Judy and the WAC were terrific. The Chinese food after the show was pretty neat, too.

I need to keep thinking about and planning for coming home, even though I know this tour is not over yet. The radio just announced that the 1st Army has crossed the Rhine river. Maybe that's the beginning of the end.

March 9, 1945

This morning we went up on a short flight to test out a new type of smoke bomb. It only took about 45 minutes. The rest of the day we spent cleaning up our barracks and chopping wood for the fire. The weather is very nice, almost springlike. The news is good, too. We're all waiting for word that Jerry has finally had enough.

We may not get finished with our missions as soon as we anticipated, as they are holding us to lead deep penetration missions. That means maybe a month or more before we can head home. They are also talking about keeping Mac, Bill, and me here to instruct. They would like me to take over the squadron gunnery officer job. I really want to come home, but this could keep me from getting shipped out to the Pacific. They would keep me with the Group for six months, then promote me to captain and send me home. We'll see how it all works out.

March 11, 1945

This morning we went on a practice mission and, since Deke had been on night duty, I did the co-piloting. I'm getting pretty good at piloting, and I get a boot from handling the ship. You'd be surprised at how well I fly our B-24. One of these times, I will take a try at landing. I have already taken off.

We have a brand new ship. It's a beauty with all kinds of new equipment, all secret of course. It may be a week before we go on another mission. We are strictly a combat wing lead on these last missions. It's one helluva responsibility, but we are up to it.

Deke and I are pretty good pals now. We just didn't understand each other. We have an incredible crew and we just could not be more closely knit. It will be really rough to leave this gang. I'm learning to make deep friendships and I have loads of them here. I don't imagine there will ever be a period comparable to this in my life again.

March 12, 1945

I write personal letters to Dad and Pooz now and then, but it seems I just take you for granted, Mom. But, that's just not so. You know that I love you very much, Mom, and whatever I am or become, it's due to you. I think about you constantly, your picture is always with me, and whenever a family conversation starts, I always want to talk about my Mom. I read your letters over and over and I treasure them more than you know. Yep, Mom, you sure are the very best!

I don't really care about the rank or medals and such as a personal thing — it's more a desire to do things right so you can be proud of me. I only hope I come out of this OK, because there's so much I owe to you and Dad. When you write how swell I am, I don't think I live up to your perceptions, but it's a goal to work for.

I have always tried to do things that I'd never be ashamed to tell you about. I have only deviated a few times, but even that wasn't too sordid, and I could still tell you, though I might be a bit embarrassed. You're one in a million, Mom, and if I ever come close to finding a woman like you, I'd really be lucky. Dad has the best compensation he needs in this world just having you.

So, Mom, this is just to you. I love you so very much and it will be the happiest day of my life when I get off the boat and kiss you. No matter whatever happens, you're number one on my hit parade.

March 12, 1945

We have been told that we will be flying our final missions within the next two weeks. Evidently they have specific plans that include our kind of know-how. I imagine such assignments could be fairly rough, but we are veteran professionals by this time and can handle whatever comes.

Even after all this experience, we must still continue to practice. We were up today working on leading the assembly and dropping a few bombs. It's the fifth day in a row of this routine, so you can see how serious everyone still is about perfection. Art was dropping most of the bombs, but I got on the sight for a few. We bet two and six pence (half a dollar) on the last two bombs. I dropped mine 200 feet short and he dropped one 150 feet short. So, I stand for a drink tonight. It's just that I haven't had a lot of bombardier practice lately (I know, no excuse, sir).

On takeoff, I flew co-pilot with Deke in the left seat, while Mac stood and watched. It's the first time I have flown our ship without Mac there, ready to grab the controls. I'm getting up in the world.

March 14, 1945

A practice mission again. The weather is turning nice and I flew in just a summer flying suit and a leather jacket. At 10,000 feet, it was only minus one degree. I flew as co-pilot. Mac is going to get me a recommendation to go to pilot's school. It's a ten-month course and I can go through in grade, without the junk that goes with being a cadet. It's something to consider, but will depend on what the colonel says.

I got three packages from you, all with good eats. I am saving them for our celebration party, when we finish our tour. Perhaps you should not send me any more packages, as I will probably be on my way to a processing center by the time they get here.

March 15, 1945

We led a big raid today. They say it was one of the most important and successful the 8th ever pulled. The command pilot who rode with us told the colonel I did a bang-up job (there's that interesting expression again). The target was in a very big place — we bombed visually and really plastered it.

Well, I might as well tell you that I have only one more to go. By the time you receive this, we may already be finished. We're going on pass tomorrow, and when we return we'll probably finish up. I think I will go to Harrogate and visit Norma. That's guaranteed fun. You can imagine how anxious I am to see all of you.

Journal Entry

March 15, 1945 – They really saved some of the big stuff for the end of our tour. Target was the German General Staff Head-quarters near Wünsdorf, intended to disrupt the command net-work of the retreating enemy forces that are being caught between our ground forces and the Russians. It would be impos-sible for anyone who could have seen us to believe that we could

fly through the walls of flak and still survive. One of the planes
was crippled and had to ditch in the Channel. The chance of
surviving in those frigid waters is almost nil. I am just hoping
and praying that we can make it through just one more.

March 17, 1945

It's true — I am on pass again! Terribly rugged life, we airmen
lead. Actually, with only one mission to go, we would rather have
stayed at the base and finished up, but it's good policy in the
army never to refuse leave when it is offered. One never knows
what the future holds.

So, I am in London. I was going to visit Norma, but the train
ride is awful long, so I came here with my crew. I wasn't anxious
to stick my neck out with the V-2 bombs, but we're still wearing
the lucky charm and, what the hell, we have fun here. We're
staying at the Red Cross Duchess Club, a great place with nice
clean beds, a congenial atmosphere, and, for 70 cents a day, we
can't go too far wrong.

Last night Bill, Deke, and I went to a movie, then had a salad
bowl at Lyon's Corner House. We can talk about any kind of
trivia and just enjoy being together. We're so close that we can all
give in to a whim of one. I have been wrong about a person
before, but never so much as in Deke's case. I'm glad I changed
my earlier judgment about him. Perhaps it was resentment
because he replaced Jim from our original crew.

Tonight, I leave the guys for my peachy little WAC from
Detroit. We'll take in a play and then some dancing at a place the
Red Cross recommended. You see, things are rough in the ETO.

March 19, 1945

I sure had fun in London, but I swear I'm not going back
there again. The V-2 bombs are just too much. I don't like the

idea that you can be standing in some nice place and suddenly a tremendous explosion wipes out everything around you. I understand that part of my life is braving flak on a mission, but asking for it voluntarily is a little dumb.

However, I had a terrific time with Wanda. We went to a play and dinner one night, then the second night, we went roller skating in a rink. You read that right — we made like twelve year olds. It was great fun, except I am still picking splinters out of my fanny. I had one other neat experience in London. I stopped in a pub for a beer and sat down next to a guy who is a captain, the group bombardier for the 452nd Bombardment Group. Before he was transferred there, he was lead bombardier in the 94th, the B-17 outfit that was one of the first to see action in Europe. He was the lead bombardier on that horrible raid to Schweinfurt. He is a real hero. His name is Cliff Bickler and he lives very near us in Chicago. In an hour of conversation, we really hit it off. Long ago, he was finished with his missions, but is just now scheduled to go home. We have arranged to find each other at the replacement depot. He has enough rank that he can probably arrange for us to be together on the way home. He's the kind of guy I would like for a friend.

Well, Mac is definitely staying with the Group as training officer after we are finished, and Harland will probably work with the navigators. As for me, I'm coming home as fast as I can make it.

March 20, 1945

It's a beautiful spring day here in England, and I am stuck at a desk as the duty officer. I answer the phone and say, "Yes, sir," or, "No, sir," and other exciting things like that.

It looks like I will get my recommendation to pilot's school The colonel is pleased with my performance, so when Mac asked him about it, he said he'd do what he could. The recommendation itself must come from Maj. Gen. Johnson, CO of the 2nd Air Division. If the colonel goes to bat for me, I will get it. Wouldn't that be something?

I came on as duty officer at 8 A.M and must stay until 8 A.M tomorrow, unless they schedule us for a mission, in which case I will get to sleep. I hope we get assigned quickly, as I am really sweating out this last one. It may be rough getting home. The replacement depots are pretty jammed. I think I will finish first, then worry about that.

March 21, 1945

They are really making us sweat. We have been riding the battle order for four days, and something always comes up to remove us. The Group has been flying like mad, but they won't let us go just any old place, so I'm afraid we will get a toughie for our last one. Good lead crews for a tough job are at a premium, and we're it.

The Luftwaffe has taken to coming over East Anglia at night, with a small force, bombing and strafing our airfields. So, the next day we send 1,000 bombers to wipe out a bunch of their airdromes, by way of retaliation. The Hun is now turning out to be a joke. As for me, I'm the air-raid shelter kid. I'm not too proud to hit it fast. The last time was after a rain, and I went knee deep in water. Some of the other guys go out to watch the show, but I'm not interested. I ask questions about what happened after it's over.

The CO talked to me last night and said he doesn't like to hand out recommendations willy-nilly, but he believes I can do a good job, so he is going to get me one for pilot's school.

What an ordeal the duty officer assignment was. I'd no sooner fall asleep than the phone would ring. I slept about 45 minutes all night, but I haven't had that job in months, so I can't really complain.

When I'm done with the missions, I will take a seven day leave and tour around to see some of the high spots in England that I have missed. Then I can come home and leave it all behind. When I set foot on the good old U.S.A., am I ever going to be thankful.

Journal Entry

March 21, 1945 – This was an incredible day! We were at dinner when in walked Jim, full of smiles. It seems he crash landed his ship on the beach in Holland. Some Dutch people pulled the entire crew out of the wreckage and took them into hiding before the Germans arrived. A few weeks later, when the Allied advances made it possible, the Dutch got him headed in the direction of American lines and he did the rest — he just walked out. Air command arranged to fly him back to the base, and here we are, together again. We're just overwhelmed with happiness!

March 22, 1945

Another lead crew was assigned today's mission. It was their last one, too. They got all the way home, and then cracked up on landing. You can imagine what that has done to our already wild jitters. I guess it's not over until both feet are on terra firma and the engines are shut down.

Damn! Here comes the Luftwaffe again ... to the shelter.

Journal Entry

March 23, 1945 – My father has the most incredible sense of humor imaginable. Today, I received a photograph he sent of my room at home, all ready for my arrival. It shows one wall that is papered, floor to ceiling, end to end, with letters, telegrams, and cables I have sent asking for money. You gotta be a really funny person to think of something like that. And, how lucky can a guy be to have a father who would answer all those requests?

I know that a few of the guys got money from home on occasion, but nothing like I did. Having ample money, to do as I please on pass, has made the time here more bearable. Like everyone, I've been behaving like there was no tomorrow, because for many there is none. Now it's time for me to settle down and be more responsible.

March 23, 1945

And still we sweat. We got bumped off the mission today, because it was a short affair. Competent wing lead crews get held out for the big ones. The days seem endless, and the nights are filled with dreams of shooting down fighters and dodging flak. This period of waiting for the last one has seemed like the longest of my life.

I know that you are the ones who really sweat out the war. I know where I am all the time, but you must continue to wonder. There's nothing I can do about any of it. We are having religious services tonight and I intend to be in the first row doing some fancy praying.

I have tried to think about the future, but I can't. All I can think about is one more, then coming home for 21 days.

March 26, 1945

This is the letter I have been hoping to write for ten long months. I hope you received the cable, so you know we're finished flying combat missions — now all of us can stop worrying. I slept the first sound sleep in a long time last night, though the raid had one last horror. During our assembly, two bombers collided in mid-air killing everyone aboard. My last mission left me with the memory of those two huge planes tumbling out of the sky.

The night before the mission we had a party going on the base. We were on battle alert, but the S-2 officer told me it would not be our type of mission, so I danced with a girl I'd met once before. We had a gay old time. I put her on the bus at 12:30, came back to the barracks at 1 A.M., and climbed into bed. Just as I started to doze off the orderly came in and said, "It's 0115 and briefing is at 0230." So, I got up and got ready — with no sleep at all. I sure didn't fall asleep on the mission though, as there were German jet fighters playing tag with us along the way.

When we landed and shut the engines down, I got out of the plane and kissed the runway. The public relations officer took a picture of me in the act and says he is going to send it to the *Chicago Sun* for publication.

We got back in the early afternoon, had our final debriefing, and I went to sleep until the evening. After chow, we went to the club where the officer in charge treated us to as much scotch as we wanted, and we wanted a lot. This morning, the guys said I was the happiest person they ever saw. I got even with the orderly, awakening him in the middle of the night, then proceeded to wake everyone else up, avoiding those who were scheduled to fly.

This morning, I turned in all of my flying equipment and checked to see that my transfer orders went in. The other guys are planning to stick around the field until after the first of April to do four hours of flying and get their flight pay for April. I'll be damned if I will, though — not for a hundred bucks. I'm not setting foot in an aircraft until after my leave at home. The Liberator is a mighty fine ship, but every time you go up, you take your life in your hands. It was built to carry a bomb load, not for the safety of the crew. I am a ground pounder now, and I like it fine. The other crews threatened to kick us out of the Officer's Mess and make us go over and eat with the paddlefeet. But, I'm happy; I don't care if they make me eat out of my flying helmet.

We have been told that the last two missions we led have been among the finest jobs the Group has ever done. We are up for several decorations, including a special commendation from the commanding general.

The few hours that I have allowed myself to look at my future have made it clear to me: I don't really want to go to pilot's school, stay here as gunnery officer, or do anything else except try to pick up my life where I left off. I want to go back to the university and finish my education. I hope I will be able to leave all this killing behind and just be a college student again.

There will be ample time for us to talk about all these things. For now, there remains just one more line, the one I have been longing to write for all these long months:

I'M COMING HOME!

Closing the Box

When the Army wanted us in England to begin flying combat missions, they managed to get us there in four days, flying our B-24. When we wanted to get home, they put us on troop ships. I was assigned to one that was part of a convoy with other such ships and a covey of destroyer escorts, that took 30 days to reach the U.S. — the war was still on and the German submarines still active.

My new friend, Captain Cliff Bickler, was on the ship and we arranged to bunk together in the officer's quarters. The first night out, I watched as he drank from a Listerine® bottle and I asked him if he often purified his intestinal tract with mouth wash. Regulations specified no alcoholic beverages allowed on board ship, so Cliff — clever, adaptive man — had emptied the Listerine and replaced it with scotch whisky. When he opened his duffel bag, it contained dozens of Listerine bottles similarly filled. Cliff was also a generous fellow, so we passed the time on the trip home in a pleasant amber haze.

After a leave at home, I spent several weeks in a rehabilitation hospital in Santa Ana, California, where I was confined and tested during the day, then turned loose on Hollywood at night. Next came seemingly endless months as a bombardier instructor in Midland, Texas. Finally the end of the war brought the arrival of my long awaited discharge from active duty.

Two months after arriving home, I received a telephone call from the War Department asking if I would be available the following day. The next afternoon an Air Force staff car, carrying a major and an aid, pulled up in front of my home. In a brief ceremony, with my mother witnessing, I was presented with the Distinguished Flying Cross. The citation read:

> For extraordinary achievement while serving
> as lead Bombardier/Navigator on many heavy
> bombardment missions to Germany and enemy
> occupied territory. 1st Lieutenant Byron D.
> Lane has displayed superior ability in over-
> coming adverse weather conditions to lead
> his formations to successfully bomb targets
> requiring deep penetrations. The skill and
> devotion to duty exhibited by this Officer
> on these many occasions reflect the highest
> credit upon himself and the Armed Forces of
> the United States.

That evening I showed the medal and citation to my father. The next morning I put them into the box marked "Byron's War."

Glossary

AA: Anti-aircraft guns, usually 88-millimeter (see 88s). A small caliber AA was anything from light artillery to machine guns and only effective against low flying aircraft.

Aachen: City in Germany, close to the Belgian border.

Adolph: Adolph Hitler, the German Chancellor from January 30 to March 23, 1933, then Dictator until his suicide on May 1, 1945, six days prior to Germany's unconditional surrender. His determination to reclaim all territories regarded as German resulted in the World War II.

Aeronca plane: A small single-engine private plane sometimes used during the war for early pilot training.

AFCE: Automatic flight control equipment.

ailerons: A movable portion of an aircraft wing that controls the lateral motion of the plane.

Air Corps: In the 1940s, the Air Force was a part of the Army and designated as the Army Air Corps. In 1947, the air forces of the United States Army became the United States Air Force (USAF), a separate arm of the defense establishment.

Air Medal: An Air Force decoration, usually given to aircrew members at the completion of five missions, but also awarded for other notable achievements.

ammunition dump: A place where ammunition and bombs are stored.

anoxia: A condition in which there is not enough oxygen or tissue oxidation.

APO: Army Post Office. An APO number is used to direct mail to servicemen without disclosing their location.

Ardennes salient: The battle line in the Ardennes forest in Belgium where the heaviest fighting occurred during the Battle of the Bulge. See also Battle of the Bulge and salient.

armorer: The aircraft ground crew responsible for maintaining the onboard artillery.

astro-compass: The navigation instrument used for obtaining location and direction through sighting the stars.

AT-6, AT-11, etc.: Designations for U.S. Army training planes.

Axis: The enemy nations — Germany, Japan, and Italy.

Battle of the Bulge: The German counteroffensive in Belgium, launched on December 16, 1944. See also Ardennes salient.

Berlin: Capital and largest city in Germany.

bivouac: Camping in the open.

blackouts: Cities and military bases covered their lights at night (were blacked out) to keep enemy bombers from targeting them.

block-busters: Large bombs, usually 2,000 pounders.

blouse: An officer's dress jacket.

Bluie West 1: The name of an air field on the south-western tip of Greenland. It was one of several "Bluie" air fields in the area.

(a) boot: [Slang] A thrill; fun; enjoyable.

bomb bay: Where the bombs were suspended inside the middle of the aircraft.

bomb bay door: Double doors in the belly of the aircraft that were opened to release the bombs.

B-17: The Flying Fortress was a famous World War II bomber. As modifications were made, a letter suffix was added. Later editions were designated B-17F and B-17G.

B-24: Four engine bomber known as the Liberator. Later editions with modifications were designated B-24J and B-24H.

B-25: Twin engine bomber known as the Mitchell.

B-26: Twin engine bomber known as the Maurader.

buzz bombs: The pilotless, German engine-driven bomb with wings, that was remote-controlled. It was used to bomb targets in England, primarily London.

Calais: This city on the northern French coast is less than 30 miles, southwest across the Sea of Dover, from Dover, England.

C'est nécessaire, n'est çe pas?: That's necessary, isn't it?

check point: A position on an aerial map that was used by navigators of a bomber formation to verify their location.

chick: [Slang] A young woman.

chicken shit: [Slang] Used by soldiers for any army order that was disliked.

chow: [Slang] Military expression for a meal and mealtime.

circular error (CE): It was the measure of the distance from the bomb burst to the actual target. Thus an average CE of 800 feet meant that the bombers hit within 800 feet of the target center.

Class A uniform: A soldier's dress uniform.

CO: Commanding officer.

coke burning stove: Pot bellied stoves that burned carbonized coal, commonly issued by the army to warm the huts where the men slept.

Cologne (Köln): A city on the Rhine in Germany near the Belgian border.

combat wing: The basic Air Force combat unit was the group, but for more detailed planning and direction of operations the combat wing controlled several groups.

combat wing lead: The bomb group that was leading the entire formation on a particular day.

Conn, Billy: A boxer who was Light Heavyweight Champion from 1939 to 1941.

Consolidated turret: Bomber gun turret manufactured by Consolidated Aircraft in Fort Worth, Texas, or Tucson, Arizona.

control point: A navigational term for map coordinates that must be reached in order to confirm that a bomber formation is on the correct course.

CQ: A non-commissioned officer in charge of soldier's quarters — in this case, a sergeant.

crumpets: A small round cake made of unsweetened batter, cooked on a griddle, much favored by the English toasted and usually served with orange marmalade.

C-2 computer: A calculator used to determine true altitude, for entry into the Norden bombsight.

Dagwood sandwich: From the comic strip, *Dagwood and Blondie.* In early cartoons, Dagwood would pile on everything in the refrigerator to make huge sandwiches.

D-Day: The June 6, 1944 beginning of the invasion of the European continent by Allied forces from bases in England.

D-8: This bombsight was a simple mechanical device.

Dempsey, Jack: A boxer who was Heavyweight Champion from 1919 to 1926.

deputy lead: Identifies an aircraft and the aircrew that fly off the right wing of the squadron lead plane.

Deutschland über alles: Germany over all others.

Dieppe: A French coastal town southeast of Brighton, England, across the English Channel.

dilly: Something delightful, extraordinary, different, or fearful. "That last mission was a real dilly!"

Distinguished Flying Cross (DFC): An Air Force decoration awarded for unusual heroism.

division: The Eighth Air Force had three bomber divisions. The descending order of command was bomber division, bomber wing, bombardment group, then squadron.

division bombardier: The top ranking bombardier in a division.

dollar slot element: Bomber formation were made up of a number of groups of three planes. The lead plane had one plane flying at the same level, just off and slightly behind its left wing and another in the same position off its right wing. Together they were known as an element. Just behind the lead element, at a slightly lower altitude, was another element, known as the dollar slot element. Two more such elements made up a squadron.

dorsal turret: The gun turret in the belly (bottom) of a bomber.

drift solution: A navigation computation that accounts for the effect of wind on the aircraft's progress over the ground.

DTs: Delirium tremens. They are hallucinations and tremors usually produced by excessive alcohol consumption. In this case, it is an acronym that means "the shakes."

dutch (in, out of): [Slang] In, or out of, trouble.

Dutch coast: The North Sea coast of the Netherlands directly east of the American air bases in East Anglia. It was on the flight path to Northern Germany.

East Anglia: The northeast portion of England that borders on The Wash. See also The Wash.

88s: German 88-millimeter artillery weapons that were used against allied aircraft with deadly accuracy.

Elgin chronometer: An instrument for keeping very accurate time. Chronometers manufactured by Elgin Watch Company were used by aircrew members.

Emerson nose turret: A later version of the gun turret in the nose of a B-24, manufactured by Emerson.

English Channel: The body of water between England and France and the Straights of Dover and the Atlantic Ocean.

E-6B computer: A calculator used to determine ground speed, wind force and other figures for setting the parameters of the Norden bombsight. Essentially an enhanced slide rule.

ETO. European Theater of Operations. In this case, the war in Europe.

feather the prop: When an engine was shot out and stopped operating, the propeller would windmill, and could cause the aircraft to go out of control. An instrument allowed the pilot to turn the propeller blades so they would knife into the wind and would not rotate.

fighter support: Most of the fighter aircraft in the Eighth Air Force were assigned to defending the bombers.

flak: Anti-aircraft fire. Usually refers to the explosive bursts of the shells and their fragments.

flak batteries: Concentrations of anti-aircraft guns.

flak happy: [Slang] An Air Force expression for the manifestation of combat fatigue.

flight officer: An Air Force rank equivalent to warrant officer junior grade in the army. While a non-commissioned rank, in practice flight officers received the same pay and privileges as second lieutenants.

fragmentation bombs: When detonated these bombs sprayed small bits of metal in all directions. They were usually used as anti-personnel weapons.

Free French Emblem: The Cross of Lorraine.

Freidrichshafen: Heavily defended German city where fighter aircraft were manufactured — a priority target of the Eighth Air Force.

FW-190: The German Focke-Wulf fighter plane.

gauntlet: Heavy fleece-lined mitten with the index (trigger) finger separate from the mitt.

GI: Government issue. Could be anything from a cot to underwear to a tank. Even soldiers were referred to as "GIs."

Gibson girl: A radio that could float and send out an SOS from a downed aircraft. It took its name from the bulbous top and bottom and pinched-middle shape made fashionable in the 1890s, and beyond, by illustrator Charles Dana Gibson.

gigs: Demerits that were given to aviation cadets for rule infractions, such as failing to salute properly and missing a formation. An accumulation of demerits had to be worked off by marching for one hour with a full pack and a rifle (a tour).

Gordo: A popular syndicated cartoon, run by the *Chicago Sun* newspaper, featuring a rotund Mexican and a dog named Pepito.

GQ: General quarters.

(the) Group: The 392nd Bombardment Group of the 2nd Division of the air command in England. See also Liberator Group.

Hamm: A town in central Germany.

Hannover: A city in northern Germany.

Harrogate: A town in northern England.

Heinie: [Slang inherited from WWI] A German.

high squadron: In a bomber formation, one squadron flew at a slightly higher altitude than the others to maximize protection against fighters.

(a) honey: [Slang] A 1940s expression used by men, often with reference to a girl. "Boy, is she a honey." It could also be applied to such things as cars, planes, even baseball mitts.

hop: A short flight.

hopped up: [Slang] Feeling really good.

HRX equipment: A radar bombsight for bombing through cloud cover.

Hun: [Slang] A German — another expression left over from World War I.

IP: Initial point. The place (or point on a map) where bombing runs were to begin.

issei: A Japanese who emigrated to the United States after the Oriental Exclusion Proclamation of 1907 and was thus ineligible by law to become an American citizen — to be distinguished from *nisei, kibei.*

java: [Slang] Same as today, coffee.

Jerry: [Slang] A German soldier.

jet fighter: In June 1944, the first rocket-engines were used by the Germans in delta-wing fighters — 350 were built by war's end.

j.g.: Junior grade. See flight officer.

Kassel: City in Germany.

knockout: An exceptionally pretty woman.

KP: Kitchen Police. A potato peeler, dishwasher, garbage remover, etc. — the assignment least desired by most soldiers.

lead bombardier: The bombardier in the aircraft leading any formation. He is responsible for using the bombsight and for dropping the bombs of the entire formation on the target.

lead plane: The aircraft, manned by a lead crew, that guides a formation (squadron, group, wing, or division) on a mission.

Leeds: A manufacturing town in Yorkshire County in north-central England.

let-down: A bomber coming down from a high altitude to the landing approach.

Liberator Group: The main combat formation consisting of four squadrons of eight to ten B-24 bombers, a total of 32 to 40 aircraft.

Liberators: B-24 bombers.

Limey: [Slang] Originally, an English soldier or sailor, but when used by Americans, it usually meant any Englishman.

London: Capital of the United Kingdom and largest city in England with a current population of 6.7 million.

Luftwaffe: The German air force.

lulu: [Slang] A 40s expression for something terrific, very unusual, or harrowing. "That mission assignment was a lulu!" (See also "dilly.")

mackinaw: A short, double-breasted coat made of heavy woolen cloth, often plaid. They were nice and warm.

(has a) mad on: [Slang] State of being angry.

Mae West: A life vest for water evacuation. It hung over the neck and was inflated when needed for flotation. When inflated, it puffed out in the chest area, which was reminiscent of the figure of Mae West, a sultry siren of the era.

Mais, c'est la guerre: But, that's war.

Marauders: B-26s.

marshaling yards: A transfer area where many rail lines came together, usually at the edge of a major city. Bombing them could create havoc with a rail system.

Medal of Honor: Congressional Medal of Honor, the nations highest award.

ME-109: The Messerschmitt, a German fighter plane.

mess hall: Soldier's cafeteria where meals are served.

mickey bombing: [Slang] Radar bombing.

Miller, Glenn: The legendary big-band leader who was one of the most popular musicians of the time. He was in the Army Air Corps and was killed during the war.

Mitchells: B-25 medium-size bombers.

MP: Military police.

Mussolini, Benito: Italian dictator who aligned his country with Hitler against the Allies.

nifty: [Slang] Anything perceived as really great — usually preceded by *boy*. "Boy, is that a nifty car."

nisei: A native American citizen born of immigrant Japanese parents and educated in the United States — to be distinguished from *issei* and *kibei*.

Nissen hut: A pre-fabricated warehouse type building which varied in size and was used for many things — in this context, housing for Air Force personnel.

Norden bombsight: See the beginning of Chapter 12 for a complete description.

Nordhausen: A city in central Germany.

Northeim: A town in central Germany.

Norwich: A town in central England.

Oak Leaf Cluster: When a medal was awarded for a second time, it took the form of a tiny metal oak leaf that was affixed to the ribbon (worn on the shirt or a blouse) to signify the additional decoration.

OD: Olive drab — the color of the clothing and just about everything else in the military.

open post: When passes were issued to leave the base to go into town.

Ostende: A city on the coast of Belgium due east, across the Sea of Dover, from Canterbury, England.

Pacy-Sur-Armancon: A small town in southern France.

paddlefeet: [Slang] Non-flying officers.

pathfinder bombing: See radar or mickey bombing.

peach of a ...: [Slang] A 40s expression describing someone or something very nice. "He's a peach of a guy." As an adjective it would become "peachy." "You have on a peachy shirt." "She is a peachy looker."

pilotage method: A navigational method for determining position and direction using sectional aerial maps of the terrain and referencing visible ground features.

pilotage navigator: Under visual conditions, the pilotage navigator directs the path of the bomber formation by reference to its position over the terrain.

Ploesti oil fields: A site in Romania of an early raid by B-24 bombers. The raid cut oil production, but resulted in heavy losses of bombers and crews.

post-hole: Massive bombing, usually with smaller 100 pounds bombs, which left many holes in the terrain, making it more difficult to traverse.

P-38, P-47, P-51: Designations for different types of U.S. Air Force fighter planes. The p stood for pursuit. The modern designations for fighter planes begin with an f (F-16).

Purple Heart: Decoration awarded to anyone who is wounded in battle.

PX: Post Exchange. The army had retail stores on many bases, where military personnel could purchase goods at very favorable prices. They exist on military bases today in expanded form.

radar bombing: Radar equipment that allowed a bombardier to "see through" the clouds.

RAF: Royal Air Force, the name of the British air force. The RAF flew, among others, the famous Spitfire fighters and Lancaster bombers.

(the) real McCoy: [Slang] A 40s expression for something absolutely authentic. Still used today.

Reich: Germany.

Rhine River: Major river that flows through western Germany.

ROTC: Reserve Officer Training Corps. ROTC programs have been conducted in universities since the National Defense Act of 1916 was passed. It was introduced later into high schools.

salient (Ardennes): The part of a battle line, trench, fort, etc. which projects farthest toward the enemy.

Scarborough: A coastal town in northeastern England.

shack: [Slang] In bombardier school, a direct hit on the bomb target.

shavetail: [Slang] A second lieutenant.

shrouds: Parachute lines attaching the canopy to the harness.

Silver Star: An armed forces decoration for unusual valor. It ranks above the Distinguished Flying Cross.

64 physical: The most intensive Air Force physical examination in World War II.

SNAFU: Acronym for "Situation normal, all fouled up." There were lots of SNAFUs in the army.

Sperry sight: The Sperry Corporation manufactured both a bombsight and a gunsight. While the latter was used extensively, the bombsight was superseded by the Norden.

Sperry turrets: The Sperry Corporation also made turrets. See turret.

squadron: The basic unit in the Air Force, consisting of eight to ten aircraft and the attached personnel. Four squadrons made up a bombardment group.

squadron bombardier: The highest ranking bombardier in a squadron.

squadron gunnery officer: The highest ranking officer in charge of all gunnery operations.

standing down (stood down): When a crew, squadron, or group was not scheduled to fly a mission.

stick time: [Slang] The time, which was clocked, a pilot or trainee actually flew an aircraft.

S-2: A designation for the intelligence division and its officers.

swabbie: [Slang] A sailor. The term comes from the swab — a mop of the type used for cleaning the decks of ships.

swell: [Slang] A 40s expression meaning very good or great — usually preceded by *boy*. "Boy, was that a swell meal."

taps: In the army, taps was a bugle call that called for lights to be put out. Taps is also played at a soldier's or sailor's funeral.

The Wash: A bay on the northeast coast of East Anglia, north of the air fields.

toggle: To release the bombs (*v.*). The lever (switch) connected to the bomb harnesses that was moved to release them (*n.*).

toggle boy: Only the lead bombardier used a bombsight. The other bombardiers moved a toggle switch to drop the bombs from their planes when the lead bombardier released his. *Toggle boy* was a term of derision most often applied to bombardiers who had not made lead status.

toggling: To release the bombs simultaneously with the lead bombardier.

tool down: [Slang] To drive slowly on a main street in order to be seen — to cruise.

tour: A punishment for cadets. It usually meant marching with a full pack and a rifle for an hour or more — depending on the accumulation and severity of demerits earned from infractions of the rules.

Tricolor: The French flag.

turret: The mechanical housing for machine guns on a bomber. It was a transparent hemisphere of plexiglass with steel ribs. The gunner sat inside the turret and could move it by hydraulic or electrical means to bring the guns to bear on a target. A B-24 had turrets in the nose, top, belly, and tail.

USO: United Service Organization. A huge national volunteer organization that supplied entertainment and services of various kinds to the troops everywhere.

Varga Calendar: Alberto Vargas was an illustrator who drew young women in sexy poses. The Varga girl had an elongated torso and legs. The pictures of Varga girl appearing in magazines and calendars were often removed to adorn walls and lockers.

Vickers ring: A metal ring surrounding an open gunner's cockpit. A .30-caliber machine gun was mounted on the ring and could be moved around a 360 degree circle.

Victrola: The record player of the times, manufactured by RCA. Originally hand wound, later electric, it played 78 RPM records.

V-mail: A form for writing a letter to go overseas that was then photographed for transport. See the introductory pages to Chapter 10 for more detail.

Vous désirez parfum?: Do you want perfume?

V-2 rocket bomb: A remote controlled rocket bomb that was used by the Germans on English targets, primarily London. It was a very advanced concept at the time and superseded the buzz bomb. See also buzz bombs.

WAAC: Women's Army Auxiliary Corps. It was changed to Women's Army Corps when it was officially made a part of the armed forces.

WAC: Women's Army Corps. This arm of the military was legislated May 14, 1942 and officially established July 1, 1943.

waist position: The middle gun positions on each side of the bomber, just back of the bomb bay. These guns were hand held and fired from open windows, not from turrets.

Waller trainer: A complex gunnery school trainer that simulated aerial combat.

weird: Expression for someone or something unusual. "He is some weird guy." "That movie was really weird."

Wendling Station: The small town between Norwich and King's Lynn in Suffolk, England, where the 392nd Bombardment Group was located.

wild blue yonder: Air Force lingo for sky.

wing crew: Crews of the planes that flew to the right and left of the lead plane in a bomber formation.

Wünsdorf: A small eastern German village south of Berlin.

Yom Kippur: The day of atonement, the holiest of the Jewish holidays.

Acknowledgments

My sister, Joan Silvern, in addition to her loving support, gave me her professional expertise as an editor, making many suggestions that enhanced my work immeasurably. Thanks, Pooz!

Ida Fisher-Lane, my wife and best friend, worked right along with me, gave many helpful inputs, and kept me going with her own special brand of emotional nourishment.

Many thanks to C.C. Dickinson who is surely the world's best designer/editor. She knew just how to get me to do things the right way rather than my way.

My friend Dan Chasman, a writer whose work I greatly admire, is the only one who read the manuscript and had the courage to tell me to my face that I had a dangling participle.

Special thanks to John B. Edwards, Archivist of The Mighty Eighth Air Force Heritage Museum in Savannah, Georgia who supplied aircraft photos, maps, helpful suggestions, and information available nowhere else.

My appreciation to my publisher, Emmett Ramey, for his continuing support and guidance through the years.

To the members of my crew and Rose and Dave — wherever you may be — you are the essence of this book.

———◆———

Index

A

AA(s), anti-aircraft fire/guns 2, 6, 107, 175, 219, 263, 269. See also 88-mm guns

Aeronca trainer 37, 263

Adolph. See Hitler

ailerons 212, 263

Air Corps 10, 17, 29, 44, 46, 98, 100, 264

Air Medal 168, 174, 190, 197, 205, 238, 264

ammunition dump 215, 264

anoxia 62–63, 264

Ardennes salient 227, 246, 264, 275

armorer 5, 81, 264

astro-compass 133, 264

AT-6 73, 79, 83–84, 264

AT-11 30, 67, 84, 264

automatic flight control equipment 100, 263

Axis 70, 208, 264

B

Battle of the Bulge 245, 264

Berlin 23, 25, 62, 210, 227, 235, 241, 246, 264

bivouac 112, 114–115, 264

blackout 69, 149, 151, 214, 237, 264

block-buster 37, 62, 265

Bluie West 1 147, 265

bomb bay 6, 95, 142, 189, 265, 278

B-17 60, 84, 105, 124, 163, 193, 255, 265

B-25 44, 52, 265, 272

B-24. See Liberator

B-26 44, 120, 239, 265, 272

buzz bomb 158, 165–166, 173, 180, 223, 226, 242, 265

C

Calais 174–175, 265

CE, circular error 101, 133, 266

check point 4, 265

Class A uniform 22, 266

coke burning stove 171, 266

Cologne 187, 266

combat wing 185, 251, 266

combat wing lead 251, 266

computer(s) 91, 98, 119

   C-2 computer 95, 266

   E-6B computer 95, 268

control point (CP) 203, 266

crumpets 248, 266

D

Dagwood sandwich 230, 267

D-Day 2, 267

D-8 bomb sight 102, 116, 267

deputy lead 184, 190, 267

Dieppe 170, 267

Distinguished Flying Cross, DFC 197, 262, 267, 275

division bombardier 222, 267

dollar slot element 184, 267

dorsal turret 82, 268

drift solution 115, 268

Dutch coast 6, 243, 268

E

88-mm guns 175, 263, 268

Elgin chronometer 91, 268

English Channel 254, 267–268

F

feather (the prop) 6, 138, 157, 243, 268

fighter support 4, 269

flak 4–6, 107, 163, 175, 181, 186, 199, 203, 212, 216, 223, 241–242, 254, 269

flak battery 4–5, 269

flight officer 43, 269

Focke-Wulf (FW-190) 269

fragmentation bomb 198, 269

Free French Emblem 240, 269

Freidrichshafen 107, 269

G

Gibson girl 144, 269

gigs 32, 45, 56, 270

Gordo 47, 132, 136, 145, 270

H

Hamm 187, 270

Hannover 175, 270

high squadron 228, 270

Hitler, Adolph 21, 52, 191, 221, 263, 273

HRX (Mickey) bombing 206, 270. See radar bombing.

I

IP, initial point 3, 203, 270

issei 70, 271

J

Jerry(s) 173, 182, 190, 206, 211, 217, 221, 223, 249–250, 271

jet fighter 246, 271

K

Kassel 187, 271

L

lead bombardier 116, 139, 153, 168, 181–182, 188, 223, 229, 234–236, 255, 262, 271, 276

lead plane 163, 195, 271

Liberator (B-24) 5, 52, 62, 73, 117, 123–124, 141, 162, 171, 199, 222, 238, 259, 265, 270–271

London 141, 151, 165–166, 173, 178–180, 187, 196–197, 199, 206–207, 213–214, 226, 235–237, 250, 254–255, 265, 272, 277

Luftwaffe 6, 9, 153, 170, 173, 175, 179–180, 206, 223, 245, 249, 256–257, 272

M

Mae West 5, 144, 272

Marauder (B-26) 120, 272

marshaling yards 190, 214, 242, 245, 272

Messerschmitt (ME-109) 6, 182, 272

Mitchell (B-25) 102, 265, 272

Miller, Glenn 40, 166–167, 272

N

nisei 70, 273

Nissen hut 167, 200, 273

Norden bombsight 30, 90, 98, 101, 219–220, 266, 268, 273

Nordhausen 242, 273

Northeim 243, 273

O

Oak Leaf Cluster 190, 197, 205, 238, 273

Ostende 213, 273

P

Pacy-Sur-Armancon 162, 273
Pathfinder bombing 191, 273
pilotage method 115, 274
pilotage navigator 5, 124, 169, 176, 181, 186–188, 190, 203, 209, 274
Ploesti oil fields 107, 274
P-38, P-47, P-51 4, 6, 274
Purple Heart 163, 274

R

radar bombing 206, 274
RAF 62, 160, 179–180, 199–200, 218, 274
Reich 179, 228, 246, 275
Rhine River 250, 275
ROTC 13, 18, 25, 31, 75, 275

S

salient. See Ardennes
Silver Star 182, 275
64 physical 44, 90, 275
SNAFU 115, 155, 275
Sperry sight 90, 105, 109, 112, 116, 275
squadron bombardier 157, 188, 276
S-2 (intelligence division) 3, 241–242, 259, 276

T

toggle 6, 116, 153, 276
Tricolor 240, 277
turret 6, 74, 82–84, 135, 138, 160, 174, 203–204, 277
    Consolidated 74, 75, 266
    Emerson 129, 131, 268
    Sperry 76, 275

U

USO 23–24, 53, 61, 65, 88, 277

V

Varga Calendar 226, 277
Vickers ring 79, 277
V-mail 149, 155–156, 227
V-2 rocket bombs 226, 235, 254, 277

W

WAAC, WAC 44, 50, 250, 278
waist position 124, 278
Waller trainer 78, 278
Wendling Station 278
wing crew 168, 278
Wünsdorf 253, 278

Y

Yom Kippur 183, 278

Hellgate Press

Hellgate Press is named after the historic and rugged Hellgate Canyon on southern Oregon's scenic Rogue River. The raging river that flows below the canyon's towering jagged cliffs has always attracted a special sort of individual — someone who seeks adventure. From the pioneers who bravely pursued the lush valleys beyond, to the anglers and rafters who take on its roaring challenges today — Hellgate Press publishes books that personify this adventurous spirit. Our books are about military history, adventure travel, and outdoor recreation. On the following pages, we would like to introduce you to some of our latest titles and encourage you to join in our celebration of this unique spirit.

Hellgate Press
P.O. Box 3727
Central Point, Oregon 97502-0032
(800) 228-2275

IN THE NAME OF ADVENTURE

GULF WAR
DEBRIEFING BOOK

AN AFTER ACTION REPORT

Andrew Leyden

Now you have access to the complete story of what unfolded during the seven months of late 1990 and early 1991, with the *Gulf War Debriefing Book: An After Action Report.* Whereas most books on the Persian Gulf War tell an "inside story" based on someone else's opinion, this book lets you draw your own conclusions about the war by providing you with a meticulous review of events and documentation all at your fingertips! Includes lists of all military units deployed, a detailed account of the primary weapon used during the war, and a look at the people, places, and politics behind the military maneuvering. This resource also gives a day-by-day chronology of the events that took place during Operation Desert Shield/Storm and afterwards.

Gulf War Debriefing Book:
An After Action Report

Available from Hellgate Press
ISBN: 1-55571-396-3
$18.95, paperback
7½ x 10", 320 pages

FROM HIROSHIMA WITH LOVE

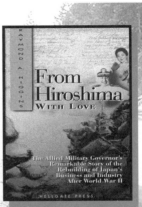

Raymond A. Higgins

This remarkable story is written from actual
detailed notes and diary entries kept by
Lieutenant Commander Wallace Higgins.
Because of his industrial experience back in
the United States and with the reserve
commission in the Navy, he was an
excellent choice for military governor of
Hiroshima. Higgins was responsible for
helping rebuild a ravaged nation of war.
He developed an unforseen respect for the
Japanese, their culture ... and one special
woman. From his research prior to his
arrival, he was able to better understand and
treat the surrendering people of this devastated
country with dignity, and the respect that they
deserved. Firsthand accounts of Japan's
astonishing defense system verify that had the
United States chosen invasion rather than the
bomb, the results would have been drawn out
and disastrous. These accounts also reveal a
secret mission to secure hidden uranium for
the making of Japan's own atomic bomb.

From Hiroshima With Love

Available from Hellgate Press
ISBN: 1-55571-404-8
$18.95, paperback
6 x 9", 318 pages

ARMY MUSEUMS

WEST OF THE MISSISSIPPI

Fred L. Bell, SFC Retired

A guide book for travelers to the army
museums of the west as well as a source of
information about the history of the site
where the museum is located.
Contains detailed information about
the contents of the museum and
interesting information about famous
soldiers stationed at the location or
events associated with the facility.
These 23 museums are in forts and
military reservations which represent
our colorful heritage in the settling of
the American West.

"Mr. Bell not only covers what exhibits and dis-
plays can be found in this collection of museums,
but gives an informative and enlightening history
lesson as well. This book is a must read for museum
enthusiasts."

> *Wayne C. Heinold, Sr.*
> *Command Sergeant Major*
> *U.S. Army Criminal Investigation Command*

Army Museums:
West of the Mississippi
Available from Hellgate Press
ISBN: 1-55571-395-5
$17.95, paperback
8 ¼ x 11", 250 pages

THE WAR THAT WOULD NOT END

U.S. MARINES IN VIETNAM, 1971-1973

Major Charles D. Melson, USMC (Ret.)

When South Vietnamese troops proved unable to "take over" the war from their American counterparts, the Marines had to resume responsibility. Covering the period 1971-1973, Major Charles D. Melson, who served in Vietnam, describes all the strategies, battles, and units that broke a huge 1972 enemy offensive. The book contains a detailed look at this often ignored period of America's longest war with photographs, figures, and maps. Melson also lists American POWs and MIAs for the period.

The War That Would Not End
U.S. Marines in Vietnam 1971-1973

Available from Hellgate Press
ISBN: 1-55571-420-X
$19.95, paperback
7½ x 10", 320 pages

Order Directly From Hellgate Press

You can purchase any of these Hellgate Press titles
at most book sellers or directly through us with this order form.

TO ORDER CALL,

1-800-228-2275

FAX **1-541-476-1479**

FOR INQUIRIES AND
INTERNATIONAL ORDERS,
CALL   **1-541-479-9464**
EMAIL   **psi2@magick.net**

Hellgate Press

P.O. Box 3727
Central Point, OR
97502-0032

TITLE	PRICE	QUANTITY	COST
Army Museums West of the Mississippi	$17.95		
From Hiroshima With Love	$18.95		
Gulf War Debriefing Book	$18.95		
The War That Would Not End	$19.95		

IF YOUR PURCHASE IS:	SHIPPING IN THE USA:
$0 - $25	$5.00
$25.01 - $50	$6.00
$50.01 - $100	$7.00
$100.01 - $175	$9.00
$175.01 - $250	$13.00
over $250	please call

SUBTOTAL $

SHIPPING $

TOTAL ORDER $

Thank you for your order!

SHIPPING INFORMATION

Ordered by:

Name:

Street Address:

City/State/Zip:

Daytime Phone   Email:

Shipped to: *Fill this out only if the information is different than above*

Name:

Street Address:

City/State/Zip:

Daytime Phone   Email:

PAYMENT INFORMATION

Indicate your preferred payment method below. Rush service is available, call for details at

(800) 228-2275. Overseas and Canadian orders: Please call for a quote on shipping.

☐ CHECK   ☐ AMERICAN EXPRESS   ☐ MASTERCARD   ☐ VISA

Card Number: Expiration Date:

Signature: Exact Name on Card:

IN   THE   NAME   OF   ADVENTURE